OUR SMALL TOWN

Our Small Town

Copyright © 2020 by James Pool. All rights reserved.

No part of this publication may be reproduced, stored in a retrieval system, or transmitted in any form or by any means, digital, electronic, mechanical, photocopying, recording, or otherwise, or conveyed via the Internet or a website without prior written permission of the publisher, except in the case of brief quotations embodied in critical articles and reviews.

ISBN: 978-1-7358263-4-9 (paperback)
        978-1-7358263-5-6 (ebook)

Printed in the United States of America

OUR SMALL TOWN

JAMES POOL

DEDICATION

To Clyde and Carolyn Ware,
without whose help I wouldn't be alive.

To the Rev. Louis Martin Jr.,
whose guidance was greatly appreciated.

And to Jameria, my inspiration.

TABLE OF CONTENTS

Dedication iv
Table of Contents v
Chapter 1 1
Chapter 2 10
Chapter 3 18
Chapter 5 32
Chapter 6 40
Chapter 8 56
Chapter 9 62
Chapter 10 68
Chapter 11 73
Chapter 12 79
Chapter 13 87
Chapter 14 94
Chapter 15 102
Chapter 16 109
Chapter 17 115
Chapter 18 122
Chapter 19 129
Chapter 20 135
Chapter 21 142
Chapter 22 149
Chapter 23 161
Chapter 24 169
Chapter 25 179
Chapter 26 188
Chapter 27 196
Chapter 28 204
Chapter 29 211
Chapter 30 217
Chapter 31 224
Chapter 32 231

CHAPTER 1

Buster slowly pulled the bra strap down as he undressed the woman standing before him. The woman in her mid to late thirties still looked good, with her short black hair that she wore flipped up in the front. She had a petite figure. In fact, just the other day, some teenagers hollered at her in the bowling alley, mistaking her for a girl half her age. Josephine Clearly, or "Jo" as her friends called her, was cocoa brown, about five feet, five inches, in her bare feet, and most men found her attractive, but she didn't like most men. They wanted to control her, tell her what to do, so she didn't date much…in fact, she didn't date hardly at all. She kept mostly to herself except when she went to work or church.

It was just her and her son, Buster, whom she had raised all by herself without the help of the father or any other man. Buster's father never came to the hospital when he was born, never sent him a birthday or Christmas card, and, to this day, was running from child support. He travelled from this state to that state, and from this job to that job, just one step ahead of the child support folks. It didn't matter to Jo; Buster was her son and her son alone.

Jo looked into Buster's eyes as she slowly undid his belt and said, "Tell Mommy how much you love her."

Buster took his right hand and slowly stroked his mother's hair. He then reached out with his left hand and pulled her toward him. "This much," he said and kissed her passionately on the lips. After a moment or so, Jo took a step backward and pushed Buster back.

With her hands still on his chest, she said, "And Mommy loves you too." She reached down Buster's unbuttoned pants with one hand and knelt down in front of him. Buster's manhood had never been more erect or harder as she put her mouth on his fully erect penis and started to move her head back and forth as Buster threw his head back and closed his eyes.

Sheriff Bill Johnson was what his friends called a man's man. He stood nearly six feet, five inches, tall, all of which was solid muscle. He spent at least two hours a day four times a week in the gym working out, partly because of the training he received as a Marine and partly because of the criticism he received as a child for being overweight. Now, at 260 pounds, Sheriff Johnson was a far cry from the "dough boy" his friends called him as a youth. He also was known for being a no-nonsense type of guy, a real straight shooter. He drank his coffee black with two sugars, no cream. None of that six-dollar latté junk they sold at the Starbucks when he went to the football games on Saturday. No, his coffee was just plain black with sugar; nothing fancy, it was about the same way in which he chose to live his life, just plain and simple. He slowly poured a fresh cup of coffee from the old Proctor Silex coffee maker in his office into his favorite mug, the big red and white cup that said "Roll Tide" on the side of it. He took a wooden coffee stirrer and slowly stirred the sugar into the coffee.

He then put the stirrer down, reached, and picked the cup up to his lips and took a short sip of the steaming hot coffee. "Ahh," he said. He was just about to lean back and put his feet up on his desk when suddenly a deputy sheriff dressed in the county's black shirt with khaki pants uniform burst into his office.

The deputy with his gray hair and deep blue eyes had a frown on his face so the sheriff knew that this meant trouble. "Sheriff," the deputy said, "there's been a shooting out on Highway 29 near the old Ford place."

The sheriff put his coffee mug down on his desk. "The crack house," the sheriff said.

The deputy nodded his head yes.

"Oh, that's just fucking great." The sheriff ran a hand through his thinning hair. "All the press, state troopers and officials snooping around. That's just what we need, damn it." He slammed his hand on his desk as he gets up from behind his desk. "Alright," he said as he reaches for his hat. "Let's go." The sheriff started toward his office door and looked back at the fresh coffee he had just made and shook his head as he headed out the door.

"Just everybody chill and don't say nothing," Dirty Red said. He didn't want his crew running off at the mouth and volunteering information to the police. Red turned around nervously as he tried to anticipate the questions the police will ask once they get there. After all, this wasn't his first rodeo. "What did y'all do with the guns?" he asked. Red looked at a young twenty-something dark-skinned black man with a bald head and a scar across his right cheek.

"We ditched them down by Jones Creek," he said.

"Motherfucker," Red said, "that's the first place them cops gonna look. You stupid son—"

"I know, Red, I know," the man with the scar on his face said. "I've already thought of that." Suddenly, Red did a 360-degree turn and puts his hands on top of his head. "That's cool, that's cool," he says, "Throw them off the trail."

Red nodded his head up and down. "Where did you put the money?" Red asks.

"It's taken care of, Red. Don't worry," the dark-skinned young black man said.

Red looked at him intently and said, "What do you mean, 'don't worry'?" Red asked. "That's two hundred and fifty thousand dollars, Bang Bang," Red shouted. Red looked down and rubbed his forehead. *Be cool, be cool*, Red thought, *the police don't know nothin'; don't volunteer any information*. Red took a deep breath to calm down and started to pace back and forth as he heard sirens growing closer.

"Okay, Bang Bang, okay," Red said as he reached into his pants pocket and pulled out a pack of Newport cigarettes. He pulled one out of the pack and put it to his lips and lit it. He took a long drag on the cigarette and then took it out of his mouth with his right two fingers. He pointed his cigarette at Bang Bang and said, "When they do find the guns, they can't trace them to us, provided you wiped them down." Red took another drag off his cigarette. "You did wipe them down," Red began, "didn't you?" Red's eyes narrowed as he looked at Bang Bang.

Bang Bang shook his head yes.

"Alright moving on," Red said as he placed the cigarette in his mouth again and took another drag off it. "What about the money? I say again."

A smallish, light-complexioned black man with a bushy beard answered, "Red, it's all taken care of, you know?"

Red looked at him and shook his head. "Yeah I know Shorty," he said. "You two fools are—" The sirens stopped as cars screeched to a stop in the front yard. Red jumped up and flicked the cigarette he was smoking, stomping it into the old wooden floor. He walked to the window and peeked out. "Alright, alright," Red said. "They're about to bust in, remember what we talked about? Don't say shit." Red looked out the window again. "Damn, there's like twenty cars out there." The other two men moved toward Red and the window. "Get back," Red said, "you dumb motherfuckers, you want to end up dead?" Red moved from the window, past Shorty and Bang Bang, and looked at the two bodies laying in a pool of blood on the floor. He pointed at the bodies on the floor. "You want to end up like these two dead motherfuckers?" he asked.

"YOU," the voice said. Red and his crew looked at each other anxiously. There was a long pause before, "YOU, IN THE HOUSE," a voice on a bullhorn said. "EXIT THE HOUSE WITH YOUR HANDS ABOVE YOUR HEAD!"

Red looked at the other men in the house and said, "Remember what I said… just shut up." Red turned toward the door. He looked at Shorty and Bang Bang. "All right, let's go." Red opened the door, there's bright light everywhere. He squinted his eyes, as he tries to see where the policemen are. "Don't get trigger happy on me," Red said. "We're on our way out."

Red and his crew walk to the end of the porch, where the stairs meet the porch. "PUT YOUR HANDS ON YOUR HEAD AND COME DOWN THE STAIRS SLOWLY!" the voice on the loudspeaker said. Red and the fellas walked down the steps with their hands held high above their heads. "LAY DOWN ON THE GROUND WITH YOUR HANDS BEHIND YOUR BACK!" the voice commanded. Red, Shorty, and Bang Bang looked at each other before kneeling down on the ground and putting their hands behind their back. The police rushed in with their guns drawn. Three of the police grabbed their hands and lassoed them with zip ties.

"Mom, I've got to go to work," Buster said as he pulled up his pants and started to button his shirt.

"Why?" Jo asked. "It's Tuesday night, everything's slow." She playfully pulled back the cover on the bed to show him what he was missing.

Buster smiled and turned away, toward the mirror. He had grown up enough to know what they just did was wrong, sinful even, but he did love her and would do anything to please her. She was, after all, his mother. "It's my job, I just started," he said as he finished buttoning his shirt. He took a final look in the mirror then turned and headed back to the bed to sit down. He reached for his shoes and slipped the right shoe on his foot. Still looking down at his shoes, Buster said, "You know mom, what we did was—"

"Wrong?," Jo answered for him.

Buster turned and looked at her. "You don't worry what other people say or think."

Jo reached out with her hand and started to gently stroke Buster's back. "Where was those folks when you needed milk or a diaper changed, needed a pair of shoes or clothes on your back?"

Buster looked at Jo and grabbed her hand. "I know you had a hard time, Mom, but…" Buster turned away. "This can't keep going on."

Jo's eyes widened and she pulled away from Buster. "Why can't it, baby?," Jo pleaded with him. "Nobody has to know. It's…" Jo propped herself up on a pillow and folded her arm so her head was resting in her hand.

Buster got up from the bed and turned away from Jo. "I don't, Mom, it just doesn't feel right."

Jo smiled to herself as she thought of a way to change the subject. "I know, I know," she said. "You have all those women at the office looking for a husband, for a man." She curled herself up on the bed as she continued, "Especially that receptionist, what's her name?"

Buster turned back toward Jo and smiled. "What are you talking about, Keisha?"

"Yeah, yeah, that's the one. The one who changes weaves every two days. What color or length of hair does she have today? Red, Black,

Blond? That girl spends three hundred dollars or more a month on hair, I don't know how she does it."

Buster laughed and Jo joined in. "Mom, I'm late," Buster said as he shook his head and headed out the door. He called back. "I'll see you later." Jo smiled as Buster left and lay back on her pillow, contemplating the future and the past as the smile disappeared from her face.

"I'll bet you Auburn doesn't score a touchdown against Alabama," a black man in his early forties with a red plaid shirt said.

"You don't know anything. That elephant gonna fall, he gonna fall," another black man in his fifties said.

"I'll tell you what, I'll tell you what," the man in the red plaid shirt volunteered enthusiastically. "I'll give you two touchdowns, fourteen points against Alabama and they still won't score."

"Hold it, hold it, any betting going on around here, comes through me. I still got ten spots left on the board," a tall, thin, and bald black man said as he headed toward the two men arguing about the Iron Bowl game. "The house gets all bets, big or small, short or long." The man reached in his pocket and pulls out a wad of hundred dollar bills and held them aloft. "Get that car, that boat, that money you need to stay afloat," he barked out. "Just one hundred dollars a square, don't worry, just hurray," he said.

The men gathered round him in the small club to place their bets. "Club" really wasn't the name for it. It was an old rundown house with a leaky tin roof, with a short porch, and old rickety wood flooring that creaked every time you moved from room to room. They played Marvin Sease blues records, sold homemade moonshine, liquor, and beer in one room, shot dice, played Pitty Pat and dominos in another. Crack cocaine and women selling their bodies operated in the back of the house, along with the prerequisite bags of weed packaged in the little red bags. All in all it was not a bad business in a poor black town that prosperity left a long time ago, along with the last of the white folks that were replaced by the poor living off the poor and with payoffs to the local police and elected officials to look the other way. Most of these folks coming in here were the locals whose families had lived here for generations

looking for a way to blow off steam from their jobs at the local auto parts supplier or escape the hopelessness of the mistakes they made as children when they committed petty crimes and got locked in the state's criminal justice system.

"Hey, Blu," a man called out. "Give me two of them squares."

Blu, the club's owner was fifty-five with a clean-shaven head and salt and pepper beard covering his face. He was rail thin, which made him look taller than he really was at six feet, two inches. He was retired from the military and, looking to supplement his income, had opened up The Cub. He was as dark as a moonless night, hence the nickname "Blu." You know, he was so dark that he looked Blue.

"I've got to go put up some of this money, wait here," Blu said. Blu turned and walked toward the back of the house to a room on the side of the house. His thin frame gave him the appearance of a man gliding, not walking, through the room. He reached the room's door and reached into his pocket and pulled out his keys. He looked for and located the key for the room and inserted it into the master lock on the door. He unlocked the door, then tugged and pulled on the lock, releasing it and then opened the door, pulling the latch back and hanging the lock on the clasp. He entered the room, quickly closing the door behind him and looked around the room. He moved toward a small safe on the floor in the rear of the room.

Blu bent down and started to turn the combination lock on the safe, suddenly there was a knock at the door. "Blu," a voice called out. Blu straightened up and moved to a desk in the center of the room. He opened the desk drawer, where he had a nine-millimeter pistol put away. "Blu, it's me, R.C.."

"C'mon in R.C.," Blue said as he leaves the desk drawer open and stood behind the desk. The door opened and in stepped a slightly heavyset, light-skinned black man in his mid to late thirties. His bald head was in stark contrast to the thick mustache on his lips. "Blu," he said as he smiled, reveling a mouthful of rotten teeth. "I've been looking for you."

Blue looked at R.C. and smiled. "The good Reverend Clark. What can we do for you, Reverend?" as if Blu didn't know. The good reverend was known as a good singer and fiery orator on Sunday, but

through the week was just another crack-head looking for credit until the first of the month.

The credit binge always began around the tenth of the month when the government or retirement checks ran and people needed "help" until the first of the month. "Well, Blu, I was wondering if I could get a dime…"

Blu waved his hand to stop the reverend before he could complete his sentence. "Okay, R.C., Okay. How much is it this month?" Blu moved away from the desk.

"One hundred, one fifty? It's just the fifteenth and you get too far behind and you don't want to pay," Blu said.

Reverend Clark looked at Blu and pleaded with him. "You know I'm good for it, Blu. I ain't never shorted you before."

Blu shook his head and said, "You better watch it, I want my money."

"I know, Blu. I know," R.C. responded. "Blu, you hear about Dirty Red?" R.C. asked.

Blu's eyes narrowed at the mention of his chief rival in town. "No, I didn't," Blu replied.

"Well, somebody tried to rob them and three people got killed," R.C. said. "They got a roadblock up there on 29."

"Oh yeah?" Blu said, trying to act surprised even though he wasn't.

He helped Red get his start when he and his son were growing up together, but like most kids his age, he didn't want to listen, wanted to do things his way, didn't want to listen to what "Old School" had to say. Blu knew that and knew he couldn't stop him from venturing out on his own. He just didn't think he'd take his son with him. "Any of Red's crew get hit?" Blu asked, knowing that his son, Bang Bang, worked for Red.

"No," R.C. said, "I didn't hear that." R.C. shook his head. "They say someone was trying to rob them and they opened fire on 'em before they got them."

Blu nodded his head, relieved that his son wasn't hurt or dead. They didn't see eye-to-eye, but he still loved him. He was, after all, still his seed.

"Blu," R.C. said as he nervously wiped his hand across his lips. "How about that hit?" he asked.

Blu smiled and waved his hand toward the door. "Tell Sneaky to come see me and we'll get you taken care of, okay R.C.?"

R.C. smiled and rushed toward the door. R.C. turned toward Blu and waved his hand. "Thanks, Blu. Thanks," R.C. said as he exited the room.

Blu smiled and looked down at the desk drawer with the gun in it. "Why won't they listen?" he said as he closed the drawer with the pistol in it.

CHAPTER 2

Sheriff Johnson and Deputy Oliver rode to the crime scene together, with Deputy Oliver driving, each dressed in there freshly pressed gray uniforms with the towns Gold emblem, embosomed on the brown Dodge Charger they drove. The emblem, which was hard to see against the brown background on the vehicle, looked strange. In fact, it was barely visible at a distance, done so on purpose so criminals couldn't tell the law from a regular driver. The county had salaries to pay and what better way for them, than with speeders, stop sign runners, and people with no insurance going through there city limits on the way to see Auburn University play. In fact, for the sheriff, that was a special delight with him being an Alabama fan.

They could afford it, not the local folks, who always opted for community service instead of paying the fine and besides, they voted—something to consider since election time was near. "The state troopers are already here," Deputy Oliver said.

Sheriff Johnson nodded his head as he turned toward Deputy Oliver. "With the entire road they have to cover in Alabama," he said. "It never ceases to amaze me how quickly they get to any emergency or incident."

"Hey, sheriff, look over there." The deputy pointed to the right. "That's Buster's car." Sheriff Johnson looked at the gray charger with the city emblem on it, parked in the yard.

"Well, well, well," Sheriff Johnson said. "I like a young deputy to show some initiative, must have been listening to his scanner." The sheriff and the deputy pulled to a stop just behind a state trooper's car. They both exited the car and moved toward the front porch, cordoned off by crime scene tape. They saw Buster standing on the porch talking to two state troopers with three young black men with hands zip-tied behind their backs, sitting on the ground next to the porch.

"Well Hello Deputy," the sheriff said as he walked past the men sitting on the ground and up the stairs to the porch. At the top of the stairs, the Sheriff flashed a smile and nodded at Buster.

"Hello Buster," he said, "I see you took the initiative to come on out here," Buster nodded his head up and down to acknowledge the sheriff. "And tell me just who are these fine gentlemen of the state that you're standing next to," he asked. The sheriff looked at the two troopers. The first one was tall at least six feet, three inches, almost as tall as the sheriff. The sheriff stood six-foot-five in his stocking feet and this trooper looked him straight in the eye.

The other state trooper was the exact opposite, short, maybe five-eight. That was if you counted the hat on his head. He had a closely cropped hairstyle, his hair cut so tight on the sides that his hat was almost touching his ears. He had brown eyes with a stocky build. In fact, he was almost as wide as he was tall, a short and powerful man. The tall trooper reached out his hand.

The sheriff reached out and shook hands with the trooper. *Nice firm handshake,* the sheriff thought. *Much stronger than what he appeared.* He smiled, revealing perfect white teeth. "Hello, Sheriff," he said, "I'm Ben Smith and this here," he said, pointing to the state trooper, "is Trooper Alex Wasson."

Sheriff Johnson turned to shake hands with the shorter trooper. But he waved him off. "That's all right Sheriff," he said, "I don't want to break your hand." The trooper smiled at the Sheriff.

Cocky son-of-a-bitch, the sheriff thought. Before he could say that, however the tall trooper spoke. "Before you go there, we've heard all the jokes about Smith and Wesson," Trooper Smith said.

Sheriff Johnson threw up his hands, "Don't worry about that," he said, "we're strictly business here." The sheriff cleared his throat before he got down to business, "Now tell me," the sheriff said, "What have you got?"

Trooper Wesson stepped forward and flipped open his notepad. "Let's see what we have here sheriff," Trooper Wesson said. He leafed through the pages until he said, "Ah, here we go. These three gentlemen," he began, "say that they were on their way home from a trip to the all-night truck stop in Dadeville when they went into their

yard and saw a vehicle parked outside the house." The Trooper cleared his throat. "They state further that they approached the house and entered where they found two dead bodies, lying on the floor of the house." Trooper Wesson flipped his notepad shut.

"End of Story?" Sheriff Johnson asked.

"End of story," Trooper Wesson said.

"Okay then," the sheriff said.

The sheriff took off his hat and rubbed his head. "Well," the sheriff said, "What happened to the vehicle?" the sheriff asked.

"Oh," the trooper said. He flips back open the notepad and flips through the pages. "Ah," he said. "Here it is. They say that they looked out the window and it was gone."

The sheriff rubbed the back of his neck and then looked at his deputies and then the State troopers. "Well," he began. "I guess the car must have been a mirage or something, since it magically disappeared." The deputies laughed. The sheriff puts his hat back on and said, "I guess we better take a look at them bodies before they disappear, huh?" The sheriff moved toward the front screen door and pulled it open. He held the door open and motioned for the other officers to come in. "Come on in, come on in," he said. "Let's see what we got here. Have the crime scene people been here yet?" he asked.

"No sir," Trooper Wesson said, "we're waiting on them now."

"Well," the sheriff said, "be careful and don't touch anything." The sheriff looked around. The television was playing on an old entertainment center against the far wall. There was an old rerun of *The Andy Griffith* show playing, with four or five beer bottles lying on the coffee table with a deck of cards. To the right of the table, two dead bodies lay in a pool of blood, sprawled on top of one another. The sheriff walked across the room to examine the bodies. He bent down, making sure not to touch anything. He looked at the victim lying on top: a young African American male in dreadlocks. He had a tattoo on his neck in the form of a dragon and another on his right forearm with the name "Shanqueisha" on it. He was dressed in a black polo shirt and khaki pants and black work boots.

The sheriff stood up and walked around to the other side so he could get a look at the other body. He was a light-skinned young black male with a closely cropped hairstyle. He also had a black polo shirt with khaki pants and black boots on. "These boys are wearing the same stuff," Sheriff Johnson said. "Is that a work uniform?" he asked. He looked at the state troopers. No reply. The sheriff took his hat off and started twirling it around in his hands.

"I think," he said, "somebody gave these boys an ambush party." He looked at the other officers before continuing. "They were waiting on these boys when they came through the door. They weren't dead when they found them. They killed them," the sheriff said as he put his hat back on. "Something happened," he said. "They either tried to rob them or some kind of deal went wrong, but whatever it was, those boys out there," the sheriff said, pointing his hand toward the outside, "aren't telling the truth." The sheriff moved toward the kitchen table and pointed at it. "The shots probably came from over here, caught me by surprise." The sheriff moved to the kitchen table. He looked at the kitchen table then turned and looked at the two dead bodies. "Yep, each one of them probably caught three of four slugs. You find any weapons?" the sheriff asked.

"No," Trooper Smith said.

"Why doesn't that surprise me?" the sheriff said. "Red is one cool son-of-a-bitch, always one step ahead." The sheriff reached into his pocket and pulled out a pack of gum. "Oliver, you and Buster call in the K9 unit and go and search the woods." The sheriff took a stick of gum, unraveled it, and stuck it in his mouth. "I think I'm going to go back and question those fine citizens sitting out there separately." The sheriff started toward the door. He turned back toward the state troopers. "You don't mind, do you?" he asked the state troopers and before waiting for a reply, stepped out the door.

Mayor Bill Heard had been mayor of this small town for three years and it was coming around election time. He'd spruced up the city by cutting down the over grown Kudzu on the city's vacant lots, while keeping the grass cut on the city's streets twice a month. He'd cut the city's power bills by turning out the lights when personnel weren't working and closed the cities lone library, kept for people or groups renting it out for meetings and such. Hell, why did they need a library? He figured it was for using public funds so kids could look at porn, rap sites, or Facebook, for their "friends" and threatened them. *Stupid kids*! he thought.

He had also made sure his town was in line for one of the Obama administration's government loans to rural communities, even though he himself was a republican. *Hey, free money is free money. You'd have to be a fool to a least not try*. Tonight, however, politics was the furthest thing from Bill Heard's mind. Betty Hughley was on his mind. All two hundred sixty pounds of brown ass he was about to get up into. "Come on baby, I'm waiting. What's taking so long?" she said from the bedroom. "All right, all right, I'll be there in a minute," Mayor Heard said. He had forgotten to order his monthly supply of Viagra so he had to improvise. He was looking for his penis pump, but had forgotten where he had put it. "Now let's see," he said as he looked in the hall closet.

Suddenly, the phone rang. The mayor ignored it. He closed the closet door and went to the kitchen. "I know it's got to be in here," he said as he looked in the kitchen cabinet under the sink. The phone rang again. The mayor said, "Fuck!" and slammed the cabinet door shut. Frustrated, he looked at the phone on the kitchen wall and decided to answer it. Before he answered it, he looked at the kitchen clock. *11:30, who could be calling at this time*? he wondered. He picked up the phone.

"Hello," he said.

"Baby," the voice from the bedroom called. "Mommas hurting, will you hurry up?"

"Shit," Mayor Heard said as he held the phone to his chest. "I'll be right there," he said. He put the phone back up to his ear and said, "Okay, who's this?"

"This is the Dadeville Press, Mayor Heard," the caller said. "Any comet on the drug-related shooting out on Highway 29?"

"What?" the mayor said.

"The two people killed tonight, Mayor Heard," the caller said. The mayor took the phone from his ear and held it against his chest. *What the fuck*? the mayor thought. Just what he needed, a murder in his town—no, not a murder, but a double murder—and he didn't have

a clue what was going on. He'd have to think of something fast. The mayor put the phone back up to his ear. "Well," the mayor began. "I'm sorry that I took so long, but I'm on my cell phone with the police chief and he's filling me in on the situation," he said. "I will have a comment on the situation later in the morning.: The mayor hung up the phone. "Just what I need at election time…" he said, "a murder in my town." The mayor shook his head. "Fuck it," he said and resumed his search for his penis pump.

Sheriff Johnson took a seat on the old wooden steps next to the three young men sitting on ground. The ABI crime scene unit had just arrived and were in the house doing their job. Sheriff Johnson looked at Red. Red, all of the tender age of twenty-one, had already been in jail two times for eluded murders. The sheriff knew him well from their previous encounters and from the looks of him and if you didn't know any better, you might have mistaken him for a college boy. With his black thick-rimmed glasses, neatly pressed jeans, baggy and sagging of course, with a fresh pair of Air Jordans on with a red neatly pressed shirt on. He didn't look the role of what people would consider a drug dealer. That was if you didn't know any better.

This "College Boy" was as cold, smart, and calculating as any criminal the sheriff had come across in all his thirteen years on the force. Red was known to have ordered hits on two rival drug dealers. The cases where thrown out, one for lack of evidence the other because the witness recanted. Red had boasted that his crew was the "Bloods" of the south, trying to strike fear in the local wannabes that he was not to be messed with. That, however, was mostly talk since the area was awash in drugs and there were new players popping up every day. Red and his crew stayed mostly out on rural Highway 29, where Red and his lookouts could see for miles in either direction, making a surprise raid impossible. Thus, they were mostly left alone, away from the town but certainly not forgotten, especially for those looking for a "bump" and didn't want noisy neighbors knowing their business. Sheriff Johnson took off his hat, sat it on the stairs, and started to rub his chin.

"How you doing Red?" the sheriff asked.

"Just fine, Sheriff, just fine," Red said and smiled, flashing two gold teeth in the front of his mouth. "Could you please tell me, Sheriff," he says, "Why the boys and I are sitting here with our arms tied behind our backs?"

"You know why, Red," the sheriff answered. "You and the boys are our prime suspects until we find out otherwise."

"I already done told you," Red said, "didn't we boys?" Red looked at Bang Band and Shorty, who nodded their heads in agreement. "We found them in the house when we came back from the store," Red continued, "and who do you think called the police?" Red said, grinning. "I did."

The sheriff stood up and folded his arms across his chest and laughed. "Is that right? Well Red," the sheriff said, "I've got a little problem with your story."

"What might that be, Sheriff?" Red asked.

"See, we found shell casings over by the kitchen table where you were drinking and playing cards," the sheriff said.

"So?" Red asked.

"So, why would shell casings be where you and the boys were drinking and playing cards and nowhere else, but you say all were gone to the all night store?"

Red smiled, flashing his gold grill. "I don't know, Sheriff," he said. "Why don't you tell me?"

"Oh, I intend to, Red," the sheriff said. "You see, I think them boys surprised the three of you and some shooting started and then you and the boys knocked over some chairs, getting out of the way."

"Echo wrong," Red said. "I say, Sheriff, if you were on a game show, you just lost first prize." Red laughed and turned to Bang Bang and Shorty who also laughed. "If we shot them, where are the guns?" Red asked.

"That, as you say," Sheriff Johnson began, "is the million dollar question." The sheriff reached down and picked his hat up and put it on his head. Sheriff Johnson looked at Deputies Oliver and Buster. "You two, take these fellas down to the jail and question all of them again, separately," he said. He then looked at the two state troopers

and said, "You think anyone can get some people out here to comb this place?" he asked.

Trooper Wesson looked at Trooper Smith. They both nodded their heads. Trooper Wesson spoke, "Yeah, I think so, Sheriff," he said. "It's probably too late to see anything, might have to do something in the morning." The sheriff started, heading to his patrol car.

"Make sure you lock down this crime scene," he said as he turned and looked at Red. "Things have a way of disappearing around here." With that, the sheriff was gone, wondering to himself what the hell was going on.

CHAPTER 3

It was a fine day in the state of Alabama, with the big game only a week away and hunting season beginning. This was the best time of year to be in Alabama and all the locals loved it. The ten or so old men that met up at the corner store in town every morning were ripe with gossip this morning about the deaths at the crack house the night before.

The women of the town dubbed the corner "The DDC," short for Dead Dick Corner because all of the older men, some retired, some disabled, and some just plain bums, gathered there every morning to rehash the day or week before, tell lies, and bargain for work that needed to be done.

These men made it a point to get their coffee, breakfast, and gossip at this corner convenience store every morning. Rain, sleet, the occasional snow, nothing could deter them except maybe a tornado warning or the every-three-month crazy bitch. Only the foolhardy would defy that and most of these men where long past that age, except, of course, when the fountain of youth or Viagra hit them.

"I heard three people got killed and one got shot up," Randolph Heard said. As a brother of the mayor, people listened to him right or wrong.

"No, I didn't hear that," Ben Allen said. "I heard that Blu's son and Red shot and killed two boys from Lee County. That's what I heard," he said.

Pete Knightly, who was busy chewing on a ham and egg biscuit, volunteered through bites, "They say they kicked down the front door and them boys was in there waiting on me." He wiped his mouth with the back of his hand and continued, "They say they used Blu's son as a hostage,"

"Blu's son?" Eric Meadows said. "I thought he was still in the Army or something."

Pete Knightly said, "He got kicked out of the army last year for drugs. They don't take that kind of shit no more like they did in Vietnam,"

"I remember when—" Eric Meadows began.

"Remember what, you old goat!" Randolph the fly said, "I remember when Auburn beat Alabama six times in a row, didn't they, Pete? And let's not talk about 'the miracle.'" Eric Meadows looked up in the sky like he was a million miles away.

"I'm just saying that was a serious time but a fun time, we all thought we could change the world. I guess in some ways we did with affirmative action and equal opportunity."

Pete spat on the ground. "Hell, affirmative action destroyed the black family," Pete took his right foot and stepped on the spit, rubbing it into the ground. "Instead of them hiring black men, they hired black women. They filled two quotas: a woman and a black."

"Yeah Pete," Eric said. "How did that destroy the black family?"

"Don't you see?" Pete said, "Black women didn't need black men anymore, especially if they didn't have a job."

"Sort of like you, huh Pete?" Ben Allen said. "Isn't that the reason Bernice kicked you out?" The fellas laughed. "Yeah," Pete said. "And maybe. The fact that I got her sister pregnant." The group of old men howled and laughed as the mayor pulled up in the city-owned white Ford F-150 truck. Ray Conley was the first to wave at the mayor. "What's going on, Mayor?" he asked.

The mayor exited the F-150, smiling at everyone. "I don't know anything, Hell y'all probably know more than me, up here at the DDC."

Everyone laughed. "Hey Mayor, I got a pump for sale. They say…" Ray said.

The mayor waved his arm. "I don't need that kind of stuff. I still got the heart of a young man," the mayor said.

"Yeah, he had the heart maybe, but definitely not the hair or body," Ray replied. The men laughed as the mayor made it to the store entrance.

He turned and said, "Well some people say that I remind them of a Billy Goat with my bald head and white beard, but just like that Billy Goat," the mayor paused for effect, "I'm just as tough and ornery when I fight for the people of this town," The mayor raised his right arm in the air. "That's what I want y'all to remember on Election Day," Mayor Heard said, "Vote for Heard, the peoples' voice!" The mayor dropped his arm, turned, and entered the store.

Sheriff Johnson walked into the county sheriff's department front door, waving his hand as he went. "Good morning," he said. He nodded his head as he made his way through the open office area. He saw one of the office girls, Keisha (he thought that was her name) as she smiled at him. "Good morning Sheriff," she said.

Keisha was a twenty-something, white, and with a smooth soothing voice. She had a shape that resembled a Coca Cola bottle, not the regular size, but the king size. No, not the king size, the extra large size, but by god it sure looked good on her! The sheriff was a happily married man but these young women would make any man think twice. "Hello Keisha," he said as he moved quickly through the office to his office door.

"Sheriff, Sheriff," the sheriff heard as he reached his office door. He looked toward the left where he heard the voice. "How you doing Ollie?" he said. The sheriff turned the handle to his office and walked in, followed closely by Deputy Oliver. An office, by any definition, was a place where you organized things, issued commands, but Sheriff Johnson's office was anything but that. Papers and files where on the floor stacked up around his desk. There was University of Alabama football memorabilia strewn around throughout the room.

The sheriff looked sideways at Deputy Oliver as he made his way through the maze on his office floor. "You get anything back from the ABI yet?" the sheriff asked as he took a seat behind his desk. Deputy Oliver stood just to the right of his desk. "Yes sir," he said. "We know the victims' names, first of all," The deputy said.

The sheriff took off his hat and threw it on his desk. "Okay, let's hear it," the Sheriff said, folding his hands in front of him as he leaned back in his chair.

Deputy Oliver took the manila folder he had in his hands, opened it, and started to read. "The two victims are as follows," he began. "James Wyatt III, of Lafayette Alabama, age twenty-one."

"Was he the one with the tattoos?" the Sheriff asked.

"No," the deputy answered. "This is the one without the tattoos," the deputy answered.

"The light-skinned one?" the sheriff asked.

"Correct," the deputy said as he nodded his head up and down. "He is the father of two young sons and employed at Kwan Tech Manufacturing. The other victim," he continued, "was Ticki Barnes, age twenty-seven of Eastman, Alabama. He also was a father of two young children, one boy and one girl and also employed at Kwan Tech." The deputy closed the folder and dropped his hands to the side, giving the appearance of being at attention as he awaited the sheriff's instructions.

"Any prior arrests on these two?" the sheriff asked.

"Just the usual sir," Deputy Oliver replied. "Both where behind on child support payments and had done a couple of months in the county jail for nonpayment. One had a few traffic violations, driving with no insurance and on an expired tag, but nothing major. No drug busts or felonies."

"Child support," the sheriff said. "It's a good idea when there's plenty of jobs, but with the economy in the shape it's in…" the sheriff started to rub his chin. "All it does is put people already in bad shape in worse shape and make an already overburdened justice system almost impossible. The county budget is strapped," he continued, "the state budget is strapped. I mean where we are supposed to put all these people, never mind feed them?" The sheriff shook his head from side to side. "Well enough of that, have you heard from Buster?"

"No sir, I haven't," Oliver replied.

"What about from the crime scene folks, and has anybody searched around the house yet?"

Deputy Oliver shrugged his shoulders. "No, sir," he said. "Well," the sheriff said. "That's what you get when you open up a shit hole, more shit."

"Sir," Deputy Oliver said, "you also have one newspaper reporter and two television reporters in the visitor's area."

"Well then," the sheriff said as he slapped his hands on his desk as he got up from behind his desk. "Let's go tell them what we don't know." The sheriff grasped his hat off of his desk and again made his

way through the maze on his floor as he slapped Deputy Oliver on the shoulder headed toward the visitor's area.

Jo Clearly sat at her desk and looked at the student sitting across from her, Nikki Flowers. She knew Nikki's mother and father, both hard working, who often took on extra work to help pay the bills. She didn't want to tell them that their daughter was caught having sex with another student behind the gym bleachers. The fact that the other student was also female made the situation a little awkward, to say the least. Both girls were under-aged, though Nikki just barely coming upon her senior year. She had been in and out of her office six times this year for cutting classes, being disruptive in class, and she was in line for suspension. The other girl's parents would receive a call. Nikki, however, was supposed to be sent home but Jo, in her job as student counselor, had to at least try and see if she could reach this girl. Nikki was a light-skinned black young lady with reddish brown hair. She had the body of a twenty-two- or twenty-three-year-old and might be considered pretty by some people.

Of course there were rumors floating around school that she drank liquor, smoked pot, and sold sex for money to some of the town's older gentlemen, but those were just rumors, as far as Jo was concerned. Her life's experience, however, had taught her that where there was smoke, there was fire and it was her job to get to the bottom of this. In fact, before this year, Nikki had never been in trouble, she made good grades, participated in various student clubs, and was considered one of the brighter students. Jo thought, *What happened? Was this girl acting out to get attention or seeking help?* The one thought that she didn't want to accept, however, the truth could be that the girl was probably was just plain wicked.

"Well Nikki ," Jo started, "this isn't the first time you've been here. What have you got to say for yourself?."

Nikki shrugged her shoulders as she slumped down in the chair across from Jo.

"I look at the past year," Jo continued as she reads from a report sitting on her desk. "Absence, fighting, smoking cigarettes on school

grounds. I mean Nikki, really?" Jo said as she looked at Nikki. "What happened to the straight-A student from two years ago?"

Nikki continued to look away from Jo and still didn't answer. Jo shook her head and got up from behind her desk and moved around the desk to be closer to Nikki. She reached her hand out to Nikki to touch Nikki on the shoulder. Nikki jerked away. "Don't touch me," Nikki snarled at Jo.

Jo pulled her hand back, surprised at Nikki's response. "Look Nikki," Jo said. "I'm just trying to help." Nikki jumped up from her chair and screams at Jo.

"Oh yeah, you wanna help? Where were you when he came over that night, when he moved in, when…?" Nikki's hands covered her face as she started to sob.

Jo moved closer to Nikki and stood in front of her, being careful not to touch her, but also trying to comfort her. "Who moved in, Nikki?" Jo asked. Nikki moved back further from her as she dropped her hands from her face.

"Don't touch me," Nikki said, still crying. "I don't want anyone touching me! I'll…" Nikki shouted at Jo between sobs. Jo, seeing how upset Nikki was, decided to take another approach. "I'm not going to touch you," Jo said. Jo moved back around to her desk chair and waved at it. "I'm gonna take a seat and I want you to take a seat also. Yes?" Jo asked.

Jo took a seat at her desk and motioned for Nikki to do the same. Nikki moved back to her chair and sat down, tears still streaming down her cheeks. "Now let's try this again. Let's reset," Jo said. "I want to recommend against suspension, Nikki, but you have to tell me something."

Nikki looked at Jo and wiped the tears from her face and took a deep breath. "Miss Clearly," Nikki said, "I don't really want to talk about that right now, it's just…"

"I know, I know, Nikki," Jo said, "you don't have to right now, but Nikki you have to meet me half way and a good starting point would be for you to tell me what happened between you and that other student?" Jo said. "What's her name?"

"Hanna?" Nikki said.

Jo looked down at her incident report, then looked up. "Yes, Hanna," Jo said.

"Oh, that's my boo. I love her," Nikki said, brightening up, smiling.

Jo noticed the rapid change in behavior that Nikki had just displayed and made a mental note of it. She pressed on. "Your boo?" Jo asked. "This is a very serious offense, Nikki. Your parents, her parents have got to be informed. There could be criminal charges filed considering the fact that your boo is underage. Don't you realize that?" Jo said, the smile on Nikki's face faded as a look of concern replaced it.

"Well," Nikki said, "we were just having fun, that's all."

"This isn't a place to have fun with your boo, Nikki," Jo said. "This is a place for education, to prepare you for the next phase of your life, not some all-night motel where you and your boo can have sex under Coach Stanton's bleachers." Nikki's face was blank as Jo continued, "I know your father and mother, Nikki, and that's the only reason that I'm willing to give you a break on this, but make no mistake young lady, this is your last chance, do you understand me?"

Nikki dropped her head down and nodded her head yes.

"Is that a yes?" Jo asked.

"Yes Miss Clearly, you won't have to worry about me anymore." Jo looked at Nikki, trying to read her.

Having no luck, Jo said, "All right, get out of here."

Nikki jumped up from her chair and rushed toward the office door. "You don't have to worry, Miss Clearly," Nikki said as turned before reaching the door. "I'm a good girl."

Jo motioned for Nikki to go with her hand. "Go ahead get out of here," she said.

Nikki rushed out the door so fast that Jo smiled and shook her head. She sat back in her chair, remembering her teenage years and the difficulties that she faced, from her being pregnant at age fifteen to her being raped by her uncle. It all seemed so far in the past now that it could pass for a dream…

CHAPTER FOUR

JULY 4, 1980

Jo ran toward the side entrance of her aunt's home. It was getting dark and she didn't want to miss one minute of the fireworks display. She had been dancing, gossiping, and playing cards with her cousins. Her aunt had recently remarried and the family reunion this year was being held out in the country at her aunt's new home. The house was a big white and green ranch style house with a huge backyard. Barbecue cooked on the grill as a mixture of rap and R&B played in the background. It was hot this day, though no hotter than usual for the Fourth of July in Alabama. "One hundred degrees in the shade," as the old folks used to say and sweet tea was being sucked down by the bucket full, thus Jo taking a quick trip to the restroom to relieve herself. Jo ran into the house not sure which way to the bathroom. She had been in the house once before. The house was shaped in the form of a horseshoe and she didn't know exactly which way to go so she decided to go right. Everyone was outside so she didn't have anyone to ask and if she was wrong, so what? She'd just back track and go the in the other direction.

Jo hurried down the hallway past one bedroom. She stopped and looked in the room to see if there was a bathroom in there. No luck. She continued on until she reached the end of the hall. There was a closed door so she reached out and turned the knob on the door and entered the door. It was dark but she could see a light on it a room off to the side. *Ah*, she thought, *that must be it*. She closed the door behind her and entered headed toward the room in the back. She turned in the room only to see... "Hey girl hold on!" a voice said. Jo had been looking down and suddenly looked up at her new uncle standing at the toilet with his long penis in his hands, urinating.

"Oh, I'm sorry," Jo said, embarrassed. Jo's eyes went straight to her uncle's penis. She had never seen a grown man's privates, but his sure was long. Her uncle looked at Jo and noticed that the young girl didn't

turn away or move from the door. Her uncle, Robert, was his name, finished urinating and turned his penis toward her. "You know what you're looking at girl?" he said.

Jo shook her head yes, then answered, "Yes, sir."

"You don't act like you've seen this before," Uncle Robert said, "the way you keep looking at it."

Jo, embarrassed, turned away. "I'm sorry, Uncle Robert, I didn't mean to." Jo felt Uncle Robert behind her, grabbing her by her shoulders, and pressing himself up against her.

"You know," he began, "I can show you more, don't you?"

Jo tried to pull away from him. "No, No," she pleaded. "I don't want to." Uncle Robert pulled her back and turns her around to face him.

"Yeah," he said, "you know you want it." Uncle Robert moved her toward the bed.

"Please no, please," Jo started to plead. Uncle Robert reached down and unbuttoned her jeans, pulling her jeans down around her knees.

"It's just you and me little one, no one has to know." He slipped his fingers inside her panties and pulled them down. "Let's keep this between ourselves, okay?" he said. Terrified and frightened, Jo unleashed the pressure that had built up in her bowels.

"Miss Clearly, Miss Clearly…" Jo straightened up in her chair and focused in on the voice calling her name. "Where have you been? Thinking about that girl?" Vice Principal Skinner asked. "I know, she's a handful, isn't she?"

"That's for sure," Jo answered. "Well tell me what have you decided? Vice Principal Skinner asked. Jo took a deep before she began, leaving the past behind and focusing instead on the now.

"Okay Buster, what you got?" Sheriff Johnson says as Deputy Buster Clearly walked into his office. Buster's lean muscular build, along with his sharply pressed pants and light gray pants, represented the department well in the field. He looked good. The sheriff thought and along with the hours the department spent training this young man, he hoped it might one day lead to a fine officer and also, more importantly, some answers to the case immediately at hand. "Well, Sheriff," Buster began. "We searched the woods like you said."

"Okay, okay," the sheriff said. "We found several tire tracks, along with some spent shell casings out in the yard." *So there was gunfire out in the yard*, the sheriff thought. "We also searched the fish pond in back of the house and found this." Buster took a black trash bag he had been holding and held it up in the air.

"Well what is it?" The sheriff asked.

"I don't know, Sheriff," Buster answered. "I didn't open it."

The sheriff looked at Buster and shook his head. "Buster," the sheriff said, "you mean you're just walking around with a bag of potential evidence and you don't even know what it is?"

"Nope," Buster replied. "I didn't want to contaminate it ."

The sheriff looked at Buster with his mouth open, wondering if the department had made a huge mistake in this young man. "You should have taken it to the forensics department," the sheriff said.

"I know," Buster said, "but I wanted to show you first."

"All right," the sheriff said, "then let's open it then,"

"Where, Sheriff?" Buster asked. "Well right…" The sheriff looked around his cluttered office. With papers everywhere, there certainly wasn't room for whatever was in the bag. The sheriff took his arm and with one motion swept the papers on his desk on the floor. "Here," he said and pointed at the spot he'd just cleared. Buster walked over to the desk, opened the bag, and poured its contents on the sheriff's desk.

In the bag where two nine-millimeter pistols, an AR-15 rifle, and another automatic rifle that the sheriff didn't recognize. "Well Buster," the Sheriff said, "it looks like you hit the jackpot." *Good*, the sheriff thought. He'd been after Red for three years; maybe he'd have something to charge him with. He should have been overjoyed, but something still didn't add up. *Red was too smart to leave weapons where they could be easily found unless he wanted them to be found or else*, the sheriff thought, *they weren't his.*

The sheriff sat down in his chair and leaned back in it. "Buster," the sheriff said, "go down to the Forensics department and bring back somebody to bag and tag this evidence," the sheriff said.

"Yes, sir," Buster said as he turned to walk out the office. Buster stopped before he exited and turned back to the sheriff. "What's wrong, sheriff?" Buster asked. "I did good, didn't I?"

The sheriff smiled. "Yeah, Buster," he said, "You did well. It's just that..."

"Yes?" Buster answered. "Where is the money?" the sheriff said. The sheriff got up and started to walk around his desk. "Dirty Red doesn't get involved with anything that doesn't involve or revolve around money," Sheriff Johnson said. "It's hard for me to think," he continued, "that here we have two murders and there's no money missing or no money found nowhere." The sheriff looked out his small office window. It was still warm outside but there had been some cool days, so winter was just around the corner. "Besides the question about the money," the sheriff said, "we really have nothing to tie Red and his crew to those murders. I mean you found shell casings in the yard, didn't you?" The sheriff asked Buster.

"Yes sir," he replied.

"Hell, he could have been telling the truth," Sheriff Johnson said as he shook his head. "I've got to have more than this. Those two boys' families are going to need answers and I'm gonna be able to tell them something other than what we think." The sheriff turned and looked at Buster. "Buster, you get back there and I want you to search until you find me some evidence tying Red and his crew to them murders, you hear me?," Buster nodded his head yes.

"Well, what you waiting on? Go on." The sheriff waved his hand at the door. Buster did not answer but turned and hurried out the door.

It was slow at The House, as Blu's place of business was sometimes called. It was near noon and most of his regulars where either sleep or at work, depending on their shift at the local auto parts supplier. Blu decided this was the perfect time to stock up at the liquor store so he had plenty of beer and liquor on hand for later that evening. People thought places like his sold moonshine but hell, moonshine cost more than regular liquor in the store so what's the point? Not to mention it was hard to make and he didn't have time for all that. I mean it just didn't make sense to fool with it. Sometimes guys would come by and give him a good deal on four or five gallons but he didn't care where the booze came from, just so it was there for his customers. Blu grabbed his keys, walked to the door, looked around, and making sure he hadn't forgotten anything, opened the door and *bam*, there she was: Gina. Gina was Bang Bang's mother. "Where you going, Blu?" she asked.

"Down to the liquor store, you wanna come?" he asked. Blu pushed past Gina, turned around, and locked the door behind him. He then turned his attention back to Gina.

Gina Tolbert was a big woman, around two hundred and sixty pounds, give or take twenty, and most of that was butt. She stood only five feet, five inches with short black hair, well at least today she was. You know women and their weaves and wigs. It could be shoulder length and red tomorrow. Not that it mattered. Most men, when they looked at Gina, automatically stopped at the butt. Not that she wasn't cute, but the way her hips went up and down, man it was something to see. The motion of her butt was known to give grown men seasickness. That's right, seasickness on dry land.

"Naw," she said. "I just wanted to know if you had heard anything from Bang."

"No," Blu said. He and his oldest son really hadn't spoken much in the last two years. Ever since, he took up with Red. Occasionally they'd see each other and nod but that was about it.

"Go down and see him Blu," Gina said. "You know how close you two once where. Maybe you two could patch things up and act like father and son again."

Blu looked at Gina and remembered the old days, Jerry Curls, fly guys and girls. Black folks where still calling each other brother back then. That was before hip-hop and crack hit, before gangs and drive-bys. Damn, he missed those days. "He'll be all right, Gina," Blu said. "He's a grown man now. He can take care of himself." Blu took Gina by the hand and walked toward his car, trying to focus on the present but no matter how hard he tried, he couldn't help but remember.

AUGUST 21, 1989

Blu was sitting on his bed. "Pass the joint man," Cheese Man said. "You gotta let the weed burn up man." Blu took a long draw on the marijuana cigarette, held the smoke in, and then passed the joint

to Cheese Man. Blu's head was spinning as he released the smoke in the air, resisting the urge to cough. Blu, Cheese Man, and Dogg were hanging out, shooting the shit, drinking a couple of brews, and smoking a blunt. "What's up, Blu?" Dogg said. "Are you gonna marry Gina or what?"

Blu shrugged his shoulders and then shook his head from side to side. "I don't know man, I just don't know."

Blu lay back on his bed. He was staying with his mom until he found something. He had worked at fast food joints all his life and wanted something better for himself. That was why he was going to go talk to an Army recruiter tomorrow. Suddenly, there was a knock on his bedroom door. He looked at Cheese Man and Dogg and they took the weed off the dresser and put it in a drawer. "Blu, you in there?" the voice asked.

"What?" Blu asked. "Go away," Blu said, "you're fucking with my high." Blu, Cheese Man, and Dogg laughed. Cheese Man passed what was left of the joint to Dogg. "I need to speak to you," the voice persisted. "Blu, I really need to talk to you."

Blu and the fellas knew who it was: Gina. Cheese Man and Dogg looked at each other and laugh. "Yo man," Cheese Man said, "we got to split anyway. Come on man." Cheese Man motioned to Dogg and the two got up to leave. They move to the door and open it. In walks Gina. "Hey Gina," Dogg says.

Gina threw up her hand and waved at Dogg and Cheese Man. "Hey," she said.

Dogg looked back at Blu as he exited the room. "See you later, Blu," he said as he shut the door. Blu adjusted his pillow as he looked at Gina. *Man oh man,* he thought. Gina was one fine girl and she was fire when it came to sex. She was everything a young man could want except Blu didn't want to commit. He figured he was too young and you couldn't pay any bills at a fast food place. "What's up baby?" he said.

"Blu," Gina said, "I need to tell you something." Blu looked at Gina and wondered what was going on. Blu and Gina had been together since high school and most of the time she had given him his space; this coming over and knocking on his door was unlike her. They usually got together in the evenings when the day was done. They would call each other through the day to profess their love and concern for each other, but their relationship was more of two friends rather than two people madly in love with each other. In fact, that was how they got together, he would tell her his problems with women and she would tell him her problems with men. It had only been in the last year or so that they had slept together.

"Blu, I don't know how to say this, but to say it: I'm pregnant."

Blu shook his head as the word "pregnant" filled his consciousness and the word echoed in his mind.

CHAPTER 5

Buster rushed through the sheriff department's front door with a cloth sack in his right hand. He headed toward the sheriff's office with a purpose. He had the evidence that was going to crack this case wide open. He got to the sheriff's office door and the door was closed. He paused, wondering if should wait until later or go in. *Go in*, he decided and he opened the sheriff's door to find the sheriff on the phone. "Sheriff," Buster said.

The sheriff raised his right hand and nodded at Buster. "I'm telling you, Chief," the sheriff said. "I don't want any drunks taking up space in my jail." The sheriffs eyes narrowed as he listened to the police chief on the other end of the telephone. He nodded his head up and down before answering. "I know, I know, but this is the situation. My jail is overcrowded and the budget's been cut. I can neither house nor feed any drunks at this time. He'll call his folks and have them pick him up and take him home. I don't care where you take him as long as it's not here,"

The Sheriff slammed the phone down angrily. He shook his head back and forth and took a moment to compose himself then looked up at Buster. "What you got, Buster?" he asked finally.

Buster held up the canvas bag he'd been carrying, "I've got the money, Sheriff." Suddenly, as if on cue, Deputy Oliver walked into the office with two or three manila folders in his hand. The sheriff looked at his other Deputy and said, "Well here's my other deputy." The sheriff smiled. "And just what have you got, Deputy?" the sheriff asked.

"Autopsy reports from the coroner's office, ballistics reports on the weapons, and some background reports on our victims," Deputy Oliver said.

The sheriff clapped his hands together and then slipped them down on his desk. "Finally," he said. "My deputies are on the ball," he said. "I just love it when the puzzle starts to come together," the sheriff

said, smiling. "Buster, you go first," the sheriff said. "You're so anxious, what have you got?"

Buster could hardly contain himself. "I found the money," Buster said, smiling and holding up the canvas bag in his right hand. "Out at the house," Buster said as he laid the canvas bag on the sheriffs cluttered desk.

The sheriff leaned forward in his chair and took the canvas bag and opened it. He looked inside then dumped the money on the desk. "Well, well, well," the Sheriff said, "let's see what we got here." On the desk was an assortment of ones, fives, tens, and twenty-dollar bills. They were folded together with rubber bands around them. "It looks to me," the sheriff said, leaning back in his chair and folding his hands behind his head, "that's probably five or six thousand dollars, what you think, Oliver?"

Deputy Oliver shrugged his shoulders and said, "Yeah, maybe?"

This here, Buster," the sheriff said, "is probably their change making money. All right, Oliver," the sheriff continued, "what have you got?"

Deputy Oliver stepped forward and laid two of the folders he was carrying on the sheriff's desk next to the money. He opened the other folder he'd been carrying and started to read from it. "First off, Sheriff," he began, "I have a little more information on our victims. Would it surprise you to know that both of our victims were at work last night? In fact," the deputy continued, "their time sheet at the plant they work in shows they both went to work last night and both punched out at the same time, which was about three hours after they died, according to the autopsy report." The sheriff leaned forward in his chair and, unfolding his hands from behind his head, picked up a pencil that was lying on his desk. "Also," the deputy continued as he laid that folder on the sheriff's desk and picked up another, "that strange looking automatic weapon we couldn't identify was a North Korean VZ-61 Scorpion Machine Pistol."

"A what?" the sheriff said.

"A North Korean VZ-61," the deputy answered. "Now how in the hell would three wood rats in Alabama get something like that?" the sheriff asked.

The sheriff's mind was racing now, trying to connect the dots but they weren't connecting. Finally, he said, "Oliver, are you sure those ballistics are right?"

Oliver nodded his head yes then added, "The shell casings we found in the yard…"

"Yes?" the sheriff said.

"Came from that weapon."

The sheriff was speechless. He went over the story that Red and his crew had told him in his mind. No way had he thought could they be telling the truth. There must have been something missing. "Buster," the sheriff said, "get that money over to the evidence locker and Oliver," the sheriff said, "I want all the info you can get on these victims. I mean I want attendance records, drug tests, and if there were any problems at work?"

"Yes, sir," the two deputies answered almost in unison as they headed for the office door, leaving Sheriff Johnson alone trying to figure out exactly what was going on in his small town.

A man walked down the center of the street as Jo Clearly pulled her car onto Fifth Street. The man was carrying a small paper bag as a dog followed him. Jo searched the house numbers for the address she was looking for. "Ah," she said, "there it is." Jo saw a stately Tudor home, freshly painted with a freshly cut lawn, probably the last cut of the season she thought since winter was fast approaching. The man on the street reached into his bag and took out two chicken wings and motioned for the dog to come and get it. The dog sniffed the air and came close but not close enough to take food from the man's hand so the man threw them on the ground and kept walking. Jo pulled into the drive and parked her car in the driveway, thinking how nice the houses were, especially in this part of town.

The dog approached the chicken wings laying on the ground, sniffed them, and, satisfied that this food was safe, picked them up with his mouth and started to trot off. Suddenly two young boys appeared and chased after the dog, forcing him to drop the bounty he just received. They quickly picked the chicken wings up off the asphalt and after splitting them between each of them, ate them.

Jo Clearly made her way down the freshly swept driveway and up to the front of the door. The house was located in the middle of this small town and dated back to the thirties when the town was more prosperous and when family farms dominated the landscape. Jo knocked at the door. She turned while waiting for someone to answer the door and looked at the two tall pecan trees loaded with nuts in the front yard. No answer. Jo turned back to the door and started to knock again, suddenly the door swung open and there was Constance Flowers standing in the door with a big smile on her face. "How you doing, Jo?" Constance said, grinning from ear to ear.

Jo knew Constance and her (she assumed) ex-husband, Frank, from the church and they said hi and bye every week at Sunday service. They talked and conversed with each other, but nothing in depth where they actually knew each other. Constance was not someone she confided in or visited; she was just a member of the congregation, that's all. Constance was a light-complexioned black woman with reddish gray hair that was also long, just like her daughter's. She liked to wear jeans since that was what Jo had seen her in most of the time around town. "Jo, how are you?" Constance asked, "Won't you come in?" Constance stood to the side and motioned for Jo to come in. Jo entered and saw papers, boxes of stuff, shoes, games, you name it, scattered around the house. *Oh no*, Jo thought, *a hoarder*. "You have to excuse the mess, but I haven't had time to clean up yet today," Jo smiled at Constance and thought today hadn't been there for years.

"Please, this way." Constance led Jo through a maze of tennis shoes, boxes of flea market goods and shoes laying on the floor, tablets and any other place that could hold junk. She stopped in what should be the living room and said, "RC." She paused. "Where are you? I have Jo Clearly with me, come here."

Jo thought to herself, *Who is RC*? But instead of asking the question, she decided to wait and see for herself.

"I'm fixing a sandwich," the reply from the other room came.

"I'm sorry, Jo," Constance said, "you know men, always feeding their faces." Jo nodded her head in agreement and smiled. She could hardly wait to see who this RC was.

"That's alright Constance," Jo replied. "I can wait a few minutes."

"Here." Constance motioned with her hand. "Have a seat."

Jo looked at the place Constance was pointing to and saw magazines and newspapers all over and shook her head no. "That's alright," Jo said. "I think I'll just stand."

Finally, RC made his entrance. *Damn*, Jo thought, *it's Reverend Clark from the church. I know this isn't her new man? Wasn't he already married?* In a T-shirt and jeans and with clearly a full week's worth of hair growth on his face, he hardly looked the part of a preacher, more along the lines of a blue-collar worker. Reverend Clark spoke. "Hello Josephine, been a while? I've missed you on Sundays," he said and started laughing.

He should laugh, Jo thought, *why in the world would I spend my Sundays listening to someone like him?* Constance laughed also, in full support of her husband. "I'm sorry that I came by out of the blue," Jo said, getting down to business. "It's about your daughter, Nikki."

Constance looked at RC, then at Jo. "What is it this time?" she said. "That girl is always acting out, she is always acting out. Ever since her father and I separated, she's just been trouble." Constance looked off in the distance and started twirling her hair. *She's nervous*, Jo thought. She didn't know the whole story, why Constance and her husband had separated, where RC fit in. Jo had heard rumors, but thought at the time, what did that have to do with her? Nothing, she concluded and had steered away from it. Besides she wasn't here to fuel the local gossip; she was here because she wanted to try and save this young girl who so reminded her of herself.

Jo continued, "There was an incident in school the other day where…" Jo paused before continuing, "Nikki was caught having oral sex at school with another student."

Constance's jaw dropped about two feet and she looked at RC and him at her. Reverend Clark seemed to sense what was going to happen and pulled Constance toward him. Constance jerked away and buried her face in her hands and started to sob. *Like mother, like daughter*, Jo thought. "Her and boys," Constance said between sobs. "I knew it was going to happen, but in school?" Constance continued to sob.

"Excuse me, Constance," Jo said, fearing what was going to happen next. "It was another female student, not a male student."

Constance looked up and stopped crying. *Here it comes*, Jo thought. "A what? Another female student? Are you kidding me? Are you kidding me?" Constance looked at RC with her hands outstretched and almost begged him when she said, "I'm not having it! I'm not having some faggot child living under my roof. When she gets home, I'm going to beat that—"

"Wait a minute Connie," Jo said. "There will be no beating of any kind. I'm here because I have to inform you about it. Not to get that child beat. We are all grown here! There is absolutely no reason for any type of violence and if there is, there will consequences." Jo looked at Constance and made sure she was following her and had not shut down with embarrassment or anger. "I'm here," Jo said, "to get to the bottom of the problem."

Constance looked at RC and said, "What do you mean 'bottom of the problem'?" Constance said.

Reverend Clark raised his hand and looked at Jo. "She means," he said. "If we, that you and I are the problem? Isn't that right, Jo?" Jo didn't answer. Instead, she observed how Constance and RC interacted, the way he comforted and held her.

Finally, Jo said, "Please don't misunderstand me. I'm not here to accuse or assign blame to anyone." Jo paused before continuing," I'm here to try and find out why such a pretty and talented young lady such as Nikki is, shall we say, underperforming?"

Constance straightened up in her seat and stopped sobbing. She looked at RC who squashed her hand for support. "Constance, has there any changes recently in Nikki's life that could explain her actions?"

Constance looked down before looking up at Jo. She swallows and takes a deep breath before saying. "I don't know if you know Jo," Constance begins, "but her father and I have separated and I have filed for divorce. If it hadn't been for the reverend here," she paused as she looked lovingly at Reverend Clark, "I just don't know what would have happened." The Reverend Clark smiled at Constance then looked at Jo.

"You see Jo," he began, "Mrs. Flowers, because of my council and my own problems with my marriage, and I have moved in together

and are contemplating a life together, but Nikki and what she does?" The Reverend shook his head.

Suddenly Constance said, "There's nothing wrong with a good old-fashioned ass whooping, Jo. If I would have come home and my mother had found out I was having sex with somebody at school! And a female student as well? My mother would have whipped my natural born…"

"We don't do things like that anymore Constance," Jo interjected. "Your daughter has a future and you don't want to destroy it by beating her to death!" Jo almost shouted at Constance as she feels the blood rush to her head. She was becoming angry at Constance and her attitude. She acted as if the girl was purposely trying to hurt her. *Well*, Jo thought as she tried to calm down, *maybe she was*. "I think what needs to happen," Jo said, "is that you and Nikki," Jo said, looking at the reverend and Constance, "need to just sit down and talk and come to some kind of understanding of what you expect of her and what she needs from you."

Reverend Clark and Constance looked at each other and shook their heads in agreement. "Yes, Jo," the reverend said, "I think you're right. We need to talk to Nikki."

Good, Jo thought. *Maybe I'm getting through to them.* "Alright then," Jo said as she smiled at the reverend and Constance. "I have to go and fix dinner for my son."

Jo turned to leave and headed toward the door. Constance said, "I'm sorry you couldn't stay longer, Jo, maybe next time?"

Jo looked over her shoulder as she reached the door and turned the doorknob. "Yes, Constance, maybe next time." Jo opened the door and started to leave but turned around to face Constance and Reverend Clark before she left. "I just want you to know that I'm available anytime so don't hesitate to call, okay?" With that, Jo stepped through the door and walked toward her car, turning once again to wave at the couple and say goodbye.

When Jo entered her car door, Reverend Clark closed the door and looked at Constance. "Nikki!" he shouted. The reverend started back toward the living room.

"RC, don't," Constance said.

"That little bitch!" he shouted. "She's been hustling on the side, she better have me some money. I know that!" He stormed toward the back of the house while Constance looked at him with a worried look on her face.

CHAPTER 6

Sheriff Johnson looked through the reports on his desk. This was one aspect of his job that he didn't particularly like, but was probably the most important: the monthly budget. The state and the people of Tallapoosa County demanded and expected to know how much of and for what every tax dollar was spent. There hadn't been the slightest rumble of any misspending in the sheriff's office since he took over and he planned on keeping it that way. He picked up one of the forms on his desk and read it. "Use of federal grant 114.7 for county purchases," he said softly. He shook his head and looked at the rest of the stuff on his desk. It was overflowing with paperwork with no end in sight.

Suddenly, he heard a knock on his office door. "Come on in," he said. In walked Mayor Bill Heard of the city of Freedom Fine, Alabama, where the murders took place. It was a small town with one gas station, one convenience store, one stoplight, but it was a whole lot of trouble. Nearly a third of the sheriff's department calls were either from there or involved making a trip there. For a small poor country town, it was one big problem and at the head of the trouble list was Mayor Bill Heard.

Mayor Heard was a fine man, but was prone to blow things out of proportion. He also somehow thought that the sheriff answered to him, which, of course, he didn't so this should be an interesting conversation, Sheriff Johnson thought. "How you doing, Sheriff?" Mayor Heard said, smiling and holding out his hand. Sheriff Johnson stood up from behind his desk and extended his hand and the two men shook hands firmly.

The Sheriff returned the smile and said, "Just fine, Mayor." The two men let their hands fall to their side as they finished shaking hands. The sheriff pointed to a chair across from his desk and motioned for the Mayor to take a seat. "Have a seat, Mayor," Sheriff Johnson said. The mayor and sheriff both took a seat.

The chair the Mayor sat in engulfed his slight one hundred seventy-six-pound frame. The large wooden chair swallowed him, making him look much smaller than he was. The mayor crossed his legs as he sat back in the chair and began the conversation. "Just wondering, Sheriff, were you on this here murder investigation?" The mayor looked down at his right hand as he rubbed his fingers together. "You know, Sheriff, it's getting to be election time and I need to stay on top of things as do you." The mayor looked up from his hand and looked Sheriff Johnson in the eye. "You know I run a law and order town, a hard working, Christian town and I—"

"Excuse me, Mayor," the sheriff said. "But we're moving as fast as we can on this and—" The sheriff looked out his office door and he saw Buster and one of the sheriff's department secretaries laughing and joking at her desk. The sheriff got up and walked across his office to the office door. "Buster," the sheriff called.

Buster stopped laughing and, with a smile still on his face, turned and looks at the sheriff. The smile quickly faded as he straightened up and ran over to the sheriff. "Yes, sir," Buster said.

"Go ahead and clock out," the sheriff said. "You put in a lot of hours, last night and today. I don't need the county auditors looking into overtime pay. Understand?."

"Okay, Sheriff," Buster said as he turned to walk away. "And Buster," the sheriff said. "You did a fine job out there today. A fine job."

Buster turned back around with a smile on his face from ear to ear. "Thanks, Sheriff," he said. He turned and walked away, waving at the secretary as he walked toward the sheriff department's entrance. The sheriff scratched his head and smiled as he turned and headed back to his office. He entered the office and looked at Mayor Heard. "Sorry about that, Mayor," the sheriff said as he headed back to his seat. "Just a little bit of administrative work."

Suddenly, Deputy Oliver appeared at his office door with some more files in his hand. "Sheriff?" Oliver said as he stepped inside the office. "Come on in, Oliver, you know the Mayor, don't you?" Sheriff Johnson said. Oliver nodded his head yes. "Well, what have you got for me?"

"The autopsy reports came in and…" Oliver began as he handed the reports to the sheriff.

"And?" The sheriff said as he opened the autopsy reports.

"Both our victims were killed by a twenty-two caliber gun." The sheriff slammed the reports on his desk and said, "So that means them boys didn't kill 'em."

The mayor, who had been sitting quietly in his chair, jumped up and said, "Now what is exactly going on here, Sheriff?"

"Hold it, Mayor, will you just hold it? I'm trying to figure things out here," the sheriff said angrily. This was the last thing he needed he thought, the mayor and evidence that didn't add up. "A twenty-two caliber gun?" the sheriff asked, sitting back in his chair. "What else you got, Oliver?"

"Well, sir," Oliver began, "it's the time record of our two victims, sir."

"Well save me some time, Oliver," the sheriff said.

"What does it say?" Mayor Heard interjected.

Sheriff Johnson looked harshly at the mayor. "Mayor Heard," the Sheriff said. "This is my office and that is my deputy, not yours, okay!"

"I mean Sheriff…" the mayor stammered.

"Go ahead Oliver," the sheriff said as he motioned for him to continue.

"Well for the last three months," Deputy Oliver started, seemingly unfazed by the conflict between the Sheriff and the mayor. "They both clocked out on Tuesdays at 8:45 and didn't return to work until 10:20 p.m."

"What?" the sheriff asked. "I thought they only got forty-five minutes for lunch, maybe an hour."

"They only get thirty minutes," Deputy Oliver said, "but their shift supervisor okays it."

"Why in the world," Sheriff Johnson said, "would these two guys take long lunches on Tuesdays and the shift supervisor would sign off on it? What about the other days of the week?" The sheriff asked. "Where they both there at the same time? Where they both in the same department?"

"Yes and no," Deputy Oliver said. "They both were there at the same time but they weren't in the same department."

The Sheriff rubbed his chin. "Well gentlemen," he said as he looked at the mayor. "It seems we have a little bit of a puzzle going on right here."

Jo Clearly checked on the meatloaf cooking in the oven, then at the time on the kitchen clock. "Well just a few minutes more," she said. She suddenly turned as she heard the squeak coming from the front door when it opened. *My, he's early*, she thought as she called out, "Buster, that you?" She very rarely locked the front door. After all, it was still a small town and everybody knew everybody and she felt safe here.

No answer.

Jo put her oven mitt on the kitchen table, turns and starts walking toward the kitchen door. Suddenly, Nikki Flowers appeared in the doorway with a knot on her forehead the size of a small egg. It was just above her right eye and Jo could tell she had been crying. "You just had to say something," Nikki said.

Jo, still studying the knot on Nikki's head, said, "Nikki, I don't…" Before she could finish, Nikki turned and walked back out the kitchen doorway. Jo followed. "Nikki," she said as she followed her toward the front door. Nikki didn't say anything as she reached the front door and grabbed the handle. Jo reached the front door before Nikki and held it shut with her right hand as Nikki tried to open the door. Nikki jerked her arm back and turned and looked at Jo with hatred in her eyes. "What happened, Nikki?" Jo asked.

"What did you expect, huh?" Nikki said. Jo looked at Nikki with a puzzled expression on her face as she tried to figure out what's going on. "You told him," Nikki said.

Oh, she thought as she began to realize what Nikki had been trying to tell her all along. It was the Reverend Clark that was the problem. "Reverend Clark," Jo said as Nikki nodded her head yes and started crying. Jo moved toward her and put her arm around her, trying to comfort her. Jo pulled her close and started stroking Nikki's long red hair and remembered. Remembers when she was a young girl and her uncle. She remembered how he forced himself on her, how she got pregnant, and how she vowed that no man would ever force himself or control her again. Yes she remembered…

It was 6:30 in the evening at a kimbap restaurant on Eastern Boulevard in Montgomery, Alabama. Jung-Hoon li was enjoying his dinner of bulgogi and cabbage kimichi in this small restaurant on the east side of Montgomery. He hadn't eaten in the past two days and was starving. He had fled here after the incident and was headed to board a flight back home, back home to his wife and two children, and the trouble he found himself in. He hoped by going to Montgomery instead of Atlanta he could avoid the authorities and more importantly, his handlers. They would be looking for answers to questions he didn't have the answer to and they didn't take excuses lightly, so retreat was the best option, at least for him. With the advent of two Korean car manufacturers relocating to Alabama and just over the border in Georgia, there had sprung up a slew of Korean restaurants and businesses to cater to the increasing Korean population in the area. Jung-Hoon had lived here in Alabama for three years and was paid a decent sum of ten thousand per month as plant manager at the Korean parts manufacturer he had signed on with.

It was enough to live on and he sent most of it back home to South Korea to his wife and two children, one boy, one girl. His missed them greatly but the expense of traveling to his homeland, twenty-eight hundred dollars round trip, was very expensive so he only saw them at Christmas because of the expense. It was a decent wage but there were other things that got him in trouble.

He took a drink of the strong Korean tea to wash down his meal when suddenly he felt a hand on his shoulder from behind. Jung-Hoon placed his tea mug on the table and turned. "My old friend, Jung," the man flanked by two other men said. "How are you?" Jung looked at the middle-aged man of Korean descent and at first didn't recognize him. "Of course, my old friend," the man said, "you haven't forgotten me?"

Jung Looked and *No*, he thought, *it couldn't be. But yes it was*. It was the captain from so long ago. Jung looked around the restaurant, making sure he wasn't dreaming. This wasn't North Korea, was it?

"May I sit down?" the captain asked.

Jung-Hoon got up from the table and bowed and motioned for the captain to sit. "Yes, yes," he said. "Please sit." The captain pulled out a chair and sat while the two other men stood to the side. Jung-Hoon returned to his chair and sat down, nervously looking at the captain

and smiling. "Perhaps you don't remember me, so let me introduce myself," the captain said, "Colonel Woo-Sung Li."

Oh no, Jung-Hoon thought, *they've found me.* The colonel picked up a menu and started flipping through it. "Aw," the colonel said. "Such good food they serve here in the US, don't you think?" Jung-Hoon shook his head yes. "Oh but I remember when such niceties where scarce. Don't you, Jung?" Jung-Hoon's smile faded as he started to remember things he had forgotten, things he had forgotten on purpose so as to never think of such things again.

CHAPTER 7

DECEMBER 7, 2003
PYONGYANG, NORTH KOREA

Jung-Hoon walked quickly through the snow as he headed to his next class. Having been a student at the prestigious Pyongyang University of Science and Technology for the last year, he knew the importance of being on time. Though only sixteen years old, he knew that this was an opportunity that he could not waste, so the things of childhood were long left behind as he thought only of his studies and the privilege to serve the great leader. He hurried past the statue of the great Kim Jong-il on the main yard toward his next class. "Excuse me, excuse me," a man with a fur cap called to him. Jung-Hoon, having no time to waste, ignored him as he hurried to class. "Excuse me, excuse me," the man said again as Jung-Hoon looked back at him. What does he want? Jung wondered as he was stopped by a large man in his path. The man pointed back at the other man and Jung, not wanting any trouble, turned and looked at him.

"Jung-Hoon Li?" the man asked. Jung shook his head yeas as he moved toward him. "How delightful," the man said as Jung came face to face with him. The man had a thick black mustache and long black hair. He had a scar over his left eye and wore the uniform of captain in the military. The military here was not surprising or shocking as it would be in western countries. Most of the students, as well as their instructors, were in the military but Jung-Hoon wasn't and he mostly steered clear of them.

"Here, take a seat," the man said as he himself sat on one of the benches along the walkway. The man sat down and motioned for Jung to join him, all the while smiling. Jung-Hoon sat next to man and looked down as his feet. "I know you don't know me," the man said, "but I know you. In fact..." Jung-Hoon looked up at the man next to him as he reached into his pocket and pulled out a pack of cigarettes. He peeled open the pack and took one from it, put it in his mouth, and lit it, taking a deep drag on it. "I have been watching you for a long time," the man said as he released the smoke from his lungs. "In fact, you could say I am the one responsible for you being here." The man spread his arm in a sweeping motion from left to right and smiles. Jung-Hoon eyed the man suspiciously. He had worked hard as a student and had never seen this man a day before in his life, so why should he believe him?

The man started to shake his finger and laugh. "I know what you're thinking," he said. "How do you know that I'm telling you the truth?" The man took another drag on his cigarette and then flicked it away into the snow. He got up from the bench and started walking back and forth in front of Jung. "You were born in the city of Chongjin," he began, "fourth of five children," Jung looked at this man intently as he continued. "In your fourth year, you showed an aptitude for languages, so you were advanced to the sixth and seventh grade level, which brings me to the present." The man stopped and looked directly at Jung. "Do you think that what you have done to this point has been because of you or because of the great leader?" he asked.

Jung bowed his head as he contemplated what to say. He knew the wrong answer could lead to a lifetime of poverty of hunger. "The great leader," he said.

"Good, good," the man said. "You have passed the first test."

Jung waited for the next move. He was not naïve. He knew that him being poor Song-bun had navigated through school, through life, were more privileged classes were denied. "The great leader," the man said, "has determined that great things lay ahead for you, so…"

The man said, "You will be transported to the south to serve the great leader. To this end you will not be in contact with anyone including your family. Do you understand?" The man reached into his pocket and pulled out his pack of cigarettes and pulled one from the pack and placed sit in his mouth. Jung nodded his head yes as the man lit his cigarette and took a deep draw. "Good," he said. "You will leave immediately with instructions to follow." Jung got up from the bench. "Follow this gentleman," the man said. "You will be informed along the way of what the great leader requires." The man took another draw on his cigarette and then flung it into the snow. Jung

turned to walk away, then suddenly turned back and said, "Please… what is your name?"

"My name," the man said, "is of no importance. Our only mission or goal is to serve our great leader." With that, Jung turned and followed the large man standing to the side to his future, whatever that was.

"So I see, you do remember me?" Colonel Woo-Sung said. The colonel smiled and reached into his pocket and pulled out a pack of cigarettes. He took one from the pack and held it his hand. "Well," he said, "as they say in America, let's get down to business." Colonel Woo-sung didn't light the cigarette but instead taped it on the table slowly. "It has come to my attention that we have some trouble, yes?" the colonel asked, looking at Jung-Hoon.

Jung-Hoon looked around the restaurant, looking to escape but found that the two men with the colonel had the escape routes covered. "We had a slight problem last night, Sir."

"Yes, I hear," the colonel said, still taping his cigarette.

"What about the payment?" he asked.

"I don't know, I…" Colonel Woo-sung looked at Jung-Huon with a cold empty stare.

"Nobody showed up last night," the colonel said. "It makes us think, that maybe…" The colonel put the cigarette to his lips. "But no," the colonel took the cigarette from his lips and smiled. "You wouldn't do that would you?" he asked.

"Do what?" Jung-Hoon said.

"Take our money and just run?"

"No, No, I wouldn't," Jung-Hoon said, frantic.

"I know you wouldn't," the colonel said and this time reached into his other pocket and took out a cigarette lighter. "But what about the girl?" he asked as he lit the cigarette, taking a deep draw of it to which he immediately coughed. He coughed for a couple of seconds before a waitress came over to the table.

"I'm sorry sir," she said, "but there's no smoking in the restaurant."

Colonel Woo-Sung bowed his head and said, "I'm sorry" as he threw the cigarette on the restaurant floor. "I didn't know." He smiled as the waitress frowned at the cigarette smoldering on the floor.

The colonel, realizing what he had just done, got up and picked the cigarette up off the floor and motioned for one of the men to come and get it. The man blocking the entrance came forth and as he bent down to pick it up. *Now's my chance*, Jung-Hoon thought as he jumped up from the table and rushed past the man picking up the cigarette. The man looked at the colonel who smiled and reached into his pocket again, drawing out a wad of American bills. He motioned for the waitress to come to him. "I'm sorry, ma'am," he said, "but I would like to pay you for our inconvenience and for my friends meal if I could." He said this as he peeled off two one hundred dollar bills. The waitress smiled and took the money, while the colonel put the money back into his pocket and looked at his men and nodded his head up and down.
    Buster walked into his house and looked at his mother, Jo, hugging and stroking the hair of a young girl on the couch in the living room. Not knowing what was going on, he grunted, letting his mother know he was there. Jo looked up and saw Buster and nodded her head to the side, motioning for Buster to leave them alone. She mouthed the words "Dinner's ready in the kitchen" silently as Buster gave her the sign up and moved through the room and toward the kitchen. Nikki turned her head and followed him with her eyes, as he entered the kitchen. She pulled back from Jo and they both sat there for a few seconds eyeing each other. Jo spoke first.
    "Nikki," she said, "I once knew a man like that, abusive. In fact..." Jo moved close so that she could whisper. "It was Buster's father." Nikki's eyes lit up as she stared at Jo. "I vowed then," Jo said, "to never let a man abuse me physically or mentally, you understand don't you?"
    Nikki nodded and smiled, happy to have found someone who might understand. "How did you stop him? I mean the man," Nikki asked.
    "The only way you can: a swift kick in the balls." Jo did an upward motion with her right arm as Nikki laughed. Buster came back into the living room with a plate of food in his hands. Jo stood up and walked over to him and grabbed him by the arm as he chewed on some food. "Nikki, this is my son, Buster."
    Buster nodded his head up as he continued to chew and swallow so he could speak. "Hi Nikki," he finally said.

Nikki smiled and with her head down said, "I remember you from school."

"Yeah, right," Buster said. "You had to be in the fourth or fifth grade when I was in high school,"

Nikki laughed and said, "You're not that much older than me."

"Sorry to interrupt," Jo said, "but Nikki and I were having a serious conversation so…"

Buster, seeing that his mother wanted to get rid of him, said, "I'll see my way out then." Buster smiled at Nikki and turned and walks down the hallway toward his room.

Jo smiled and took a seat back down on the couch next to Nikki. Jo looked at Nikki and said, "You know, Nikki, we could have child services look into—"

"No, No, No," Nikki said, "they won't do nothing but take me someplace and put me around people I don't know and someplace I don't wanna be."

Nikki grabbed Jo by the hands and said, "Please don't, Miss Josephine, please don't!"

Jo looked at Nikki and decided to just let this thing just play itself out. She could always intervene if the situation became too critical. If she called child services, the girl was right, there was no telling where she would end up. "Okay, okay, don't worry," Jo said, smiling. "We'll just play it by ear and see how it goes, okay?"

Nikki's face burst into a big smile as she jumped off the couch and headed toward the door. Jo got up and follows her trying to keep up with this bundle of energy. "Nikki," Jo said as they reach the door. "The reverend is not abusing you or having sex with you, is he?"

Nikki turned and looked at Jo with a quizzical look on her face. "Oh no," she said. "Why would you think that? He just tries to be strict that's all."

Nikki opened the door and headed out lightning fast but Jo was right behind her. *This girl*, Jo thought, *what is it with her or she thinks is she being played*? Nikki suddenly stopped and whirls around and put both arms around Jo and hugged her. Jo, surprised, said, "Well, Nikki" as Nikki hugged her hard. Nikki pulled back from Jo and before Jo could react planted a passionate kiss on Jo's lips.

Jo was shocked, but didn't pull away as Nikki tried to tongue her. Nikki finally pulled back and looked at her and smiled. She then turned and as she was walking away said, "Thank you, Miss Josephine." She lept down the steps and then ran down the sidewalk. Jo, still in shock, touched her lips, then turned and entered the house, closing the door.

Jung-Hoon looked at the GPS navigation screen in his car. *Good*, he thought, *they won't know where to find me.* He headed down Interstate 65 toward Birmingham. He would drive to Birmingham, he thought, and catch a flight there. They wouldn't think of looking for him there. *I wonder how they found me in the first place*, he thought. No matter, maybe they had been watching him. Well there was no maybe to it; they had to be watching him, he thought. And the more he thought about it, they had probably been watching, controlling him all his life. The state didn't leave anything to chance. He looked at the gas gauge on his car and saw a little less than a quarter tank.

He was going to have to stop and get gas if he was going to make it to Birmingham, he thought. He looked at the exit sign coming up on his right. "Exit 34, Bay Minette," it read. He saw the gas symbol on the sign and decided this would be a good place to stop. Small town, hardly anyone around, he would gas up quickly and leave. No problem. The sign said three miles away. He would be there in no time. His mind drifted as he thought about his time in America. At first he was excited; the opportunity to go to a new place but the long hours at the plant and the other duties he had become expected to perform had worn on him. He had become lonely, isolated. He missed his wife and family, though arranged by the state as part of his cover. He had fallen in love with his wife and he adored his two children. That was part of the reason he had been drawn to the young women in that small town. She provided a distraction, an outlet for him and yes she was beautiful. The exit was less than one mile away and he started to slow his vehicle down. He didn't want to miss this exit because the next exit might be ten miles or more up the road so he needed to focus, not let his mind wander.

Many thoughts raced through Jung-Huon's head as he turned off the interstate and onto the exit ramp. He looked at the sign showing where the gas station was and see he had two choices, one to the left and one to the right. He'd take the one to the right that would be fastest. He came to a stop at the bottom of the exit ramp and made a turn toward the right and seen the gas station sitting on the right. He pulled into the service station and came to a stop at the gas pump closest to the door of the gas station. He turned off the car and got out. He looked around and saw no one, so he decided to go in and pay for the gas instead of at the pump.

It was nine o'clock at night and Jung-Hoon was surprised that the gas station was still open since most of these small town gas stations closed up early, so he was fortunate, he thought—very fortunate, he thought, to be alive with the people he was dealing with. The state didn't take failure lightly or at all and he, for all practical purposes, was a failure. Jung-Hoon walked toward the front door and walked in. The clerk, a black woman in her thirties, was heavyset with short hair and large hoop earrings. She was dark and her hair was short and dyed black and red.

"Hello," she said as he walked toward the counter. Jung-Hoon nodded his head as the women said, "What can I do for you?"

"Just gas," Jung-Hoon said as he reaches into his pocket and pulled out his wallet. He took out one of his credit cards and handed it to her.

"How much?" she asked as she chewed on some gum. "Twenty," Jung-Hoon said. He didn't see the need to get anymore. He was going to leave the car at the airport and he wasn't coming back so no need to fill it up.

The woman took the card and asked, "Credit or debit?"

"Credit," he said as he looked around the store. It was stocked full of snacks and cold drinks in the coolers but he wasn't hungry, having just eaten at the restaurant. The woman ran his credit card and handed it back to him as she waited for the receipt to print. Jung-Hoon waited patiently as the woman tore off the receipt and handed him a pen and paper to sign. Jung quickly signed and handed her back the recipe. "Thank you now," the woman said as she smiled, revealing two gold front teeth as Jung turned while raising his hand to say goodbye.

"Bye," he said as he headed out the door toward the gas pump.

It was a cool night and Jung-Hoon thought that maybe he should put on a jacket. He got to the pump and started to pick up the hose

but remembered he hadn't pressed the gas cover so he headed to the driver's side door instead. He grabbed the door, when suddenly he felt a sharp pain across his shoulders as he lurched forward. He tried to catch himself on the door but fell on the ground. He was immediately kicked in the ribs and he moved his arm to his side as he recoiled in pain. He rolled over on his back as tried to identify his attackers and saw Colonel Un and his two associates. Colonel Un smiled as he said, "You disappoint me greatly, Jung Huon" as both of the men with him reached down and pulled him up from the ground.

Jung Hoon was paralyzed with fear as the colonel reached into his pocket and pulled out his pack of cigarettes. He pulled one from the pack and lit it and inhaled, coughing. Instead of putting the cigarette out, he held it in his hand as he looked at Jung-Hoon. "You think we are fools?" the Colonel asked as he continued to hold the cigarette. "You can never escape us. You were implanted with a tracking device the moment you were smuggled into the south and you have always been under surveillance. Do you think our great leader a fool to risk so much on you?" The colonel's eyes narrowed as Jung-Hoon breathed deeply, still writhing in pain from the blows he received. He looked back at the store and saw the girl looking out the window. *Good*, he thought. *Maybe she will call the police.* The colonel followed his eyes to the window and motioned for one of his men to take care of the woman in the store. He released his grip on Jung-Hoon as the other man grabbed his arms and pinned them behind his back. "I'm afraid, Jung-Hoon, there's no escape for you, you'd best corporate, No," the colonel said.

Jung-Hoon, afraid and in pain, could not believe the situation that he found himself in. He thought of his wife and two children and what would become of them if something happened to him. He thought of his family back in North Korea and how he may never see them again.

Jung-Hoon nodded his head up and down and said, "Yes, yes," as the man that went in the store came back out. He looked at the colonel and nodded his head, signaling that the situation was handled. "Good," the colonel said as the cigarette continued to burn in his right hand. "Where is the money?" the colonel asked. Jung-Hoon shook his head from side to side. "I don't know where, I swear," he said as the colonel

signaled to the man who just came out of the store to move closer. The man took the gas pump from its cradle and started pouring gasoline onto Jung-Hoon. The cold gasoline sent a chill through Jung's body as he realized what was about to happen. "No, no, please don't," Jung-Hoon said as he begged for his life. "Now, now," the colonel said as he took a puff on the cigarette. The embers on the cigarette glowed as the colonel once again coughed.

"I have given my life to the state," Jung-Hoon pleaded. "I have done everything asked of me," Jung-Hoon said as he gagged at the taste of gasoline seeping into his mouth.

"You have," the colonel said, "but where is the money?"

"I tell you I don't know," Jung-Hoon shouted. "I just don't know!" Jung-Hoon broke down sobbing. He was not the crying type but now faced with his demise over something he had little or no control over left him feeling helpless and desperate.

"No need to worry Jung-Hoon," the colonel said, "maybe what you say is true. Maybe not. But you are, as you say, a good asset." The cigarette had almost burned to the end but the colonel continued to hold it. "I must, however, ask about the girl," the colonel said.

"The girl?" Jung-Hoon repeated. Jung-Hoon thought of the girl who befriended him, who gave him comfort when he needed it. Surely she didn't have anything to do with the money. "We are friends," Jung-Hoon said, "that's all."

The colonel leaned closer to Jung-Hoon, only inches from his face. "Do you think we can walk away from a half million dollars after all the state, the leader, has done for you?"

Jung-Hoon dropped his head. "No," he said.

"Well then what do you purpose we do about this then?" the colonel asked. Jung-Hoon knew that the answer he gave next could either save his life or end it. He took a deep breath and said, "We find the girl and question her."

The colonel stepped back and laughed. "Of course, of course, why didn't I think of that? In fact, that's exactly what we will do." The colonel motioned for the man holding Jung-Hoon to let him go. The man released his grip and Jung-Hoon dropped to the ground. The colonel turned and started to walk away.

"What about me?" Jung-Hoon asked as the two men with the colonel walk past him.

The colonel turned and with one flick of his finger, sent the last of the still burning cigarette in Jung-Hoon's direction. The cigarette ignited the gasoline poured earlier on Jung-Hoon. Jung-Hoon screamed as the flames shot up around him, engulfing him in flame. He tried to roll and put out the fire but it only makes it worse. Through the pain he could hear the colonel's final words to him. "Yes," he said, "what about you?"

CHAPTER 8

Sheriff Johnson walked in the front door of his modest three-bedroom ranch style house. Sitting on five acres, he had enough room and space to where he could relax and not have to worry too much about his neighbors. Heck, his nearest neighbor was half a mile away and he was an old retiree with too many cats.

"Hey babe," he called out. "I'm here," he said as he walked in and closed the door. He looked around the neatly kept house and not seeing the television on, he began to wonder where his family is. He walked through the great room and to the hall leading to the bedrooms past the kitchen. While passing the kitchen, he saw his wife and youngest daughter sitting quietly at the kitchen table. He knew they heard him calling out. *Uh oh*, he thought, *something's wrong*. He stuck his head cautiously through the door. He glanced at the clock on the wall, 7.30 p.m., and thought, *Well I'm not that late, and so it's not me*. Before he spoke, he took one final read on his wife and daughter, both of them silent, looking away from each other.

"Hello, my two beautiful women, what's up?" he says smiling trying to lighten the mood. "The television's not on and you two look like someone died, what's going on? Joyce, Lilly," he said as leaned against the kitchen door. Lilly, his wife of twenty years, looked at him. Because of his work, he saw his wife less than he wanted these last few years, but he still loved her as much now as he did when they first dated in high school, him with his high tops and her in those jeans. She could still wear those jeans and it was a miracle to him that after all these years, she had still kept her figure. Twenty years, three children, and enough ramekin noodle nights to last a lifetime. She certainly didn't marry him for his money and she had stuck with him through thick and thin, so he knew when she was worried and this was one of those times. "Our youngest daughter here," Lilly said, "got sent home from school today."

"Is that so?," Sheriff Johnson said.

"Yes," Lilly said and got up from the kitchen table. "It seems she and another girl were caught having sex behind the gym bleachers."

Sheriff Jonson looked at his wife to make sure she wasn't joking and then at his little girl with her head held down. She was just entering her teen years when kids experimented with all kinds of things to find themselves. Heck, as a teenager he did it. He drank, smoked weed, even tried cocaine, but he didn't expect this. His first thought was to be angry and come down hard on her, but from all his years in police work he knew better.

How many kids had he locked up who had rebelled against their parents and spent their lives in jail, when a little patience and understanding would have gone a long way in fixing their problems? He wouldn't come down hard on her, get angry, or panic, and make the situation worse. Instead, he would listen. "Well young lady," he said. "What happened at school today?"

Joyce looked into the table, never moving her head. "Nothing," she said, "Nothing really." Sheriff Johnson, with both of his hands on the table, leaned over the table.

Lilly looked at her husband, then her at her daughter. "You call having oral sex with another girl at school nothing?" she asked.

"Yeah, I guess so?"

"Joyce," the sheriff said as he got down on one knee in front of her and laid his left hand on top of hers. "Joyce, you know how your mother and I feel about you." The sheriff looked at his wife. "To us, it was only yesterday that we were helping you slide down the jungle gym in the park. I just want you to know that—"

Joyce looked up from the table and looks directly into her father's eyes. "That you love me?" Joyce said. "

Well yes," the sheriff stammered.

"She said that you would say that," Joyce said.

"Who, what?" the sheriff said.

"The girl at school. The other girl," Joyce said. She stood up, pulling away from her father. She turned around with her back to her father and her mother. "It was nothing dad, see it was a bet," Joyce said, "Nikki said that if we got into trouble, that would be the first thing you'd say, how much you loved me."

The sheriff stood up, all six feet, five inches of him. His eyes narrowed as he grew angry. *A bet? A bet about how much he cared and loved his own flesh and blood*? "You mean you and this girl had a bet about what I'd say if you got into trouble? Is that what I'm understanding, Joyce?" the sheriff asked.

Joyce sat back down at the kitchen table. "You see, Dad, me and some friends were listening to some music at lunch, when Nikki..."

"Who's Nikki, baby?" he asked as he looked at his wife.

"The other girl at school," she said, "the one that went down on me."

Lilly interrupted, "Okay, okay."

The sheriff waved both of his arms and said, "You listen to a couple of songs then what?"

"Nikki said that if we did that and we got into trouble, that you'd get us out of it, that nothing would happen to us."

Sheriff Johnson looked at his wife with his eyes wide and with his hands on his hips. He looked at his wife then his daughter and finally he said, "Baby, tell me. I'm not hearing this, not what I just thought I heard. This must be some kind of dream." He paused, trying to figure out what he just heard. "I must be having some sort of dream or something, Lilly," he said. "Tell me I'm not hearing what I just thought I heard," He paused. "That our little girl gets sent home from school and that we're standing here worried about her and that it's all because of some stupid bet?" Sheriff Johnson grabbed his daughter by the arm, bringing her from the kitchen table and closer to his face. "Let me tell you something, little girl," he said slowly. "Don't let you let anybody from outside this house, question your mother's or my love for you. Do you hear me?"

"Bill, Bill," his wife called out to him.

Sheriff Johnson looked at his wife and with his free arm, motioned for her to calm down. "Don't worry, baby," he said, "I've got this." He looked at his daughter and said, "Now you go to your room and look at that pink Zebra and pink bed spread, that zebra wallpaper that your uncle, Fred, and I painted and all that other stuff that you wanted. That your mother and I paid a fortune to do, because our little girl just had to have it, and," he paused, "think about how somebody you don't even know, came this close," he said as he squeezed his first two fingers together until there is but an inch apart, "from taking that away from you." The sheriff released Joyce from his grasp and pointed her toward her room without another word. Joyce headed toward her room without uttering a sound. She looked back as she neared the room's entrance and looked at her mother.

Her mother shook her head no, not wanting the conversation to continue, so Joyce opened her room door, entered, and slammed the door shut. With Joyce gone, Sheriff Johnson turned to his wife and shook his head from side to side, calming down from the anger he felt just moments before and said, "Is it me or has the whole world become just one big hustle?"

Blu looked at the television playing in the corner of his club. Tonight, ESPN was doing a review of the upcoming rivalry weekend and he wanted to see what they said about the Auburn Alabama game. He also wanted to see if there was any mention of the murders that had just occurred in his town. He definitely didn't want to miss that. The time at the bottom of the ticker was 9:37 p.m. *Good*, he thought, *plenty of time before the news*. The place was packed tonight with the regulars and a couple of newcomers. The people at the plant had been paid the night before so they still had some money. "Hey Blu," someone called out from across the room. "Who you like? Auburn or Alabama?"

Blu looked across the room and saw RC, who was in for his evening hit. Blu waved and smiled, "I don't care, as long as they bring their money here," he said. RC made his way across the room.

"Hey Blu," another voice said, "the man is here to see you." Blu turned to his left and saw one of his workers, Gooseneck, pointing toward the back of the room.

Blu nodded his head and leaned over the bar where he was sitting. He looked at Gooseneck and said, "Give RC his usual and none extra," Gooseneck shook his head yes. "He don't want to pay and I don't want no shit," Blu said. Blu made his way toward the back office. When he got there, standing in front of him was Mayor Bill Heard waiting for his weekly payment. Blu wasn't naïve and he knew new going into business in a small rural county required that he make certain payments and Mayor Heard was one of them. The one thing about

politicians in Alabama that you could be certain of was that they were always on time for their money, regardless of what they had done for you. It never failed.

Blu reached into his pocket and pulled out three crisp one hundred dollar bills. He folded up the money and put the folded up money into the breast pocket of Mayor Herd's suit jacket. Mayor Heard smiled at Blu and said, "Good doing business with you," and turned and walked toward the exit. Blu smiled and followed him toward the exit only to see three Korean gentlemen standing at the front door. It surprised him. No, not the fact that they were Korean. He had Koreans in here all the time looking for drugs, liquor, and women. That was universal in any language or culture. The Koreans, however, were just a little more discreet about it. They usually came in the back door or sent one of their black "friends," in to get something. These three, however, weren't regulars and actually looked like tourists on vacation, not like the guys who worked at the plant. They had flowered shirts on, khaki pants, and two of them were plenty big by Korean standards—about six feet, two hundred fifty pounds or so. The smaller one of the two seemed to be in charge with his dark Ray-Ban sunglasses on.

He started walking toward them when he thought, *Damn, I'm missing the news.* He switched direction and stated walking toward the bar. He motioned to Gooseneck. "Give me the remote," he said. Gooseneck flipped him the remote control. Blu quickly turned to the Montgomery channel since they ran local stories on that channel. Blu motioned for Gooseneck to get him a beer and settled down to watch the television. Blu looked at the bottom of the screen for recent news flashes. The little ticker running across the screen said, "Employee at local car supplier burns to death in rural town." Blu read the ticker out loud. "Another murder?" Gooseneck said. "Turn up the volume," Blu demanded. Gooseneck hit the remote control for the volume.

"This just in, from channel 11 eyewitness news. Jung-Hoon li, plant manager at Kwansung Manufacturing, was burned to death at a gas station in Bay Minute."

"Bay Minute," Blu said, "where's that?"

"An employee of the gas station was found tied up and police have taken her into protective custody. This brings to count three employees of Kwansung that have died in the past two days. Anyone with information about these murders is encouraged to call crime stoppers at 334-567-8965."

Blu looked around and for the three Korean men he had seen earlier. No sign of them. "What happened to our Korean friends that were here?" Blu asks.

"Don't know," Gooseneck answered. "I was looking at the TV like you." Blu shook his head. "And here I thought we could get some fresh money tonight," Blu said as he shrugged his shoulders and walked away from the bar.

CHAPTER 9

Sheriff Johnson exited his patrol car and walked quickly past the reporters and television camera blocking the entrance to the sheriff department's doors. "Sheriff, Sheriff," a voice called out, "anything new about the crack-house murders?

"What is the involvement of the plant manager?" another voice called out. The sheriff said nothing and reached the top step of the entrance before he turned and faced the crowd.

"Okay, Okay, ladies and gentlemen," he said, "could you please calm down?" The crowd noise calmed down. "This is an active murder investigation and as news becomes available, we will release it to you, okay?"

"Sheriff, Sheriff, Liz Nixon from Channel Eight News." The sheriff looked into the direction of the voice and saw a small black woman with long hair. She pushed a microphone into his face as she said, "What connection to the crack-house murders does the plant manager have and have you charged the three young men now in custody with the previous murders?"

The sheriff shook his head from side to side. "Like I said before, as soon as we have anything, the press will be the first to know." The sheriff quickly turned and entered the sheriff departments doors as two deputies kept the news media out. *Good questions,* the sheriff thought as he headed toward his office, *I just wish I had some answers.* He headed quickly toward his office where he was met by Deputy Oliver.

"I see you've gotten past the first hurdle, sir," the deputy said while smiling. "I'm afraid," the deputy continued, as he reached for the door handle. "There's more waiting for you in your office." The deputy opened the door and sae\w five men crowed into his small office. Four men were standing around his desk while the fifth man was sitting in his office chair.

"Well hello," Sheriff Johnson said, forcing a smile. He walked in slowly and took off his hat, throwing it on his desk.

The man sitting at his desk jumped up and said, "I'm sorry, Sheriff, we didn't know when you'd be here so I just made myself comfortable."

The man smiled, one of those politician smiles, the sheriff thought and he was sitting in his chair! His chair! The man moved quickly around the desk and extended his hand. "I'm State Representative Sam Jackson and these four gentlemen are…"

The sheriff ignored the man's handshake and moved to his desk and took a seat and leaned back in his chair with his hands folded behind his head. He instinctively didn't like these gentlemen so he wasn't going to offer them a seat or even send his deputy on a hunt for some chairs. He just wanted to get down to business and get these gentlemen out of his office as quickly as possible. "You were saying?" Sheriff Johnson asked.

Representative Jackson pulled back his hand and turned toward the other men in the room, not being flustered one bit and continuing on, "This here is Richard Davis of the governor's office," he said as he pointed to a middle-aged white man with a bald head. "This is Todd Sinclair of the ABI." He pointed to a tall dark haired white man with deep blue eyes. "And these three gentlemen are company representatives of the Kwansung Corporation." Two of the three men were of oriental heritage, probably Korean, and the other was a young looking white man with blond hair.

The sheriff took a minute to study each of the men he'd just been introduced to. The first one, the one who was sitting at his desk with the full head of jet black hair, Sam Jackson, well he definitely was a politician with his whitened teeth and snake skin boots, color washed jeans with a silver belt buckle, probably had his family's farm insignia on it. Now what else he was, only heaven knows, but he bet this guy could tell a lie faster than a rattlesnake could shake a rattle. Now, the other gentlemen, the older one, with the bald head, what was his name? Davis. *Yeah*, the sheriff thought, *Richard Davis of the governor's office*. What did that mean exactly? The sheriff wondered what office, division, well whatever… he'd soon find out.

The tall dark one, Sinclair from the ABI, he didn't know. Good looking guy, probably one of those ass kissers who moved up the ranks saying to anything his boss said and finally, the two Koreans

and the young looking blond haired white guy. Well the white guy was probably the company lawyer and the Koreans, who knew? They both had dark hair and wore glasses but one was taller and heavyset while the other the looked mousey. "Well," the Sheriff said, "I can't think of anything interesting to talk about so how about we get down to business. To what do I owe the pleasure?" he asked as if he didn't know. The sheriff unfolded his hands from behind his head and waited.

"Well," Mr. Jackson said. *The first one to speak, the politician,* Sheriff Johnson thought. "We understand that you're busy, so that's why," Jackson paused, "that in the spirit of corporation between the state and county governments, we have sent both Mr. Davis and Mr. Sinclair to help you in your investigation." Mr. Jackson looked at the sheriff and smiled that politician smile. "These three gentlemen—"

"What are their names?" the sheriff asked. "They do have names, don't they?" Jackson laughs.

"Well of course they do, Sheriff. This here is Mr. Pak," he said as he pointed to the shorter of the two Koreans. "And this here is Mr. Chang-bok li," he said as he pointed to the taller heavyset man.

"And I am," the white man with the blond hair spoke up, "Jerry Connelly, chief counsel for the Kwangsung Corporation."

Uh, oh, Sheriff Johnson thought, *here we go.* "As I was saying, Sheriff," Jackson said. "These gentlemen and I are here to lend assistance to your investigation and that the state and the company are not negatively impacted by the results. Sheriff," he said as he started to pace the floor. "We have a weak economy and people are going hungry. We want to put the events of the last two days to rest."

"To rest?" the sheriff asked.

"Yes," Mr. Jackson said. "You have the murder suspects in custody and we are here to make sure that whatever charges the county comes up with will put these criminals behind bars and convict them of their crimes."

Just what I need, the sheriff thought, *a lot of help.*

"Yes, Sheriff," the bald guy from the governor's office chimed in. "We want to make sure that you have all the resources available to you here at your disposal, so me and Mr. Sinclair here…" he pointed to the ABI guy, "… are going to stay here and lend a hand with this."

"Now you hold on there," the sheriff raised his hand in protest. "I don't need nobody from the state or the ABI looking over my shoulder while I'm conducting a murder investigation."

"No, no, no, Sheriff." Sam Jackson said, "that's not the case at all."

"Well, what do you call it then?" the sheriff said. "You post two of your men down here in my county?"

Sam Jackson smiled and flashed those bright white teeth. "I remember when," he said, "when I was a little boy, my daddy, God rest his soul, used to work in the textile mills to help support my brothers and me. He would get up early and go work his twelve hour shift and come home dog tired." The sheriff nodded his head as Jackson continued. "He did that for thirty years all the while saving money and buying land so that he could leave his family better off than he." Sam Jackson looked at the other men in the office as they shook their heads in agreement. "I also remember," Jackson continued, "that when those mills closed and put people out of work how my daddy was almost devastated and a lot of people were, but he had that farm to lean on, to help him in his time of need. Just like you, Sheriff, we want to be that farm that you lean on in your time of need."

Sheriff Johnson looked at Jackson as he finished his little speech and got up from his desk. He pointed a finger at the door and said, "The only thing that I need you to do is for you gentlemen is to leave my office."

"Sheriff," Mr. Jackson said, "you are taking this entirely the wrong way."

"Let me tell you something," the sheriff said, seething in anger. "This is my county, my men, and by last resolution, my murder investigation, okay!"

Jackson smiled and turned away from the sheriff and looked at the other men in the office. "Gentlemen," he said, "I think maybe we should leave and give the sheriff some space." He then turned back toward the sheriff, "while he sorts some things out."

The other gentlemen started walking toward the door except for Connelly, the lawyer for the company. "Just one moment of your time, Sheriff?" he asked as the others exited. The sheriff, starting to cool

down, nodded his head yes as he took his seat. The other men exited, led by Mr. Jackson.

When the last of the men had departed, Mr. Connelly spoke. "I just want you to know, Sheriff," Connelly said. "that the company is willing to pay a substantial reward for the capture of whoever perpetuated these crimes against the company's employees."

The sheriff smiled as he looked at Connelly. "You're not offering a bounty on their heads are you Mr. Connelly, are you?"

"No, Sheriff, that's not what I'm saying. It's just that our company wants to make sure that our employees can not only work in a safe environment when they come to work, but also a safe community where law and order can be respected and that is something that we do not take lightly and we are here to support you in that endeavor."

Some more help, the sheriff thought. This case had certainly gone from two black boys being murdered at a crack-house to something else on somebody's radar. He just wasn't sure whose. "All right, Mr. Connelly," the sheriff said. "We appreciate whatever help you can give us. Oliver?" the sheriff called out. "I want you to get Mr. Connelly's number if we need any other information or help. Okay, Mr. Connelly?"

"Thanks, Sheriff," Mr. Connelly said as he turned and headed out of the office. Oliver started to follow until the sheriff motioned him back. The sheriff motioned for him to close the door, which he did.

"Oliver," the sheriff said, "check the telephone records of all the victims and see what we get. Let's see who they've been talking to."

Deputy Oliver shook his head yes and opened up the office door and headed out. He looked back at the sheriff and said, "Smooth, Sheriff. That went real smooth." He then disappeared through the door and the sheriff smiled as he looked down at the piles of paper work on his desk.

The men of the DDC were on their second cup of coffee and the conversation was red hot with gossip about the murder. Ray Conley looked at Peewee. "You know those people work twelve hours a day, seven days a week, with no benefits. I mean none." Ray took a drag on his Newport cigarette. "They hire them temp so they don't have to pay them no benefits. They just drug test them and background check 'em

and keep them on minimum wage until they point it out or just don't care 'cause there never gonna hire them."

Shorty jumped up. "The way I hear it is that half them boys on meth and that the company gives it to them, to keep 'em working."

"That ain't true, that ain't true, that ain't true, Shorty," Ray Conley said. "You just mad because your nephew got fired for stealing up there."

The men argue as Josephine Clearly drove by on her way to work. She thought about last night when Nikki kissed her. Her not being unattractive and single, Jo had been approached before by other women at the school, but had politely refused. One, because she had something at home and another because she really didn't find another female her age attractive. This, however, was different. She felt herself drawn to this young girl for some reason. She was excited by her. Maybe it was her youth that intrigued her.

The men on the corner waved at Jo as she drove by and she returned the wave with a smile as she continued to drive down the street. She continued to think about the night before. Why did she do that? What made last night any different than any other night? It was just one kiss. Just one kiss, what was so special about that? It was special; Jo just didn't want to admit it. That one kiss had made Jo feel two things she hadn't felt in years: wanted and needed.

CHAPTER 10

Colonel Un looked out the window of the all-you-can-eat sushi buffet as he drank his tea. He really didn't like sushi, but being this far from a big city he had to settle for it. He really wasn't that hungry but he decided to try and eat something while his men searched for the girl. It was almost noon and they still hadn't found her. He still didn't know if she had any information or even knew anything but he knew he had to be through. The great leader himself was involved in this enterprise so he could not make any mistakes. If he did, he could end up like his nephew, Jung-Hoon. He wondered if Jung-Hoon ever knew that he was his uncle or not, probably not since he never told him and he was sure his sister never did.

He had watched Jung-Hoon for months, years actually, since he was his handler but he was surprised when he took up with the girl. He started to intervene then but decided against it and looks what it lead to: Jung-Hoon's death. What a pity, he had such promise. He had run their meth operation well. Had contacted the right people and was making the people a lot of money until he took up with that girl. The colonel looked at his watch. He still hadn't heard from his men and time was running out. He'd have to explain to certain people why the money was late. What had happened to Jung-Hoon and he'd also have to find a replacement for him, all for which he'd better have an answer... or else. The colonel took another sip of his tea, resisting the urge to smoke. He liked to smoke and drink his strong Asian tea, but smoking was not permitted and the last thing he needed to do was draw attention to himself. He looked out the window again, thinking about how much Jung-Hoon had told the girl, the little whore, something—maybe nothing—but he was sure he would find out. *The sooner, the better* he thought for time certainly wasn't on his side. The colonel saw the rental car he and his men had rented pull up outside the restaurant. *Good*, he thought, *some news.*

The two men got out of the car and headed into the restaurant. They came into the restaurant but one of the men took the lead and headed straight for the colonel. He bent over toward the colonel and whispered something in his ear. The colonel nodded his head and said, "Good." The man stood back up as the colonel said, "Let us go. " The colonel got up from the table and headed for the door, preceded by his men. *Now maybe,* he thought, *I can get some answers.* He needed to know how much the girl knew and more importantly where was the money.

Blu walked into the county jail and encountered two guards at the entrance. The sign said, "Remove all items from your pockets and place them in the container provided. Then proceed through the doors." Blu reached into his pockets and took out his keys and loose change and put them in the plastic container provided. He knew the routine. He'd been in enough jails to know the drill. How many times had he been here because of his son? Lately, it had been more times than he cared to remember. He passed through the doors and reached into the plastic container the guard had pushed through and retrieved his stuff. He started walking and turned toward the left, knowing that was the way to the cellblock. He didn't need a sign telling him which way to the prisoner lockup. "Hey, Blu!" Blu looked up, hearing his name called. It was, as you could you have guessed, R.C. The one thing about the good reverend: if there was something to be gained by his appearance, he would be there. "Talk to you later," R.C. said as he passed Blu on the way out. Blu proceeded down the hall to the prisoner lock-up. He looked at heavy metal doors with iron bars. Stenciled in black were the words "Section A."

Blu stopped and looked through the bars at the guards looking at the video camera of the jail. "May I help you?" one of the guards asked. He had long dreadlocks and you would think him from Jamaica or the West Indies, not West Lowndes County. "May I help you?" he asked again.

Blu looked at him and said, "Yes, I'm here to see my son, Robert Norris the Third."

The guard entered the name into his computer. He sees the prisoner listed plus allowed contacts and what he had been sentenced for. He

looked up at Blu. "Sign in please," he said. Blu took the sign-in sheet and signed it. He looked down the sheet and saw the Reverend Clark's name as a visitor for his son. "Wonder what he wanted," Blu said as he signed the sign-in sheet and handed it back to the guard.

The guard was a woman with long black and green streaked hair. *Another weave maiden*, Blu thought. Women who, ten years ago didn't have five inches of hair, now had long following locks. *Black women have made India rich*, he thought. Not that it made a difference to him. A woman was a woman, dark, light, short hair, long hair—they all had something about them that was beautiful. The guard looked at the sheet and told Blu, "Step back please." She then nodded at the other guard sitting behind a bank of cameras. Blu heard the whine of motors and locks being released as the doors to the jail cell came alive and unleashed. The door opened and Blu stepped in. "Follow me," the guard said as she started walking briskly down the corridor. Blu's eyes automatically looked at her ass. *Damn*, he thought, *no ass*. Didn't matter to him, he thought; he was just visiting. The doors whined and two doors swung open as two sheriff's deputies and the sheriff emerged. Blu knew Sheriff Johnson from the old days when they both played high school football. They were teammates. Blu was a running back while Sheriff Johnson played both sides of the ball, offense and defense. Heck, Johnson was the biggest kid on the team and they sure needed him, as the rest of the team was skinny and let's just say light in the ass. "Blu, Blu, Blu," the sheriff said, "what's going on?" The sheriff ran up to him and grabbed his right hand.

"Good to see ya, Blu, what brings you up here?" Sheriff Johnson asked. Blu smiled and returned the handshake. "Down here to see my son," he said.

"Your son?" the sheriff said.

"Yeah," Blu answered.

"Gina Tolbert's and my son," Blu said.

"Bang Bang's your son, really?" the sheriff said. "I knew that they said you and Gina had a son years ago, but after you left…"

"Yeah," Blu said. "I had to see the world, Johnson," Blu said, "and since I've been back, we haven't seen each other." *It's a funny thing about people from the past. You either try to impress them with what*

you've done or you agree with everything they say because you really don't remember them or the event, Blu thinks.

"Well you know people go this way and that," Sheriff Johnson said, "No telling where they end up."

Sheriff Johnson and Blu looked at each other, sizing up each other. Blu knew what he knew and Sheriff Johnson was the same. They both recognized that whatever they knew about each other was immaterial to the present, what was going on now. Sheriff Johnson said, "Well, good to see you Blu, we've got a big case we're working on,"

"Yeah," Blu said, "I know."

The sheriff smiled and said, "You need to stop by the house, Blu, have a drink, just for old times' sake, okay?"

The sheriff patted Blu on the shoulder, turned, and walked away. Blu returned the smile and shook his head and walked toward the double iron doors, knowing the closest he and Bill Johnson would come to sharing a drink was right here in this hallway.

Reverend Clark snagged his head on some sticker bushes, "Shit," he said. He backed up and looked for a way around the sticker bushes. He saw a small opening over to his left, so he moved that way. *What in the hell has that girl got him into now*? He thinks. Ever since he hooked up with this girl's momma and her, it had been one thing after another. Hell, he wasn't complaining, but it was just thoughts that ran through his head. She kept him supplied with meth and crack, but hell what was all this secret stuff she had been involved with lately, with that Korean dude? *Yeah, yeah*, he thought. That's when all this shit started when she started fucking this Korean dude from the plant. Reverend Clark moved through the small opening, coming up on a patch of rusted tin lying on the ground, covered by leaves. He reached down and pulled back the tin to reveal a small handgun. "Shit," Reverend Clark said. "This is what the fuck she wants?"

"So I saw the Reverend Clark in here earlier," Blu said. "What did he want?" Blu asked Bang Bang sitting across from him.

"Oh, you know," Bang said. "He just wanted to save my soul and read me some Bible verses. You know," Bang Bang said, looking away. "Just talking bullshit so as to make him feel good."

"Just like this bullshit that you've gotten yourself into?" Blu asked.

Bang Bang shrugged his shoulders. "I guess," he said. "It's what you want anyway. For me to go away. It's not like we're that close knit have-dinner-every-Sunday-type-of-family, now are we?" Bang Bang smiled as he looked at Blu.

Blu looked at his son, wanting to be angry but couldn't be. Every word his son said was true. What was he doing there? "You're your mother came by," Blu began.

"And what?" Bang Bang said as he started to grow angry. "You got to remembering when I was a baby, Dad? Well I got news for you I'm a grown man, now." Bang Bang's eyes narrowed as all the hurt and disappointment through the years came out, the disappointment of a son in his father and the disappointment that a father has for his son and all his dreams for him, all come out. Band Bang rubbed his hand through his long black dreads as Blu said, "It is what it is. Son," Blu said. "I don't blame you or mother for anything I did, Everything I did was more about me, than you," Blue said, "you understand?"

Bang Bang nodded his head yes as Blu turned away from him then back. "I will say this, son," Blu said. "No matter what you do son, or say," Blu said as he looked at Bang Bang, "I love you and there's not anything I wouldn't do for you." Blu slapped his right hand on the table as he jumped up from the booth. Before he hung up the phone, Blu looked deep into the eyes of his only son and said, "I mean if that's alright with you?"

Bang Bang looked at his father and said, "Yeah Dad," he said, "I guess it is."

CHAPTER 11

"Look Daddy," Sam Jackson's son said as he rode a two-year-old mare around the fenced-in barn area of their one hundred fifty-acre farm. Sam smiled and waved at his son from the front porch of their ranch-style home. It was five thousand square feet and painted white with green trim. Not flashy, but well-kept and more importantly, Sam thought, paid for. His father had bought this land and had passed it down debt-free to his son and Sam was as proud of it as anything he'd ever done or accomplished, him winning the state senate race was just gravy on the biscuit and Sam had every intention of representing his constituents as best he could as his father had taught him to do. To do the best job he could and to represent everyone fairly and believe that hard work paid off. The problem was Sam thought the world was going to hell in a hand basket faster than anyone could keep up with it. Every new leap in technology led to a new problem when the old problems weren't fixed yet.

With the global economy, your neighbors were strangers, who you rarely saw as they commuted to their jobs and the people who were your business partners lived two thousand miles away, but provided you and your neighbors with jobs, something every county in the U.S. needed and wanted, especially in the middle of nowhere county. "Daddy, Daddy!" his son called. "Company's coming." Sam looked up and saw a black SUV racing up the road. Dust was flying from the tires as it slowed down and came to a stop. *Wonder who this could be*, Sam thought as the SUV's engine turned off. Suddenly, the doors flew open and three people exited. Sam squinted, his eyes, as he tried to see who it was.

The three gentlemen emerged from the vehicle. One was Chang-Bok li, the other Mr. Pak and the third was Jerry Connelly. *I wonder what they want*, Sam thought as the three men approached him. "Hello, how are you doing?" Sam said. You see with a politician greeting people was second nature. Some you liked, some you didn't

as long as you met them with a smile on your face maybe you could count on their vote or in this case corporation.

"Hey Sam, how you doing?" asked Jerry Connelly as he thrust out his hand. Sam shook his hand vigorously all the while smiling. Sam looked at the two Koreans who politely smiled and nodded their heads. "Sorry to bother you Sam," Jerry said, "But we hand to talk to you about what was going on in the murder investigation."

Sam smiled as he said, "Well come on in Jerry and you, Mr. Pak and Mr. Li," He motioned for the men to enter his house as he opened the front door. The men walk through the door as he said, "Martha, Martha, we have company!" The three men stepped into the immaculately kept house. Even though they lived in the country, Sam and his wife Martha believed in a clean house and theirs certainly was.

Sam led the men through the front entrance and into the living area. There sat couches and chairs all centered on the fireplace, where a flat screen television hung over the fireplace. Sam motioned for the men to take a seat. "Please gentlemen," he said, "please take a seat." The three gentlemen took a seat as Sam's wife made an entrance. Dressed in a white dress and with her red hair pinned up, Martha was a southern beauty.

"Hello," she said behind her perfect white teeth.

"Honey," Sam said, "I would like you to meet Mr. Chang-Bok li, Mr. Pak, and Jerry Connelly."

Martha smiled again and looked at her husband. "Pleased to meet you gentlemen," she said. "But as you gentlemen know, time stands still for no one and I simply must run," Martha smiled and nodded her head at the gentlemen in the room and made a quick exit. *Perfect Martha*, Sam thought, *she's always on point. She knows when to stay and when to go, perfect*, he thought.

"Well, gentlemen," Sam said, "what can I do for you?" Sam looked at the gentlemen seated before him. Mr. Pak and Mr. Li looked at him and smiled. Finally Mr. Connelly spoke. "As you know, Sam, The Kwangsung Corporation has been an active participant in the community since they arrived in 2002. We have provided jobs and have actively participated in community projects aimed at helping the less fortunate. With this in mind, we have a couple of concerns we would

like to communicate to you." Sam looked at Jerry and thought, *Yeah, here it comes, the offer.* "The recent murders involving our employees we would like you to expedite. We all know that the company will be exonerated and the quicker this is put to rest the better. Secondly," he continued, "the company would like to offer a work release program with the county where prisoners charged with non-violent crimes will be able to pay their fines or restitution and provide for themselves by working for our company, and thirdly the company will plan an expansion of our existing facility, which will provide an additional five hundred jobs." Sam looked at Jerry. He wanted to jump up for joy with this good news but decided to play it cool.

Everything sounds great, he thought, *but what is the end game? Why this generous offer unless the company had something to hide?* The only that had changed since yesterday was the work release program. "I get what you're saying as I did yesterday," Sam said. "But why the work release program?"

"Well," Jerry said, "that's a little incentive for the sheriff and as a little incentive for you, I want you to read this." Jerry handed him some papers folded up from his breast pocket. Sam took them and opened them up to revel a contract. Sam quickly read through the document. It offered him the sum of one hundred fifty thousand dollars a year as a lobbyist.

Lobbyist? Sam thought. That would mean he would have to give up his state seat at the house which paid twenty-one thousand a year and required a whole bunch of his time and work for Kwangsung full-time. *Am I missing something?* Sam thought. This was a deal beyond a deal for him. "Well Jerry," Sam said. "This is some kind of offer, but what are the strings attached to the offer? And why," Sam began, "is this so important today after we just met with the sheriff yesterday?" Sam didn't like being so direct but he had learned that the best way to do business was up front and direct so that there was no confusion or misunderstanding. Each party needed to know exactly what it was getting.

Jerry got up and started walking around the room scratching his head. "Good question Sam," Jerry replied. "I think I'll let Mr. Li answer."

Mr. Li stood up. Dressed in an orange shirt and khaki pants, he looked no different than any other employee of Kwangtung. "Mr.

Jackson," he began, "first of all, we would like to thank you for all the help you have given us," and Mr. Li bowed his head toward Sam. "Secondly, let me try to explain the situation that we are in," Mr. Li stood and walked over to Sam. "We are a multi-billion dollar corporation that has come to the conclusion that in order to exist, that we must grow, and the United States is a major part of that growth strategy." Sam looked at Mr. Li. He wasn't a big man but he was about average size and again he wore glasses which conveyed to him that he was smart and had better listen. "We must increase sales against our competitors as they experience setbacks and in order to do this we do not need to create distractions. Do you understand? "Mr. Li asked. "We are prepared to do whatever we have to do to minimize the damage this incident has caused us."

Mr. Li stopped and took off his glasses. He took his shirt and wiped the lenses against hid shirt then put his glasses back on. "That is why we must impose on you the upmost importance that this matter must command."

Sam looked at Mr. Li and smiled. "You know I have been on board and out in front of this matter since it began," Sam said. "I will continue to direct all of my efforts to resolving this situation as quickly as possible." Sam looked at the group of men and smiled that politician smile of his. Jerry looked at Mr. Li and the two men nodded in agreement.

"Well then, since we're in agreement," Jerry said as he and the Koreans headed toward the exit. "We won't take another minute of your time and we will be in touch with you soon. The three quickly made their way toward the front door and exited the house quickly. They jumped into their SUV and started the engine and drove off. Sam waved as the SUV backed up then sped down the road. Sam watched and then thought to himself, *What the hell just happened here*? Why had these guys come to his home and admittedly offered at least two things they hadn't offered before, the work release and the lobbyist job, and essentially go over what was agreed on from the start, only with more whistles.

Now, Sam, being an old country boy, could only figure two things. One, that they were guilty of something, and two, that whatever it was they were afraid of they didn't want anyone to know.

Sheriff Johnson rushed into his office followed closely by Buster and Oliver. He looked up and saw Johnson of the ABI standing there with his hands folded behind his back. "Hey Johnson," the sheriff said, "What have you got for me?" the sheriff said as he sat down in his chair. "I need some..." The sheriff slapped both of his hands on his desk, "answers."

Johnson smiled and unfolded his hands letting them fall to his side. "Well," he said, "some of this you'll like and some of this you won't."

"Go ahead, shoot," the sheriff said.

"First off," Johnson began. "We haven't found the gun that killed the two victims at the crack house."

"Yes," the sheriff said, "go ahead."

"And the victim killed at the gas station was burned to death."

"How do we know that these murders are connected?" the sheriff asked. "The murder at the gas station was four counties away. The only thing that connects them is that they all worked for the same company."

"We don't know," Johnson said, "but it's a mighty big coincidence don't you think? And also," Jonson paused, "what you don't know, which I'm about to tell you, is that we checked the cellphone records of all three of the victims and that was where we found some interesting results."

The sheriff laughed. "Quit playing, Johnson," the sheriff said, "Just tell me and stop playing with it." Johnson smiled.

The sheriff didn't know Johnson well or really at all but this guy sure had a strange sense of humor. "It seems that Dirty Red and all three of the victims were regular phone buddies. They were in constant communication with each other for the last three months."

"Now," the sheriff said, leaning up in his chair, "we're getting somewhere. I knew Red was mixed up in this somehow," Now the sheriff was getting back to a more familiar place, of getting Red.

"However, Sheriff," Johnson said. He then took a sheet of paper from a folder that had been sitting on the sheriff's desk. "There were some unexpected numbers that also showed up," Johnson handed the paper to the sheriff. Sheriff Johnson scanned the paper until finally he saw it. "You've got to be kidding me!" he said as he jumped from his

seat. He slammed the paper on his desk as he turned and looked out the window.

Buster and Oliver looked at each other and finally Oliver said, "What is it, boss?"

Sheriff Johnson turned and looked at both of them and said, "My cellphone number's on that sheet."

CHAPTER 12

Jo looked out the window of her small kitchen. It was getting near dinnertime and she had a hungry boy coming home. Well he really wasn't a boy anymore, she thought and he was getting to be less and less of "Momma's little boy." Jo sighed, wishing for the old days again and then went to the refrigerator and opened it, looking for some lemons to make a pitcher of lemonade.

Suddenly, the doorbell rang. Jo closed the refrigerator door headed to the front door, wondering who it could be and hoping it wasn't one of those door-to-door salesmen. Jo opened the front door and there stood Nikki. "Hello," she said as she pushed her way into the house. Jo closesd the door then turned and faced Nikki, placing her hands on her hips. "Well Nikki, what brings you by?" Jo asked.

"Well, t's me and my stepdad," Nikki said. Jo looked at Nikki and could see where she had been crying. Suddenly Nikki lunged forward and hugged Jo.

Jo, surprised, returned the hug and said, "What's wrong?"

Jo pushed Nikki back then took her by the hand and led her to the living room couch. They both sat as Nikki said, "He just won't leave me alone, and he just won't."

Jo looked into Nikki's watering eyes while holding her right hand. "Can I get you anything?" Jo asked. Nikki shook her head no. Jo got up from the couch and started heading for the kitchen. "Come on," Jo said. "I was just about to finish making dinner."

Jo headed toward the kitchen and Nikki got up and followed her. Jo motioned for her to sit at the kitchen table and headed back to the refrigerator where she pulled out four fresh lemons. "I'm about to fix some lemonade, Nikki," she said, "I don't know but there's something about fresh made sweet lemonade that just washes your problems away, don't you think?" Nikki nodded her head as she looked down at the kitchen table. Jo opened her kitchen drawer and took out a sharp knife. She carried the lemons and the knife over by the kitchen

sink. She sat the lemons on the counter and then took the knife and carefully started to cut them in half. "Nothing wrong with that, now is there," Jo said as she looked at Nikki.

"No, nothing wrong with that," Nikki said as she smiled at Jo.

The sheriff looked at the call list on the printout. There was no mistake about it; it was his number and… "Wait a minute, wait a minute," the sheriff said, "that was the day before yesterday when the first murders occurred," he said.

He handed the sheet to Deputy Oliver, who quickly scanned the sheet and said, "Right, Sheriff," he says, "it was."

"My daughter was at home that day." The sheriff picked up his office phone on his desk and punched in his telephone number. The phone rang. "Hey, baby," he said, "is Joyce there?" He looked at the other men and nodded his head yes. "Well baby, could you put her on the phone, please?" The sheriff waited as his wife called his daughter to the phone. "Listen baby," the sheriff said, "what was the bet you made between you and that girl, what's her name? Nikki? Okay, Nikki Flowers." The sheriff listened as his daughter told him the details of the bet. "Okay, thanks baby," he said. "Tell your mom I'll be working late, all right? Okay baby." The sheriff hangs up the phone. He looked at Johnson, Deputies Oliver and Clearly and said, "She said the girl wanted to use her cell phone for the day." The sheriff looked at Deputies Oliver and Clearly. "Find out," he said, "who this Nikki flowers is."

Blu saw Reverend Clarke getting out of his car. Blu pulled his car in behind him. Both Blu and Reverend Clarke got out of their car together. "Hey, Rev," Blu said, "I need to talk to you for a minute." Blu started walking toward R.C.

R.C. started backing up with his hands in front of him. "Now look here, Blu" R.C. said, "I don't want no trouble, I was just doing what they wanted me to do. That's all." Blu tried not to act surprised, since he didn't know what the reverend was talking about. "It's in the trunk, here," he said as he tossed Blu the keys. Blu instead of asking what was going on, Blu decided to play along and pressed the open button for the car trunk. The trunk opened up and Blu saw a black backpack. Blu

grabbed it and opened it up. In the bag were stacks of one hundred dollar bills along with a twenty-two-caliber revolver.

"You know Nikki," Jo said, "You don't really have to stay there," Jo said as Nikki finished up her lemonade.

"Well," Nikki said as she looked at the just finished lemonade glass. "It's really not what you think," Nikki said.

Jo looked at Nikki with a puzzled look on her face. "What do you…" Jo started.

Nikki suddenly looked up from the glass and said, "I mean he's just nosey as hell and all the time begging me for rocks." Jo's mouth opened slightly as Nikki got up from the table. "I'm sorry Miss Jo, to involve you in any of this, but the last few days have been…"

"Have been what?" Jo looked for the voice. In her doorway was a man. "Excuse me," Jo said as she got up from the table. The man stepped forward and Jo could see that he was a Korean man with a gun in his hand. Jo looked at Nikki who had a terrified look on her face.

"My apologies please?" the man says as he walked toward them. "But me and the young woman have some unfinished business,"

"Go ahead, finish your story," the man said as he motioned the gun at Nikki.

"Wait a minute Nikki," Jo said, "Who is this man and what is he doing holding a gun in my house?"

"I don't know," Nikki said as the man with the gun smiled.

"Again, I apologize," the man said, "My name is Colonel Un." The man smiled again. "And my two associates," he said as his two henchmen step from behind him.

"Who are they?" Jo said, "Your backup singers?,"

"Very funny, miss?" the colonel said. "And you are?" he asked.

"Clearly," Jo said, "Josephine Clearly."

"Good, good, good," the colonel said, "now that we have introduced ourselves, we have many questions to ask and little time for answers from your little friend, Miss Flowers."

Sheriff Johnson looked at Buster and shook his head. "You mean this girl was in your house the other night?"

"Yes," Buster said, "she came over there to see my mom. Something about school."

Sheriff Johnson slapped his hands on his desk. "That girl got my daughter into trouble the other day at school," the sheriff said as he leaned back into his chair. "Then the day of the murders, she placed a call to our Korean victim, what's his name, Oliver?" the sheriff asked.

"Jung-Hoon," Oliver said.

"Yeah, him," the sheriff said. Sherriff Johnson rubbed his chin as he contemplated the latest chain of events. "What about you, Oliver?" the sheriff asked. "You know anything about this girl?"

"Well," Deputy Oliver began, "there are rumors that…"

The door to the office suddenly bust open and in walked State Senator Sam Jackson. "Hello, Sheriff," he said as he walked to the sheriff's desk. The sheriff's mouth opened as he looked at the senator. First off, nobody came into his office without knocking or unannounced and this guy just did. Secondly he really didn't like people just dropping in. The sheriff looked at Buster and Deputy Oliver and said, "What can I do for you, Senator are you here on business or were you in the neighborhood and just happened to stop by?" The Sheriff tried to let the sarcasm cut the intended victim, but he seemed unfazed.

"Sheriff," Sam began, "I have such good news for you that I had to just drop on by and tell you about it. Sorry I rushed in, but I just couldn't keep it to myself."

"Oh really?" Sheriff Johnson said. Sam looked around at the deputies and said in a low voice, "I must say Sheriff that this is of a confidential nature and maybe we would require some privacy?"

Sheriff Jonson motioned to his men. "All right, y'all know what to do. Let Mr. Jackson and me have a moment."

Both Buster and Oliver nodded their heads at the sheriff and headed out the office. Sheriff Johnson said, "I want to hear what you have to say, Oliver, just give us a few minutes, okay?"

Oliver said, "Yes sir," and closed the door behind him as he exited the room.

"All right Mr. Jackson," the sheriff said, "what have you got?"

"Sheriff, I have the best news ever," Mr., Jackson said excitedly. "The Kwansung Corporation has decided to start a work release program with your county jail, where some of your minor offenders can work for Kwansung on a temporary basis and maybe gain full-time employment with the company while of course paying off the debt to the county and state."

Sheriff Johnson looked at the senator and picked up his hat on the desk and started twirling it around in his hand. "Well," the sheriff said, "that certainly sounds good to me. And tell me," he began, "what must we do to initiate this program?"

"Nothing, nothing, Sheriff," Sam said, "Just what you're doing now only quicker."

The sheriff stopped twirling his hat and laughed as he laid it back on his desk. "What? You want me to pin three murders on three black boys because it would look good?" the sheriff asked.

"That is not what I meant, Sheriff," Sam said, doing his best to look hurt by the question. "I mean that we have to move quickly on this or else this opportunity will disappear," Sam said.

The sheriff looked down at his hat then back at Sam. "Well I tell you what," Sheriff Johnson said, "I'm sure you have things to do like I have things to do, so will just leave it at that, okay?" The sheriff smiled at Sam who smiled back.

"I'm just here to offer you my help, Sheriff," he said. "That's all." Sam turned and headed toward the door then turned back toward Sheriff Johnson. "I just want you to know," he said, "that time is of the essence." The sheriff nodded his head as Sam Jackson headed out the door.

"Well the main thing I want to know," Colonel Un said, "is what happened to all the money?" Colonel Un reached into his pocket and took out a pack of cigarettes.

"Ain't no smoking in this house," Jo said.

The colonel turned to his two men and laughed. "May I remind you," he began "who has the gun?" Jo looked at this strange looking Asian man. She thought he was Korean but she wasn't sure.

"I'm sorry," she said, "but I don't allow smoking in my house."

The colonel took a cigarette out of his pack and put it to his mouth and lit it. He took a long drag off the cigarette and immediately started coughing. His men moved quickly to his side but he shoed them away. "Miss Clearly," he said, "I must assure you that my smoking days are nearing an end, but nonetheless, the point I want to make is that, this is my house now, not yours." Colonel Un threw the cigarette onto the floor and stamped it out. "Do you understand?" he said. Jo and Niki looked at each other not knowing what to think. Jo thought that Nikki was just as frightened and surprised as her by this turn of events so she thought she'd best be quiet and see what the hell was going on. "Now," Colonel Un said, "I need answers to questions," He glared at Nikki. "Questions that only you can answer," he said. Colonel Un pulled a chair from the table and took a seat.

"Now young lady, if I might take a minute of your time," he said. "I know that you were a companion of a Mr. Jung-Hoon." Colonel UN took out his pack of cigarettes and pulls one from the pack. He took one out of the pack and put it into his mouth. "What I need to know is where the money is?" Jo looked at Nikki since she didn't know the answer.

Nikki, looking lost, answered back. "I don't know."

Colonel Un smiled and lit his cigarette, immediately choking on it and coughing. "Ah I see," he said, "Now you're Miss Poor and Innocent." He motioned to one of his men who grabbed Nikki by the hair, jerking her head back.

"Ah!" she cried out. "I don't know, I don't know," she cried.

"Now, wait a minute," Jo called out, jumping out of her chair. The colonel's other associate moved toward her. He looked at the colonel who motioned to him to slow down. "Now, once again," he said, "where is the money?"

Nikki looked at the colonel and tears came to her eyes. "I don't know, I don't know," she said. "All I know is what he told me, that's all." Nikki sobbed as the colonel looked at her.

"And what was that?" he asked.

"That," she said, "he was afraid."

"Afraid of what?" he asked. Nikki, with her red hair and her bright brown eyes, looked every bit the naive girl. too young to know the big picture and only looking at the here and now. The colonel looked at Nikki and tried to understand what he was dealing with. Maybe she didn't know, he thought, or maybe she did. Maybe she did and she didn't know it. It was up to him to decide or maybe she was just lying.

"Oh, come on," he said. "You know something, don't you?" Colonel Un lit the cigarette he was holding and took a deep puff. "You were sleeping with him, weren't you?"

Nikki bowed her head and looked off. "Yes," she said.

"And you're going to tell me that you don't know anything?" the colonel asked. "Surely he told you something."

Nikki got up from the table and started walking around with the ten or so bracelets of various shapes clanging on her arm. "He only told me that he was married and that he was lonely," Nikki said. "And how he was going back home to be with his wife and kids."

The colonel took a long drag on his cigarette and laughed. "You mean to tell me that all the time you were sleeping with him, the subject of money never came up?" the colonel asked.

Nikki smiled at the colonel and said, "Well we did talk about the money he would give me but..." Jo, hearing that Nikki was selling herself for money, was surprised but not shocked. *This little girl*, she thought, *is a lot more cunning and devious than what she appeared.*

"But what?" the colonel asked.

"But that was it," she said. "I knew he had a good job so I didn't question or know where he got the money from. I just knew he had it."

The colonel studied Nikki then got up from the table, cigarette still smoldering in his hand. "Well then," he said, "I guess my business here is concluded then."

The colonel dropped the cigarette on the floor and before Jo could say anything and stamped it out on the floor, he looked at his two associates and said, "We will be taking our leave then, ladies." He nodded to his men and they make their way toward the door. The colonel started to follow then stopped and said, "I like for you to know that we will find the money or who took it and one way or another," he said. "That money will be returned to us." The colonel smiled then turned and left.

"Blu," the reverend said as they both looked at the bag containing the money. "I've never seen so much money," he said with eyes as big as saucers. "What you think we oughta do with it?" he asked.

Blu looked at the money and the gun and then at the reverend. "Who gave you this?" Blu asked.

The reverend looked at Blueand then ran his right hand through his thinning hair and turned away. "Like I said Blu," R.C. said, "I was just doing what Bang Bang told me, that's all."

"Bang Bang?" Blu said. Blu knew that he had seen the reverend at the jail but didn't know what he was there for and come to think of it, the reverend had rushed past him and really didn't stop and have a conversation like he usually did.

Blu looked at the money again and said, "How did she have all of this?"

The reverend shrugged his shoulders and said, "I don't know." He paused then looked at Blu and said, "How far is Wetumpka from here?"

Blu laughed and said, "What you want? To go to the casino and gamble with it?"

"Yeah," the reverend said, "Why not? Them boys in jail and they going to need some money for lawyers and such. If we go to the casino we could double that money."

Blu looked at the reverend and instead of dismissing the idea because knew someone was looking for this money and that the reverend certainly wasn't telling the whole story said, "Well we can't go to Wetumpka, 'cause too many people know us there." Blu thought on it some more and said, "Biloxi."

"Biloxi?" the reverend said.

Then they both say, "Biloxi." They laughed and Blu shut the trunk of the reverend's car as they both headed for Blu's car.

CHAPTER 13

Jo and Nikki looked at each other and neither said a word about what just transpired. Jo, not knowing what to say, got up from the kitchen table and headed out the door of the kitchen. She went to the front door and opened it. She opened the screen door and looked out in her yard, making sure that the men that were just there had left. Satisfied that they were, she closed the screen door and the front door and this time, she made sure to lock it. She didn't want any more surprises. "Well," she said as she turned to see Nikki standing in the living room.

Nikki, twisting her arm bracelets, looked down.

Jo, knowing she needed to say something, said, "Well that was interesting. Let me know when you want to begin?" Nikki shrugged her shoulders as Jo walked up to her. "Here," Jo said as she led her to the couch. "Sit down." Nikki and Jo sat as Jo held Nikki by the hand. "I knew that..." Jo began but she is interrupted by Nikki suddenly hugging her. "Well, Nikki," Jo started, as Nikki pulled her tighter. Jo finally raised her arms around Nikki as she tried to comfort her, but Nikki drew back. The two locked eyes as Nikki moved in and kissed Jo on the lips. Jo could feel Nikki's tongue penetrate her mouth and to her surprise, she welcomed it as she opened her mouth a little more and the two shared a deeply passionate kiss.

Jo pulled back. "Nikki," she said, looking Nikki in the eyes. "You and I both know this is wrong now, don't you"? Nikki smiled but didn't say a word. Instead she got up off the couch and, still looking at Jo, started to undress. With skin -ight jeans and a white tank top on, it didn't take her long to disrobe. Jo looked at her remove her clothing and saw her light brown body come into focus. Her medium sized breasts, along with a nicely formed butt, came out of the clothes she was dressed in.

Jo knew she should say something but didn't. Instead, she stared, transfixed at this young girl. *This girl is a student,* she thought, *I could*

lose my job or worse go to jail. And still, she said nothing. After Nikki had shed all her clothing, she moved back to the couch and moved in to kiss Jo again. Jo felt she must be in a dream as Nikki kissed her and then moved her hand to her crotch area. Jo felt her hand massaging her vagina as her internal juices started to flow. *This feels good,* Jo thought. *Too good.* Jo pulled back again. "No," she said.

Nikki, undeterred, took Jo's hand and moved it toward her vagina. "Just do this," she said as she took it and inserted in and around her virginal. "Just rub it like this," she said as she moved Jo's hand up and down as she lies back on the couch.

She released Jo's hand and Jo took over. "Yeah," Nikki said. "I like that." Nikki squealed out in pleasure as Nikki grinded on the couch. Finally, Nikki said, "Yes, yes, I like that. Momma want to play?" Nikki grabbed Jo by the other hand and moved it up to her breasts. "Like this," she said as she took her first and second finger and fondled her nipple. Jo complied, knowing that this was wrong but was becoming more and more excited by the moment. It was wrong, but she felt so right. "C'mon Jo," Nikki said. "You take off your clothes." Jo looked at Nikki and slowly got up off the couch and started to disrobe with all thoughts of this being wrong slowly vanishing with the night.

"Sheriff," Deputy Oliver said, "what charges are we going to bring against our..." The rest of the sentence never left the deputy's mouth as suddenly into the office walked Deandre.

"Deandre, how you doing?" the sheriff asked as a short woman in her mid-twenties walked into the office. It was a week from game day and the sheriff was hoping for some clues or a resolution at his daily morning briefing and in walked Deandre.

"Why are you holding my clients in jail, Sheriff?" Deandre Amay asked.

The sheriff looked at this attractive, professional young lady. Deandre was legend around these parts. She was young, white, and attractive with a never quit attitude, which made her formidable for any judge, lawyer, or jury. She had won quite a few cases and the ones he didn't, her clients usually received a lighter sentence.

"What client might that be Deandre?" the sheriff asked.

"Quit shitting around, Sheriff," Deandre said. "You know who I'm talking about." Deandre looked at the sheriff with the contempt that a serial killer would show a preacher.

"You mean Red?" the sheriff asked.

"Yes," Deandre said as she paced around the room. "Along with Mr. Josh Wiggins and Trammel Howard," she snorted as she waited for a reply.

The sheriff, familiar with her tough talk and antics, decided to slow this exchange down a bit. "How's your family, Deandre?" The sheriff asked, "And what about Willie."

Deandre smiled. She knew what the sheriff was trying to do. "Oh, everyone's just fine, Sheriff," Deandre said. "And what about your family?"

Sheriff Johnson looked at Deandre and smiled. "Everything's just fine."

"Sheriff, we can play this everyone's fine and everything's fine game all night but what about my clients? Their families want to know everything is all right with them and they miss and need them just like you and me with our families."

The sheriff contemplated what Deirdre has said and said, "I know what you are saying, but right now there are too many questions. If I let your clients go, am I releasing innocent men or killers into the population? Are these boys innocent and are victims of circumstance or coldblooded killers trying to work the system? This is what I have to ask myself."

Deandre listened to the sheriff and sighed as she replied, "I know what you're going through Sheriff," she said, "I really do. But unless you have some charges against my clients, then by law you have to let them go."

The sheriff looked at Deputy Oliver and said, "What do we have, Oliver?"

"Well, Sheriff, this is it." The deputy cleared his throat. "This is what we have: possession of illegal and non-registered firearms, suspected money laundering, and possession of an illegal substance."

Deandre turned around in a circle as the charges were read. "I hear you, Sheriff, but what about the murder charges?"

The sheriff looked at Deputy Oliver who shrugged his shoulders. "We are still investigating the other charges," Oliver said.

"And what is that?" Deandre asked.

"Suspects in a murder investigation, including aiding and abetting said murders, which includes committing or knowing who committed these murders," Deputy Oliver said.

Deandre folded her arms across her chest and said, "So that means you won't bring the charges that you think they're guilty of until you find out what there guilty of?"

Sheriff Johnson looked at Deandre and said, "Look, counselor, we are trying to be fair here. We have not charged your clients because we either A, we don't have the evidence, or B, have some evidence and want to make sure it sticks so that we can lock your clients up for a long time," Sheriff Johnson wasn't usually this direct with a defense attorney, but Deandre was aggressive and the best way he found to deal with aggressive people was to be aggressive.

Deandre laughed. "Well sheriff at least you're honest and I have to honest with you," she said. "Unless charges are brought against my clients within..." Deandre checked her watch, "... the next two hours, I'm afraid you are going to have to release them, understand?"

The sheriff knew what Deandre said was true but of course he wouldn't admit to it and he always had a way to stall for time. "Well counselor, we appreciate you stopping by and believe me we do everything here by the rule of law, so feel free to check back with us in two hours."

"Two hours? Deandre said.

"C'mon, Sheriff, you can do better than that."

The sheriff looked at Oliver who shook his head no. "Look, counselor," he said, "that's the best that I can do,"

Deandre shook her head and said, "You know you don't have any murder charges against my clients, let's just cut to the chase and you charge them and we can move forward," Deandre said.

Damn, the sheriff thought, *this woman was like a dog in heat. Attack and then fall back until you got what you wanted.* "Like I said, counselor," the sheriff said. "Get back with me in a couple of hours and we will have some answers for you." The sheriff pushed back in his chair and then folded his hands together.

Deandre looked at the sheriff and laughed. "Sheriff, you and I have played this game too many times before. You stall, I wait and in the end you release the prisoners, or a better description would be my clients. So…." Deandre put her right hand on her chin and rubs it, "why don't you cut the bullshit and let my clients go?"

"Let my people go!" the sheriff said and laughed.

"What's so funny, Sheriff?" Deandre asked.

"I know you're too young to know," he said, "but that's what Moses said to the Pharaoh to let the Israelites leave Egypt."

"Well this ain't Egypt," Deandre said, "this is Alabama and no one is going to the Promised Land unless you release them, okay?"

There she goes, he thought, *this annoying woman would just not let go*. "Okay, Deandre," the sheriff said, "let me take thirty minutes to talk to my men then I can tell you something, okay?"

Deandre smiled, knowing that she had won. "That's all I was asking for sheriff," she said. "Fairness and justice for my clients, that's all I want."

What a pain in the ass, the sheriff thought. "I'll have something for you in an hour or so, okay, Deandre?" the sheriff asked.

Deandre turned and started toward the door. "All right, Sheriff," she said. "I expect to hear something." With that, Deandre was out the door and out of the sheriff's life, at least for the moment.

"Shorty," James Heard said, "I heard that that Korean dude that got killed was tied up with them two boys that got killed the other night."

Shorty looked down and reached into his pocket and pulled out a can of Shoal wintergreen chew. Shorty opened the tin can and took a pinch of the tobacco and put it into his mouth. "You know," Shorty said, "I heard that too. Them Koreans got money."

The sun had been up for a couple of hours now and the men on Dead Dick Corner were busy reviewing the previous day's events. Hollywood had *Entertainment Tonight*, but this town had Dead Dick Corner where no gossip, big or small, escaped without at least some kind of comment. "Now see, ever since Obama been President, people can come and they can go over here as long as they got money or some big company backing them," Charlie Longhead said. "The state of Alabama had the toughest immigration law in the country until the police started stopping those Germans, Japanese, and Koreans, and guess what?" he said, "Now you don't hear about it anymore. Once that law was starting to fuck with the state's money, it disappeared."

"Yeah, yeah, real talk," Youngblood said, "those Koreans at work can go into any place and they automatically get a thirty percent discount. I mean on food, furniture, homes, or whatever. I mean they're the new plantation owners. They have purchased the state of Alabama for a bunch of eight-dollar-an-hour jobs."

"But the American companies got to pay union wages and union health care why these folks are protected by not only the state but federal trade laws as well. I mean what the hell we are doing to ourselves?" James Heard says. "The young workers can't retire because they have no pension. They can't save no money because they have none, I mean they can't even buy the car that they helped build."

"But that's alright with them," Lou Angle said, "It is their world, let them make the choice of what it will be, not us. We done lived our lives and did what we could so let it what it be."

"Hey, anybody seen Blu?" James Heard asked. "I went by there last night and the place was closed up."

The guys on the corner looked at each other and either shrugged their shoulders or shook their heads no. "I hope he's alright," Bill said. "That place is always open; I just wonder if he's alright?"

Blu and RC looked at the road sign as they passed by. "Biloxi, 40 miles." "We're almost there," RC said.

Blu smiled as he looked at the reverend. "RC," he said, "how you always get tied up in a bunch of mess?"

Reverend Charles shook his head back and forth then said as he snapped his finger. "I almost forgot, Blu. Bang Bang told me to give you this." RC reached into his pocket and pulls out a letter that said "Dad" on it. RC handed the letter to Blu.

"What am I going to do with it?" Blu asked. "I'm driving. Just stick it in the bag."

RC opened the bag that separated them and put the letter inside while looking at all the money in there. "Blu, this sure is a lot of money isn't it." Blu nodded his head yes and said, "Sure is, RC and I bet somebody's looking for it now."

The colonel looked at his men as they walked into his motel room. "What are you doing here?" he asked. "I told you to watch that girl and to follow her wherever she goes," he said.

"She's in school," the larger of the two men said as he closed the door behind him. "So?" the colonel said. "She might have the money hidden there."

"Colonel," the shorter of the two said, "we can't go on school property."

The colonel reached for his pack of cigarettes on the table in his room and took the last one out of the pack, lit it, and crumbled the pack and threw it toward the trashcan. The ashtray was overflowing with cigarette butts. "Yeah, I didn't think of that," he said as he lit his last cigarette. The colonel took a deep puff then said, "You two go to your rooms and rest up then. I have a lot to think about." The two men started out the door. "And if you please gentlemen, would one of you get me some cigarettes out in the motel lobby?"

The big one shook his head yes as they exited the room. The colonel was feeling tired. He had been up for two days without much sleep and wanted to lie in his bed and sleep but instead got up and walked over to where his overnight bag was and reached down and pulled the zipper open. He reached inside the bag and pulled out about an ounce of pure white powder in a plastic bag. He took it to the table that he'd been sitting at and threw it on the table. He looked at it. "Methamphetamine," he said, "our leader's great hope."

With that, he took a seat and reached into his pocket and took a small knife out and carefully cut the top part of the bag open. He reached the blade of the knife into the bag and withdrew a small amount of the crystalline substance. He carefully pulled the knife toward his nose and took his finger, clamping the other side of his nostril shut. He snorted the powder up his nostril. He put the knife back on the table and tilted his head back, momentarily forgetting his current predicament.

CHAPTER 14

The Gulf Stream G550 sliced through the air as the chairman looked at the computer readout on his screen. They had just launched a new model car and where anxious to see if it sold. Evidently it did. Sales forecasts where from five to six percent above the previous year's sales, which would certainly be good news. Chairman Ji-Kwang-ho was traveling to the United States to check on his company's major investment. Although everything was a subsidiary of the parent company, his Chaebol. He still had to make sure everything was running smooth, according to plan.

"Would you like some tea?" the flight attendant asked as the airplane struck through the sky. The chairman smiled at the attendant and said, "Yes, thank you," He looked at the young woman and thought about his youth and the young girl with whom he was madly in love.

APRIL 7, 1984
JINNAH NAVAL PORT FESTIVAL

"Ji, Ji," the young woman said, "why don't you want to go to your father's birthday party?" *If only she knew,* he thought. His father already had his life planned out, who he would marry, how he would carry out the family business and who he would and wouldn't associate himself with. Ji looked at his future life and didn't want any part of it. He had told his father of his feeling but that was to no avail.

"Hyn-woo, that is of no concern to us," Ji said, "let us just be happy here and now and not worry about what other people think or plan for us." The cherry blossoms where in full bloom and why waste this beautiful moment thinking of other people? Instead, he was with a woman he loved with all his heart, but his family was having none of this. They had already arranged a marriage to one of his father's associates daughters and that was it, or so they thought.

Hyn-woo, caught up in the moment, danced around happy and laughing, ready to make fun of anything. "This year at the festival," Hyn-woo began, "I think you should be a donkey and I his master?"

"And why is that?" Ji asked.

"So that I may tell you everything to do and you must follow me forever," Hyn-woo said as she fell into Ji's arms. "Oh, my love," Hyn-woo said, "I wish this could last forever."

Ji laughed as he kissed Hyn-woo and thought of what must be done. He pulled back from her and said, "Next week I travel to America with my farther for some potential new business," he said.

Hyn-woo sighed then frowned and said, "For how long?"

"One week, maybe two," he said, "It is very important business,"

"Well," Hymn-woo said, "so is mine, I must inform you," she said, smiling, "that I am with child." Hyn-woo hugged Ji as he laughed. "Oh now really?" he said as a worried look came over his face as he hugged her tightly.

"Mr. Ho," the flight attendant said, "we shall be landing shortly, is there anything that I can do for you?" The chairman drew back into the present and smiled and said, "No, I'm fine," and again turned toward the window of his airplane to think of things that might have been and things he must do.

Jo woke up as her cellphone alarm went off. She shook her head, still sleepy. "Damn, I don't want to go to work," she said. She said this everyday but today the urge to not go in is almost overwhelming. She thought of the events from the night before, her and Nikki. She knew that she would never submit to a man, but to a woman? The Bible said that what she had done was a sin, but how could something so wrong feel so right? She hadn't felt this way in a long time. What she and Buster did was satisfying, especially so since she controlled everything but this the new nest, the simple pleasure that she received instead of giving out made her feel empowered.

Jo sat up on the side of the bed having reached the conclusion that whatever this day would bring, that she would face it head on, and not hide away at home, becoming a prisoner of her own doubts and fears.

RC and Blu drove down I-10 and they turned on to the street leading to Beach Boulevard. They were armed and loaded for bear.

They had a bag full of money and were ready to go. They drove the length of the boulevard and surveyed the scene. The beachfront fronts were beautiful to the point that one forgot where they came from but appreciated where they were.

Blu and RC looked at the names on the hotels: Beau Ravage, Grand Biloxi, and marveled at their opulence. They decided to pull into the Grand Biloxi Casino. It was nice, but it didn't look too expensive.

"Hello," the greeter said as they exited their car in the casino parking lot.

Blu tossed the keys to the valet. "Keep it warm," he said. "We'll be leaving here soon with a lot of money."

Blu and RC walked into the casino and looked at all the people scurrying here and there. "Yeah RC," Blu said, "I can just see everything going well tonight."

RC looked at Blu then did a three-sixty as a pretty girl walked by. "Well," RC said, "I hope something good happens tonight, that's for sure." They laughed as they headed toward the Blackjack table.

Red didn't really mind jail, especially the county one. His hoes and baby mama could get him anything he wanted and wasn't nobody in there that was going to mess with him. He was on his home turf. He was waiting for the guard to escort him to meet with his lawyer up at the inmate center. He'd been in the game long enough to have planned for any screw up and was confident he was going to beat whatever the local police would come at him with. Hell they had no evidence and he had a lawyer that had and would get him out of anything. The only thing he was worried about was what that young bitch, Nikki, was goanna do.

He knew she was trouble from the time he met her, but she could be mighty persuasive and besides she was bringing him some new business from them Koreans so no matter how much trouble she caused, he could always count on the money.

"Red," the county corrections officer said, "let's go." Red got up from his bed in the jail cell and headed toward the cell door as it opened. He walked through the jail door entrance and turned back and looked at his cell, confident he wouldn't be in here much longer.

Sam Jackson sat back in his chair and nodded as he talked on his phone. "I know, Governor, I know," he said as he nodded his head back and forth. There was a knock at his office door. "Come on in," he said as he continued to listen to the governor. The door opened and in walked his wife. He smiled at her as he said, "Yes, Governor, I understand that there's an election coming up." Sam cupped the mouthpiece on the phone and pointed for his wife to take a seat.

She moved to one of the two chairs in front of his desk and sat in the one to the right of the desk. "Well, Governor," Sam said, "I think I know what you want and believe me, I'm doing everything I can to get to the bottom of this situation and to try and speed things up." Sam looked at his wife and smiled. He didn't care what was going on in this world. He knew his wife would be there right with him as she had been since the fifth grade when he'd follow her home from school every day. She was so beautiful then and was still so. "Okay, Governor," Sam said. "We have everything covered down here." Martha got up from her chair and moved around the desk and moved behind him, putting her hands on his shoulders and gently massaging them. He looked up at her and smiled almost forgetting who he was talking to on the phone. "Like I said, Governor," he said, "we got everything covered down here." He nodded his head one last time before saying, "Alright, bye," and then hanging up the phone.

"Whew," he said, "what in the world is going on? Why in the world is everybody so concerned with a couple of boys being killed at a crack-house."

"I don't know honey," his wife said as she started to rub his head. "Maybe the governor wants to make like he's tough on crime while providing jobs for the people of Alabama."

Sam turned his chair and pulled his wife into his lap. "Yeah," he said, "that could be it, Lord knows this state needs all the jobs we can get, and I just hope," he said as he hugged his wife, "that we're not selling our souls to satisfy the flesh." He embraced his wife and kissed her, not concerned at all about what anybody else wanted, at least not at the moment.

Jo looked at the clock on the wall. It was three o'clock and the day had gone pretty good. She had almost forgotten about the previous

night and had had a pretty production day. She had almost finished her recommendations and evaluations of the tenth grade class and was doing some follow up work to see which students she still needed to see. That was the one thing about work she thought. It could definitely take your mind off your problems at least for the time you were at work.

Suddenly, there was a knock at her office door. "Come on in," she said as she continues to work on her laptop.

"They followed me to school."

Jo looked up and to see Nikki standing in the door. Her mind reeled with the fact that this girl stepped into her life and instantly all these problems appeared. The fact that didn't escape her was that she was enjoying every minute of it. "Nikki," Jo said, "what is going on? There are two people that have been killed, some strange North Koreans looking for money and then you and I make love." Jo pulled back from her laptop and folded her hands in her lap.

Nikki walked into the office, closing the door and taking a seat across from Jo. The way she sat down, Jo thought, was like a cat, you know how they turn around in a circle then sit. This cat, Jo thought, was turning out to be one hell of a bitch, or so she thought. "Tell me the whole story, Nikki and start from the beginning."

Nikki sat back in the chair and sighed. "Well," she started. "I was at the spot and he walked in," she began, "I had seen the Koreans here with their hurrying about and talking in Korean at the grocery store with my mom, but I didn't know any, anyway he walks in," Nikki said as Jo studied her face to see if she was lying. "He orders a beer and to me seems a million miles away, you know like he's here but not here, just sitting there staring ahead, not really sipping his beer at all,"

Jo shook her head up and down then said, "Yeah, so?"

"Well I thought, maybe these Koreans got some money to spend; lord knows them Niggas up in the club didn't. You'd have to fuck them all night and suck their dick to get twenty dollars out of them. I wasn't having any of that so I approached him and introduced myself." Nikki paused and said, "What you got to drink? I need something to drink."

Jo said, "I don't have a refrigerator in the office. Girl, here." Jo opened her desk and got two dollars in loose change. "Here," she said,

"there's a drink machine down the hall. You go and get me and you a couple of Dews."

Nikki jumped up from her chair and took the money then headed toward the door but before she leaves she turned and said, "You know I really liked Jung-Hoon, I really did. I'm sorry that he didn't get—k"

"Get away," Jo said, finishing her sentence. Nikki smiled and headed out the door.

"Yeah, I guess so," she said as she closed Jo's office door.

Damn, what a piece of work, Jo thought. *And to think that I let myself become involved in this shit. What if Buster found out? Hell what if anybody found out? What then?* Jo sat back in her chair and closed her eyes. *Maybe I'll get lucky she thought and this girl will just disappear from my life*, she thought as she waited for Nikki to return.

Sheriff Johnson looked at his radio in his car and decided he wanted to hear some golden oldies circa 1980 or 1990. He flipped through his satellite stations until he got a song he recognized. It was Steely Dan's "Deacon Blue." *I just know how I feel; they call Alabama the crimson tide, call me Deacon Blue.* The sheriff nodded his head in time as the music played. He thought about the case he was presently on and compared it to things he had learned in his past. He remembered himself and how he felt about his parents, how they didn't understand him and how he wished to be respected just like them. Then he thought of his own daughter and what she must be feeling. He knew from experience that it wasn't easy being a teenager.

The Sheriff turned his car onto the main street leading to the high school where he would pick up his daughter and maybe have a long talk with her.

Jo waited as the school clock reached the 3:30 mark. School was about to be dismissed and she was certainly looking forward to it. The last twenty-four hours had been rough and she needed to be alone. She needed to think about everything and figure out where she stood, and about how if the previous hours were a blip on the life screen or a life-changing event. "Where is that girl?" she said as she began to wonder where Nikki was.

"Sheriff," the radio in the sheriff's car said, "we have to bring charges against the prisoners or release them. Can you come by and talk about

it?" The sheriff had been thinking about it. In fact, he couldn't think of anything else. He had received calls from the governor, the mayor, and got personnel visits from both the mayor and the ABI. That was why he was ratcheting it back just a bit, take his mind of the case a bit, and especially to see where his daughter fit into all of this. Then there was this girl Nikki. He definitely needed to meet her. What part did she have to play in all this?

"Oliver," the sheriff said, as he picked up the microphone on the radio. "I'm picking my daughter up from school and I should be there shortly—" the sheriff pressed on his brakes as a black SUV raced across his path. "Damn it ," he said as he slammed on his brakes. Now if he wasn't on his way to pick up his daughter he would turn on his sirens and put his foot to the pedal and been after this law breaker, but today they were lucky, extremely so. The sheriff grunted and shook his head and continued on toward the school.

Jo, tired of waiting, opened her office door and looks down the hall. No sign of Nikki. "Now where can that girl have gone off to?" she asked. Jo closed her office door and walked down the hall to the drink machine. No sign of Nikki. "What in the world could he have got to so fast?" Jo says. Jo looked at the drink machine and noticed a drink in the machine. Her mind sees this and says. "There's a drink that nobody has claimed. What if that was Nikki's drink?

Jo rushed down the hall looking left and right. Still no Nikki. What if she was telling the truth? What if somebody was following her? What then? These thoughts raced through Jo's mind as she headed to the front entrance. She opened the door and ran into... "Sheriff Johnson," Jo said as they practically ran into each other.

"Hey Jo," the sheriff said, "just who I was looking for."

Jo, surprised, put her hands on her hip and said, "Wow, really? And to what do I owe this great pleasure?" The sheriff and Jo had been friends for years. She was a couple of classes behind him when they were in high school but he had always looked on her fondly.

"Yes," he said, "I want to see if I can talk to one of your students,"

"And who might that be?" she said.

"Nikki," he said, "Nikki Flowers."

Jo looked at him and smiled. That was the only thing she could do to keep her jaw from dropping down. "Well," Jo said, "she is a student here, would you like for me to send for her?"

The sheriff came into the front door and let it close. "Yes, I would," he said, "and I also would like to talk to you about my daughter."

Jo looked at the watch on her arm. "Sheriff, I would like to address all the issues that you are concerned with but the time," she said, "In two minutes the bell will ring and the students will be leaving for the day. So if you want to see or pick up your daughter, you'd best get her out at the bus pickup."

The sheriff nodded his head and turned to exit, but then turned around. "You do have an address on Nikki, don't you?"

Jo smiled and said, "Of course I do. You just go ahead and pick up your daughter and I'll run and get it for you, okay?"

The sheriff smiled and said, "Okay, Jo. I'll be waiting for you," and then turned and exited the door.

Jo heard the door shut then turned and headed toward her office. *Where in the hell could that girl have gone?* she wondered. *Where could she be?*

CHAPTER 15

RC and Blu headed toward the hotel's front desk. "Hello," Blu said, "we would like to book two rooms for tonight."

"Would that be single or double?" the clerk asked.

Blu looked at RC and said, "Well it really doesn't matter, we'll take whatever you got."

The clerk checked her computer. "Well gentlemen," she said, "we only have two rooms available and that's two deluxe at one hundred forty-six per night."

Blu looked into the backpack and took out five hundred dollar bills and handed them to the clerk. "Hope that's enough to cover that," he said.

RC looked at Blu as he counted the money out. "Blu," he said, "let me talk to you for a minute," as the clerk took the money and started typing up the invoice. "Blu," he said, "you wouldn't happen to have a hit on you, would you?"

Blu looked at RC and shook his head no. "You know I don't walk around with that shit on me, RC," Blu said.

RC turned his head to the side and turned around in a full circle. "I mean," RC said, "I really need something, Blu."

Blu looked at RC and shook his head. He really didn't like dope heads, alcoholics, or anybody else who had a habit they couldn't pay for. At the same time, those same people paid his bills and put food on the table so he'd best get on to providing an answer and no certainly wouldn't be the right answer. RC would just walk the entire city of Biloxi until he found some, so he might as well help him.

"Let us check in first RC," Blu said, "Then I'll take you to find some." Blu smiled and RC smiled back. Blu turned and walked back to the check-in, firmly gripping the bag.

The colonel took a seat in the dimly lit room. "I don't want to continue to ask the same questions," he said, "but I must have answers,

okay?" The colonel reached into his pocket and took out his pack of cigarettes. He had long run out of the cigarettes from his country but the South Koreans had a few good brands, This, This Plus, and Airing, so he had stocked up on them but now. He was into search-and-find with the American brands.

He had watched Westerns as a little boy and saw the Marlboro ads so he knew he couldn't go wrong with any Marlboro cigarette. He had his men pick up a pack of the Marlboro menthol blacks. He took one out of the pack, lit it, and inhaled. Immediately he started coughing. He coughed so long that his eyes turned red. "Whew," he said, "that's just how I like them, good and strong."

He looked at Nikki all tied up with a gag in her mouth. She was so very young and pretty. She was about the age of one of his granddaughters he thought. The thing was, however, that this young girl had gotten herself involved in some serious business and when it came time for her to answer some questions and be held accountable, she had better. She would not only answer his questions truthfully and without hesitation, but she had better do it quickly for after all her life was on the line.

"Young lady," the colonel said, "Nikki, if I might, you have said before that you don't know where the money is and may I also assume that you don't know who killed our people?" Nikki shook her head yes. The colonel nodded his head and smiled. "You're lying, young lady," the colonel said. "I don't know why, even though it's easy to assume it's for the money." The colonel took another puff off of his cigarette. Again, he coughed. I think I'll let my associates talk to you for a minute and see if the answers aren't more readily available."

The big guy grabbed Nikki's hair and pulled it to the roots, jerking her head back. Nikki screamed. "Stop," she cried. "I'll tell you. I'll tell you."

The colonel looked at Nikki, then at his big associate. He shook no and the big one let go of her hair. "Now, let us begin again," the colonel said, "where is the money?"

Nikki, trying to buy time and keep herself alive, said, "I have to show you. I have to take you there."

The colonel looked deeply into Nikki's eyes, trying to see the deceit that he knew was there. "Alright then," he said, unable to see the obvious lie. "Why don't you take us to where it is then?" The colonel knew this was a lie, but what choice did he have? He had to find the money or at least where it was in order for him to live.

Sheriff Johnson looked at his daughter as they ride home. "Baby," he said, "I want you to know that I'm willing to work with the counselors and teachers to get this all back right." He smiled at his daughter. He knew that…

"I don't care what you do, Dad," she said, "I'm goanna enjoy my life and do what I want to." Sheriff Johnson looked at his daughter with a blank face. He didn't know what to say. He knew whatever side of the argument he took, he was going to be wrong so he decided to shut up and let her talk.

"Me and Nikki," she began, "we're gonna do a lot of things together, you know?"

"No, I don't know," the sheriff said, "Why don't you tell me"?

"We're gonna go to Atlanta and get an apartment and be in some of those music videos," she said. The sheriff nodded his head and continued to play along with his daughter, to see where this was going says.

"Y'all got a place to stay?" he asked.

"No," she replied. "But Nikki's got an aunt there or something."

The Sheriff had asked Jo about Nikki at the school but she wasn't there. Jo had seemed busy so he just let it drop. This girl's name, however, just kept popping up all over the place. He made a mental note to see her first thing in the morning. "What about school? Baby, don't you want to graduate and go to college?"

"Oh dad," his daughter said, "I'm not talking about now, but after I graduate…" His daughter looked out the window of the police cruiser and said, "You know what I want for Christmas?"

"No I don't," the sheriff said.

"One of those new iPhones. You know what? You can…" His daughter continued to expound on the virtues on the newest gadget to hit the masses, while he just smiled and felt at least some relief that his little girl was still just that: a little girl. And maybe with a lot of

patience and a little understanding, they could both make it through this phase of her life.

The colonel looked out the window of the SUV they drove, looking at the country landscape. The trees and bushes, along with all the cows and goats and other various farm animals, really made this quite a beautiful place, not the hustle and bushel of the big city. *Just a quiet and peaceful place*, he thought. He almost smiled as his mind started to drift back to home and how he was raised—the good old days. "Sir," the driver said, "We're almost there."

The colonel turned his head and looked at Nikki, his mind back to the present situation. "I hope for your sake," the colonel said, "that you are telling the truth."

Nikki stared at the colonel with those dark brown wide eyes of hers. *She really was quite pretty*, the colonel thought, *it would be a shame to...* "We're here, sir," the driver said as they made a right hand turn into the driveway where Nikki said the money was.

The colonel said, "Stop the car," as he proceeded to check out the place. It was a deserted old wood house with a stack of firewood on the front porch. The house was sort of a military gray color with a satellite dish on the side. There were no cars parked outside but the grass was cut and had the appearance of being kept up though no one seemed to live there. "Alright," he said. "Let's proceed."

The car moved forward into the yard and came to a stop in front of the front porch. The colonel nodded at the driver and said, "Get out and check it out." The driver nodded his head up and down then exited the vehicle. He closed the door then reached behind him and pulled out his gun and moved to the front porch. "Ki-swan," the colonel said as he turned in his seat and looked at his other associate seated next to Nikki. "You circle around the house and make sure no one is here." Ki-swan, the biggest of the colonels two associates also nodded his head yes and exited the vehicle. The colonel looked at Nikki and said, "Very soon we'll find out if you're telling the truth." Again, Nikki said nothing as she continued to stare straight ahead.

The Gulf Stream jet came to a stop on the Montgomery, Alabama airport airstrip as two SUVs with dark windows approach the airplane.

The chairman looked out his window as the airplane came to a stop. He looked at his head of security. The man in a dark suit and with dark shades on said, "Chairman, we are here."

The chairman nodded his head as he unfastened his seat belt. He had a lot to do in short period of time. His life was on a strict timetable from beginning to end. There was no stopping what had had to be done, both for his country and for his family. The path that he chose was one few traveled and fewer still committed to. The chairman rose from his seat, directed by the security force of young men all around him.

"This way sir," the head of security directed him. The chairman stood and was hustled down the exit ramp toward the SUVs. He barely noticed the increase in temperature as he exited the plane. It was hot. He noticed as his team rushed him toward the waiting vehicles. The Alabama sun was hot in November like it was in July. It just depended on what day you caught it. The chairman, as he walked down the exit ramp, feeling the change in temperature from the climate-controlled airplane, thought about his mission. His goal for this trip and the consequences it could have on the future.

The colonel's men circumnavigated the house, looking at every possible angle. They looked at each other and nodded. They were certain that no one was there. They both walked back toward the vehicle. The big one opened the car door and looked at the colonel. "Everything's clear," he said.

The colonel opened the car door and said, "Get the girl" and then exited the vehicle. Nikki, sitting in the right hand side of the vehicle, stared straight ahead as the bigger of the two Koreans grabbed her by the arm. Instead of walking around the vehicle to open the door, he pulled Nikki across the seat, making her exit on the left hand side of the vehicle.

Everyone was out of their vehicle as the colonel looked at Nikki. "Okay young lady," he said. "Where do we go from here?"

Nikki looked at the colonel then said, "Straight ahead into the house."

The colonel nodded at his men. "Okay," he said, "let's go." The shorter of the two associates led the way toward the house. He walked

up the steps and went to the door. He turned the doorknob. The door was locked. "The door is...," before he could finish his sentence, a shot from a gun rang out. The three Koreans dropped for cover.

"What's going on?" the colonel asked. "I thought you said everything was clear!" he shouted at his two men. "Nikki merely smiled and instead of ducking for cover, walked up the stairs and smiled.

"Nikki!" a voice called out. "You alright?"

The colonel and his two men scoured the landscape with their eyes. They saw nothing. The colonel's two associates had their guns drawn but with no place to target. The colonel looked at Nikki. "Please," he said, "you may answer."

"Yeah, it's me," Nikki said as she stood up and started to move away from the colonel and his men. The big Korean pointed his pistol at her. "I wouldn't do that if I were you," a voice from the woods said. The colonel and his men swept the woods still looking for the source of the voice. Nothing. The colonel motioned for his men to lower their weapons. Once they lowered their guns, they saw some tree branches moving not twenty-five feet from them. Out of the bushes walked a man covered in camouflage gear. He was carrying a Black Rain BRO-P69 rifle.

They then heard more bushes moving and snapping. Suddenly, they saw three—no, six—men move from the tree line, all in camo gear and each carrying some sort of semi-automatic weapon. A man to the right of them emerged with Bushmaster MOEM4 rifle drawn. The first man moved forward toward Nikki. Nikki ran toward him. The colonel cringed, wanting to stop her but when faced with overwhelming firepower, the best thing to do was to stay put.

"Uncle Bug," Nikki said as she hugged the tall black man in the camo gear.

"Hey baby," he said as he hugged her back. "What youyou're your friends doing out here?" Bug asked.

"Oh, they don't matter," Nike says. "You can kill them if you want. Nobody would miss them."

Uncle Bug looked at Nikki then at the colonel and his men. "Naw," he said, "that would be a waste of good ammunition. We are hunting deer right now."

The colonel studied the situation. He was always used to holding the edge especially with just common people. But, he marveled that the United States was one of those few, if not the only, countries where the general population was as well armed, often better than the authorities. He wondered how they ever kept order in this country when Nikki said, "I know what you mean Uncle Bug" Nikki smiled at the colonel and then said, "I don't want you to kill them, especially when we got money to talk with."

The colonel looked at Nikki and wondered what he had gotten himself into. He had seriously underestimated this young woman. He just hoped that it wouldn't cost him his life.

CHAPTER 16

Jo looked at the clock on the wall. It was six o'clock and she hadn't heard anything from Nikki. What a day! She was so filled with anxiety that she didn't know what to do! She was lost in her thoughts about what to do next when she heard footsteps on the porch. She heard a key in the lock and the door opened. It was Buster. She smiled as he walked through the door. "Now that's what I want to see," she said, "somebody I love walking through the door." Buster smiled that illuminating smile of his. She was glad that she had spent the money she had at the time on his teeth instead of the latest television set available.

"Hey, Mom," Buster said as their eyes met. Jo could tell immediately that something was wrong as Buster ducked his head down. "Mom," Buster said as he looked around the room. "They're investigating this girl down at the station."

"Yes," Jo said.

"The girl who was here the other night."

"Who?" Jo said as if she didn't know.

"Nikki," Buster said.

"Nikki," Jo said. "You mean the student that I was counseling the other night?"

"I guess," Buster said.

Jo smiled as she looked at Buster. "Buster, I counsel all the students at school. I have an open door policy. They're free to stop by at any time to discuss their problems. You know that."

Buster looked at his mom and narrowed his eyes. He knew that there was something that she was hiding. He just didn't know what.

"What was she here for, Mom?" Buster asked. "She and another student where having a problem at school," Jo said.

Buster knew that the sheriff's daughter and Nikki where involved in something. He just didn't know what. "But why was she here?" Buster asked again.

Jo stopped smiling at Buster and looked at him straight forward in the eyes and said, "She has problems, son," Jo says. "Just like me and you."

Buster nodded his head up and down. "Just like you and me, huh?" he asked. "Would having sex with your son qualify?"

A shocked expression came over Jo's face. "What do you mean?"

"I mean what I say Mom," Buster said. "I mean it just isn't right."

Jo looked at Buster wide-eyed and said, "I know it's not right just like all the other stuff that's happened to us, Buster. None of it's right, none of it."

Buster looked at his mother, the woman who raised him, with nothing. "I guess this is where I feel guilty, Mom, for all the sacrifices you made and all. I know that's what you told me when I was young but I'm grown now. So tell me who my daddy is?" Jo immediately turned her back to Buster. "Ready to run, huh Mom?" Buster asked. "Not today, Mom. Not today." He grabbed his mother by the shoulder and forcibly turned her toward him. "Why, Mom?" Buster asked. "Why all the secrets, why all the silence?"

Jo looked at Buster and just like all the other times he asked who his father was, she did not answer. "Mom," Buster said, "Nikki is under investigation. That means anybody that had contact with her these last few days is too." Buster released his mother from his grip and looked at her. He knew she was scared and confused or thinking of another lie. "It's time, mom," he said. "It's time for us to be honest with each other, to be real." Jo looked at Buster and decided it was time to tell him, tell him of her shame and the past, about how he was born from a relative who raped her and afterward talked about her, about how the young people were lost, about how all they needed was a good butt whipping, everything but the truth of the matter. About how they caused most of the problems that their children caused or were in.

"I was young," Jo began, "and I was unaware about life. I was just a young girl who fell into a situation that I had no control over." Buster looked at her, looking for the stutter, the look down or look away that most people did when they were lying. He saw none of that. "We had a family gathering and a step-uncle of mine forced himself on me, that's it," Jo said as Buster studied her response.

Buster compared this response with the other answers he had been given through the years. "Then he left town and he died in Iraq.".

"What did the DNA test say?"

Jo looked at him wide-eyed. "There weren't any DNA tests then," she said, "I cut off all contact with them after that and buried it deep in my memory."

Buster believed that his mother is telling the truth, or at least what she thought was the truth. "Mom, we need to end this," he said. "We need to put it behind us."

Jo knew what was coming next. "Why don't we have a DNA test to tell us the truth?" Buster said.

Jo stepped back from Buster, searching for the right thing to say. She hadn't been in contact with her relatives in years. After she went to college, she never went to another family reunion even though every year she received an invitation in the mail. "I just don't know Buster," Jo said, "I haven't been in contact with those people in years." Jo walked back toward the kitchen. She suddenly turned and said, "Why is that so important? That was years ago and a long time ago. Just forget about it, baby. It's just you and me."

Buster looked at his mother and felt what she was feeling. He knew that a lie was always comforting. It hid the truth and what the reality was in any situation. It just made you feel so much better. "Let's put it to rest, Mom, while we still can. If not for you, then for me," Buster answered back. "Can you tell me that was the only one? The only person you had sex with?"

Jo had been telling the same thing to people, to Buster through the years that she had almost forgot about… "I'll try to get in touch with them," she finally said. "I guess it is time we find out the truth," Jo said as she thinks back about the day after, about the boy she was sure was to be with for the rest of her life.

Blu and RC rode around the streets of Biloxi. Biloxi was a beautiful place right off the Gulf of Mexico. The streets were clean but they knew how to find trouble. The first sign of an abandoned home, of people walking the street with no place to go would lead them to what they wanted. "Over there, over there," RC said as they roll down Division Street in Biloxi. Blu looked at a sign off the road he was on

and made a right-hand turn onto it, Main Street. RC said, "Yeah, this is the place. I can just feel it." RC and Blu looked at the streets. They looked for a young man standing on the corner alone smoking a cigarette or talking on his cell phone, the kind of young men that populate the streets of America, the kind of men they used to be.

"Pull over, pull over!" RC shouted. Blu looked at where RC was pointing and turned the car in that direction. Blu saw the person that that RC was pointing to. It was an Asian man with a semi-Mohawk, dressed in all black, talking on a cellphone. They pulled up to the young man and RC rolled down the window.

"What's up, bro?" he asked.

"What is it looking like?"

The Asian man looked at Blu and RC. "What ya'll looking for?" he asked in a perfect Southern drawl.

"We looking for a hit," RC said.

"Don't anybody around here sell a hit," the man said as he held his cellphone to his chest.

RC looked at Blu and Blu looked at RC. "This ain't Alabama, RC," Blu said, "you got to get out the car and tell the man what you want."

RC nodded his head as Blu came to a stop. "All right then," RC said as he exited the car. He walked across the street to the Asian man. They engaged in some kind of conversation and walked down the street to the ranch style house. They walked up the drive as Blu watched what was going on. He thought about how many times in his life that he had been in similar circumstances and how they had turned out bad.

He didn't have his gun, but he did have the gun that was in the bag, the twenty-five caliber. Blu looked at the time on the clock in his car. It was exactly 6:45 p.m. Suddenly he saw RC running across the street. "Blu!" he yelled, "let's go! Let's go."

Blu looked at RC running across the street and saw two Asian men chasing him. RC grabbed the door handle of the car and opens it. He jumps in to the car and looked at Blu. "Punch it ," he said. Blu floored the 1968 Plymouth Barracuda with its 426-hemi engine. The car roared as if shot out of a cannon. Blu does a U-turn and headed back up the street the way they came. The two Asian men leapt from in front of the car as it headed toward them.

They turned and look at the car as it roars past them. They shook their fists at them as they pass them. "What in the hell is going on, RC?," Blu asked.

RC laughed as they sped up the street. "Oh nothing," he said, "Let's just say I made a withdrawal without a deposit."

Blu shook his head. They sped up Main Street and made a wide turn back onto Division Street. "Why didn't you just pay for the shit?" Blu asked.

RC smiled and said, "I pay for what I got to pay for. If I can find a way out of it, I do."

Blu shook his head as the car sped down the street.

Red grinned as he walked out of the jail. "Those folks ain't got nothing," he said as he looked at his attorney, Deandre with her coal black eyes and long black hair, who might remind someone of a sorceress. In a way she was, getting Red out of the mess that he was constantly involved in. To him it might have meant being free and able to make money and see whatever women of the week he might be involved with, but to her it meant work, billable hours that must be paid for.

"I know that you're happy," Deandre said. "But we have a long ways to go and that means more..." Deandre let it hang for a moment for effect. "What is the term I'm looking for?" she asked.

Red smiled, revealing the gold and diamond grill that he liked to sport. "When has that been an issue?" he said, "You've always gotten your money."

Deandre flashed that pretty white smile of hers and said, "Look Red, let's not bullshit each other. I'm here for the money, point blank. I don't care if you're guilty or not. I just have to be paid." Red threw his head back as he heard the cold hard truth of the situation. He knew Deandre. In fact, they both went to high school together, but he knew everyone wanted to be paid, especially with the economy the way it was. There were no freebies. "Look Deandre, you know you wouldn't be here and I would still be in jail if we didn't trust each other." DeAndre frowned. "You know what I mean," he said, "You know that I'm a winner and you will get paid, so stop the bullshit, okay?"

DeAndre looked at Red and smiled. She had known him since grade school. The other kids picked on him, calling him names such as "Four Eyes," "Poor Mouth," or whatever. The kids always had something to say about Red. That is what fueled him, what drove him. The negative. The downright words that told him that he wasn't fit to live, that he didn't deserve a place on this earth. The people that were judging him? Red knew that they were no better than him and in a lot of cases, a lot worse. The fact that most of them were black in this situation didn't bother him. These people didn't pay his bills, or live his life. This fact didn't escape him, though he didn't consider this a problem. Whatever anybody did was cool to him. He just had a problem with what he did to survive and live was a problem to them even though not a one of them would ever lift a hand to help him, he knew it wasn't their fault and it wasn't his. It was just the way it was.

"Deandre," he said, "I have an off shore account that has been deposited in your name. The amount is three hundred thousand dollars and that is to use to pay you are agreed upon fee and also for you to provide for my family in case everything doesn't go as planned."

"What plan?" Deandre said.

Red grinned and looked at her and said, "It's best you don't know everything just yet. There's a fact of law that any court will stand behind."

"And what's that?" Deandre asked.

"Plausible deniability."

Deandre shook her head and looked at Red, wondering what the hell she has gotten herself into.

Sheriff Johnson sat in his chair with his hands folded together, twiddling his thumbs. He looked at what he was doing and laughed. "This case," he said, "has got me twiddling my thumbs." The prisoners had been released. Not enough evidence. He had to start from scratch building a case against someone. He just didn't just know who. He also thought about his daughter and what she was going tomorrow. He leaned back in his chair. He thought about everything that was going wrong and what direction this case was leading then he thought, *Damn, the game is in two days.*

CHAPTER 17

It was a beautiful morning. The sun was shining and it was about time for the pecans to fall. Pecans had always been big business in this part of Alabama, and people were already looking at which trees had a lot of fruit and which ones didn't. It was funny. In years when there was a lot of rain, the trees didn't bear a lot of fruit or pecans, but in years when there was hardly any rain, it was a bumper crop. Farming was funny that way. When you expected a big year, it didn't happen but when you didn't, you could hardly keep up with the demand.

The fellas had gathered at the corner on this cold crisp November morning ready for gossip. They had heard Red was out and nobody had seen RC and Blu. Most of all, however, was that the game was one day away and everyone had to get in last the taunting. The last of bragging that lasted day in and day out about who was better: Auburn or the University of Alabama.

"Shorty," Ray Heard said, "Alabama got more championships than Auburn and then played in bigger games." Ray spat on the ground for effect and plus the fact that he smoked a lot and had a lot of film built up. "Alabama got the best recruits, the best defense and they got history." Ray smiled as he said this. He didn't want shorty to know the other side of being a fan. You where one hundred percent for your team and you knew they were the biggest and baldest in the land but what if they lost? After all, anything could happen and with Auburn it most certainly would...

Shorty laughed. "You bamas always talking about your tradition and the bear, but the bear been dead for thirty years... ain't no bringing him back," Shorty looked down and kicked the ground. "Y'all are the worst fans in the world," Shorty said. "If you win it's not enough and if you lose you want to kill somebody." Shorty shook his head. "Welcome to Alabama."

"Fuck that, fuck that," Knothead Barnes said. Knothead came and went on the corner. He showed up on at the end of the month but disappeared on the first when the government checks rolled in; he owed too many people money. "Red then got out," he said. "He too smart for them white folks, they can't hold him." Knothead threw his fist down emphatically as he makes his point. "They always looking too lock up ant Black man that fits their description, their profile. They don't know who did it just that he's poor and black enough for them."

Ray Heard looked at Knothead then the rest of the fellas. "Yeah Knothead, a lot of what you saying is true but," Ray paused, "what that got to do with the game?" The fellas on the corner laughed as other arguments erupted about who would win Auburn or Alabama at this year's Iron Bowl.

Sam Jackson rushed through the door of the Kwantung automotive plant. He was a little late by five or ten minutes, but hey, this meeting was called at the last minute. The chairman was in town and he was to be snoozed and impressed about the investment his company had made in Alabama. He made the trip there every two to three months. Sometimes he took a full tour of the facility, other times he made it to the fence of the property turned around and left. You never knew, but whatever. The state, city, and county had a lot riding on the jobs that his company provided and the money it brought into the state so he was more than happy and eager to appease him.

Sam stopped at the guard's shack and said, "State Senator Sam Jackson."

The guard looked at his guest list and said, "I'm sorry, Mr. Jackson, but your name isn't on the guest list."

Sam looked away from the security guard. "I'm sorry," he said, "I'm State Senator Jackson."

The guard flipped a few pages on his sign-in roster and said, "I'm sorry. I do not see your name on the sign-in."

Sam's mind was reeling. What the hell did they call him here for if he would not be admitted? "If you just contact Mr. Jimmy Cane," he said.

The guard smiled at him and said, "Okay Mr. Jackson, I'll call him immediately." The guard picked up his radio and said, "Jimmy, Jimmy, come in!" The guard waited for a response. No answer. "Jimmy, Jimmy, come in!" the guard reiterated. Still no answer.

Sam waited and threw his back as the guard continued to try and get in touch with Jimmy Cane. Sam snapped his fingers and pulled out his iPhone. He scrolled down the menu to access his contacts. He clicked on Jimmy's name and pressed the send button. The phone rang once then twice. Jimmy answered the call and said, "Yeah, Jimmy! I'm at the gate, but they won't let me in."

"Sam," Jimmy said, "something has come up and the meeting has been cancelled."

Sam paused. Well he thinks something must have happened and the chairman was needed elsewhere. "All right," Sam said, "just let me know if I can be of any help to y'all."

"Sure Sam," Jimmy said, "we'll be in touch."

Sam pressed the off button on his iPhone, turned, and started to walk away.

"You all right?" the guard said as Sam walked away.

"Sure," Sam said.

"I'm getting better every minute," Sam glanced at the guard as he exited the entrance. He walked briskly toward his car thinking about what just happened and what the kids wanted and what he was supposed to do for his wife when suddenly his phone rang. He was about halfway to his car but stopped and looked at the number and who was calling. It was the governor's office. "Shit, just what I need," Sam said as he pressed the receive button on the phone. "Hello?" he said.

"Sam," the voice said, "what the fuck are you doing?"

"What?" Sam asked.

"You're fucking up. Those niggas are out of jail and you're fucking up our business," the voice said.

"Who is this?" Sam said, his face turning red and starting to burn with anger.

"You dumb fuck, don't you know that's why the Koreans cancelled your meeting? Do you know how much money they bring in? You had better tighten up!" The phone went dead as Sam took the phone

from his ear and looked at it. Finally he shook his head and continued walking toward his SUV. *Racism and money*, he thought as he opened his car door, *would Alabama ever change?*

The colonel sat in the motel room, seething. The girl had certainly pulled one over on him and he didn't like it. *This young girl*, he thought. He should have killed her when he had the chance. Now he had lost his only lead about where the money was and the people in the community knew he was there. They didn't know he was North Korean or whatever nationality. They just knew he was there. His government's plan to saturate America with drugs had hit a snag. *That's all*, he thought, *things would be going smoothly soon enough.* His cellphone rang. He looked at it on the table of his motel room and debated whether to answer it or not. It went off again as he stared at it, thinking about who it might be. He got up off the bed and moved to his cellphone and looked at it. He grabbed it off the table and looked at the number.

"Okay," he said. It was another agent assigned to this endeavor. He wondered what he wanted since the two of them barely communicated, much less talked on the phone. He pressed a button and was connected. "Yes," he said.

"Un, my friend comes" was the reply. Colonel Un recognized the voice. It was Colonel Li. *Uh oh*, Colonel Un thinks. This man was hardly his friend, more like a dreaded rival looking to capitalize on mistakes both real and imagined, just to let you know that they were there waiting to take your spot. "This is Li," Colonel Li finally said. "I just wanted you to know that our contact, Red, has been released from jail."

Colonel UN raised an eyebrow, surprised that Red was released and also that Colonel Li knew about it. "What do you want, Li?" Colonel Un asked. "We already know that and I am working on it." He was lying of course but he knew Li was fishing for something. He just didn't know what.

"I just wanted to make sure," Colonel Li said, "that you knew. That's all. I might need you to share some of the information you have in the future, okay?"

Colonel Un smiled and said, "Of course. I would be most glad to," We'll be in touch." Colonel UN hung up. Red was the contact—no the lynchpin—of all these endeavors in Alabama. That Colonel Li knew more than he and that the home state intelligence was funneling the information to him more than hurt his feelings. He knew that the exalted one had lost confidence in him. That meant he would have to excide the mission, make this into something that nobody could dispute. Not a failure by any means. In other words, he would have to hit "a home run" to use American vernacular. Something he had no idea of what or how he would do to accomplish this.

Sheriff Johnson sat at his desk and thought about his situation. He had a teenage daughter who was being a teenager, a case without any answers, and a mess of people looking for answers. The fact that Red and his crew had been released didn't help matters. *Beep, Beep, Beep,* his cell rang. "Who in the hell was that?" he asked. His mind raced as he thought who it could be. "Fuck it," he said as he pressed the receive call button on his cellphone as he puts it up to his ear.

"Daddy," the voice said. *Ah,* he thought, *someone he knew.* "Frankie and I are going up to the mall in Auburn," she said. "Can I use the credit card you gave me?" she asked.

"What do you want to buy, baby?" he asked.

"Well I want to…" there was a knock on the door of his office.

"Come in," he said as the door swung open and Samuel Jackson walked in.

"We need to talk," he said as the sheriff nodded at him.

"Okay, baby," the sheriff said, "you know we set a limit. Let's stick to it, okay?" The sheriff nodded his head as he looked at Sam. Sam seemed worried or bothered about something, or so he thought. He didn't know the man, but he knew how to read people. After all, he was in law enforcement. He knew when people where bothered or lying. Sam's rapid eye movement, the way he moved quickly into the office, told Sheriff Johnson that something was wrong. "Okay, baby," the sheriff said, "I've got to go."

"Daddy," his daughter said, "I love you."

From the age of three to her now teen years, when your daughter tells you she loves you, it meant something. "And I love you too," he said as he hung up the phone. Sheriff Johnson looked at Sam Jackson and Sam looked at him. Both of them where sizing up their opponent. Sheriff Johnson knew this would not be good.

"Well, Sheriff," Sam said, "it seems our prime suspects are out on bond, and after all, the help and resources the state of Alabama has provided to you," Sam paused, "there still hasn't been anybody charged in the murder of these two young men gunned down as they visited the home of the suspects."

Sheriff Johnson smiled as he looked at Sam. "Sam, this is the United States of America. Everybody has rights and if they have enough money and a good enough attorney, they can and will defend themselves against any and all allegations," Sheriff Johnson said.

Sam, beet red, threw a temper tantrum. "God dammit, Sheriff," he said, "do you know what's at stake here? Jobs, jobs, jobs, and more jobs. What this country needs and Alabama desperately needs," he continued. "Do you know," Sam said as he bent over the sheriff's desk, "that Alabama is one of the leading states in America in automotive jobs? Not Michigan or California, but Alabama."

Sam said this emphatically, pounding his fist on Sheriff Johnson's desk. Sheriff Johnson raised an eyebrow. He knew how important jobs were. Hell, the country was in a recession, jobs were scarce, but did that mean he was convicting anybody and everybody because they threatened the system that was in place? Or did he do what he thought and what he believed: convict the people or person responsible beyond a shadow of a doubt? Damn the consequences. What was wrong with the truth?

"I know how you feel, Sam," the sheriff said, "but what about the parents of those boys killed? Don't they deserve the truth?" Sam nodded his head yes. "And what about the parents of them boys charged?" he asked. "Don't you think they deserve the truth?" Again, Sam nodded his head in agreement. "I know it may seem to you and your higher ups that we are just dumb niggas in east Alabama that you got to cover for and make sure you do their job for them, but believe me," the sheriff began, "Mama and Daddy didn't raise any fool, and

I know if you keep hunting around in the field, something's going to run." The sheriff smiled as Samuel Jackson looked at him. To him, the sheriff was either the smartest son-of-a-bitch he ever met or one stupid mutherfucker who didn't know when to take what was given to him. He just really didn't know.

"Sheriff," Sam began, "I've got pressure from my side and you've got pressure from your side so why don't we…"

"Work together," the Sheriff said, completing his thought.

Sam shook his head up and down. "Yeah," he said. "How about that?" he said. "A southern Republican and a Southern Democrat working together." They both laughed. "Okay," Sam said. "What's the plan?"

"The way I see it," the sheriff said, "is that you take what you know and I take what I know and we put them together. The way I see it," the sheriff continued, "this is more than two black men gunned down at a crack house, much more."

"Why do you say that?" Sam Jackson asked. "Why all the pressure on both you and me? From the governor's office, no less," Sam said and then thought a second. He then said, "I can see where you're coming from. These things happen in every neighborhood in Alabama every day, what makes this one so special?"

"Exactly," the sheriff said, "Why is this case any different from any other? Ding, ding, ding, ding! The answer is," the sheriff began, "the money."

Sam Jackson looked at the sheriff. His mind ran through the calls from the Koreans and from the governor's office and he saw a pattern developing in his mind. People were either trying to protect money or make money; there was no question about that. He just had to find out who had the most to gain or the most to lose. "I agree, Sheriff," Sam said, "but what can we do about it?"

"Recheck the facts and work together," the sheriff said. "In fact, let's start now. What do you know that I don't know?" They both looked at each other, intently deciding if they should trust one another or not.

Finally Sam said, "Well, Sheriff, when I first heard about the situation…" The sheriff leaned forward in his chair listening intently.

CHAPTER 18

RC and Blu were sound asleep. They had spent the previous night gambling and living with any kind of debauchery they could find. They both lay fast asleep as there is a knock at their door. RC stirred from his sleep, got up, and walked to the door. He rubbed his head as he yawned and looked out the peephole. "Yeah," he said, "Room Service,"

"Room Service?" RC asked as he opened the door. "I didn't order no room—"

Suddenly, three men rushed into the room and one of them grabbed RC and slammed him on the floor. Blu, hearing the commotion, woke up.

"RC," he said, "what the fuck is going on?" Blu turned over and pulled his pillow upon his head. One of the three men ran to Blu and stuck his nine-millimeter pistol in his ear.

"Get up," he said.

Blu, still groggy from sleep said, "What?" as he turned and looked at the man holding the gun to his face.

"Get up!" he shouted at Blu. Blu jumped up out of bed and saw RC lying on the floor.

"Over there, over there!" the man with the gun motioned to Blu to join RC.

"Lay down, lay down," he said. Blu complied, still wondering what the fuck was going on.

"You think you can rob me and get away with it?" the man with the gun asked. Blu and RC look at each other, each wondering what the hell the man with the gun was talking about. "Get up, get up!" the man with the gun said. RC and Blu rise slowly to their feet.

"What in the hell is going on here, bro?" RC asked. "We didn't rob nobody."

The man with the gun dropped the gun to his side and walked closer to RC. "Still don't recognize me?," he said.

RC looked closely at the Asian man then slowly went over recent events in his mind and realized it was the drug dealer on the corner yesterday. The one he ran out on without paying. "Oh," RC said, "you the guy from yesterday, right?" RC smiled and said, "I'm sorry, I had to get back to the hotel and pay the clerk before they kicked us out. If you let me get my wallet…" RC started toward his pants laying on the couch in the suite.

One of the two men on the side of Blu and RC grabbed RC by the arm. "Stop," the drug dealer said, "get his pants."

The man walked to the couch and picked up RC's pants and took them to RC and handed him the pants. Blu reached into his right rear pocket and pulled out his wallet. "Here is…" RC said as the man snatched the wallet from his hand and took it to the man with the gun. The man unfolded the wallet and took out all of RC's money and counted it. "Let's see here one, two hundred dollars?" the man said, then looked at RC and continued, "I guess that would just about cover your bill." He smiled. "But how much more," he paused then said," for your life?" He raised up the gun at RC as a look of fear crossed RC's face.

Blu raised his hands up and said, "Wait a minute, wait a minute! You got what you want, your money, right? Why you want to add murder to it? Here," he said as he motioned to his wallet lying on the dresser. "I've got a couple of thousand in it, just take it and go."

The man with the gun motioned to his associate to get the wallet. His associate retrieved the wallet and handed it to him. He lowered his gun as he pulled the money out of the wallet and began to count it.

Jo hurried down the hall as students called out her name. "Hello, Miss Clearly," a student with a multicolored weave said. Jo nodded and smiled as she continued to her destination. She had an appointment with a college recruiter to recommend which of the senior class students might be a good fit for their school. She turned the corner and almost ran into Nikki.

"Slow down," Nikki said as Jo stopped. They both looked at each other, studying one another. Nikki said, "Hi, Jo."

Jo looked at Nikki and with that smile of hers that could light up a city and shook her head and said, "Hi," as she continued walking down the hall.

Nikki followed. "You know what happened?" Nikki started.

"No," Jo said, shortening her strides so that could listen to what Nikki had to say.

"Those Koreans took me hostage and—"

Jo stopped and looked at Nikki, putting her hands on her hips. "Now Nikki," Jo said, "this isn't just another one of your stories, is it?" Jo knew that the Koreans were after Nikki and the information that she might have about their money, but kidnapping her?

"Don't tell me you didn't miss me yesterday, Jo," Nikki says. "Where did you think I went?"

Jo frowned and dropped her hands from her hips as she resumed walking toward her appointment. "Well, I don't know?" Jo said, "What I do know, however, is that I'm late for an appointment and that you have to go to class." Jo looked at her wristwatch. "Let's meet in my office at let's say, noon?"

"Lunch?" Nikki said. "You treating?," Nikki asked.

"Yeah," Jo said as she turned to walk down a hall on the left. "To whatever the school cafeteria has to offer," Jo said as headed away from Nikki down the busy hallway.

The drug dealer-turned-robber (now working on murder) counted the money over again as Blu and RC looked at each other.

Blu, impatient and eager to get this shit over with, said, "Look, you've got what you wanted and more. Just go ahead and take the money and go. What else do you want?"

The man looked at Blu then took the money from the wallet and put it into his pocket. He then aimed his gun at RC and said, "You two think you can come into my town and take from me? It wasn't nothing but a twenty dollar hit," RC said, almost pleading with the gunman. "You two search the room," he motioned to his two associates.

"Yeah," he said, "you two took what you wanted from me so the least I can do is the same to you, no?" His two associates fanned out

across the room, searching for anything they could find of value. Blu and RC remained silent hoping they wouldn't find the real money.

Jo closed the door of the meeting room and looked at her watch. 11:45. She was nearly exhausted. The past two days with both Buster and Nikki had left her mentally tired. She was, after all, a country girl at heart. She was used to people acting the same being the same every day, and people pretty much leaving you alone, if you wanted to be alone. Now all these questions especially from Buster and the unpredictability of Nikki had her worried and what about the involvement of those Koreans? She had much to think about as she walked to the cafeteria and then back to her office.

"Hey Jo," the voice said behind her. Jo turned and it was Sheriff Johnson, all six feet, five inches of him. *Of all the people,* Jo thought, *him.*

"Hey, Sheriff Johnson," Jo said as she smiled and extended her hand.

Sheriff Johnson grabbed her hand and with a quick firm grip, released her hand and said, "That student of yours? Nikki?" the sheriff began, "I definitely would like to see her if I could, please." *Uh oh,* the alarms went off in Jo's head, *this is it. This is where everyone finds out about her. About how she's fucking both her son and an underage teenager and a girl at that. Fuck me! It's over. I'm caught.* "Do you know where she at is?" Sheriff Johnson asked.

"Yes, I do," Jo replied, "In fact, I'm fixing to meet her for lunch." Jo smiled at the sheriff, never letting on to the fact about how worried she was.

One of the drug dealer's associates searched under the bed, where he saw the backpack holding all of the money. Not knowing what was inside, he pulled the backpack from under the bed and opened it revealing the money. "Damn," he said, "look at all this money!."

"What?" the man with the gun said. "Bring it here." The man brought it to the drug dealer, who opened it and said, "Wow! What do we have here?." He started pulling money out of the bag and finally decided to quit because it was too much to count. He shook his head. "Where the hell did you guys get this?" he asked. RC and Blu remained silent, not saying anything. Meanwhile the other associate searched Blu's jacket pockets. He pulled out the envelope addressed to Blu.

"What's this?" the drug dealer said. Blu and RC both looked at each other, watching all of their hopes and dreams going out the door. They had to think of something or else… "I'm sorry to inform you, but we are federal agents and the money that you have taken procession of is US taxpayers' money," RC said.

The drug dealer and his men looked at each other then simultaneously laughed. "That's good, really good," the drug dealer said as he laughed. "You two broke down niggas ain't heard of the federal government unless it's from the IRS." He and his two men continued to laugh. He looked at the letter and threw it to the side, on the floor. "It's funny," the drug dealer said, "but I was going to kill both of you Niggars and take every cent you got, but now," he said, "I think I'll let you live and deal with the repercussions." He looks at his men then said, "Let's go." They took the backpack and all the cash they had and went through the door, the drug dealer stopping at the door. "Dude," he said, "If you haven't, read the letter," he said as he smiled and exited the room. The door closed as RC and Blu looked at each other. They both knew that of all the things that could have happened, this was the absolute worst!

Jo and the sheriff reached Jo's office with two trays of food. The sheriff, being a big fellow, had ordered a lot of food. "Damn, Sheriff," Jo said, "two slices of Pizza, an order of chicken tenders and fries, an extra-large Coke, and a slice of cherry pie!"

"Yeah," the sheriff said, "I hope that's enough to hold me until dinner."

Jo smiled and shook her head. She opened the door to her office to see Nikki sitting in her chair with her back turned and looking out the window. "Nikki," Jo said.

Nikki turned around in the chair and seeing Sheriff Johnson, jumped up. "Hey, Miss Clearly," Nikki said.

Jo looked at the sheriff then at Nikki and said, "Nikki, the sheriff would like to ask you a few questions."

Nikki and Jo looked at each other, each wondering where this would lead but they knew they had no choice. "Well, Sheriff, would you like to begin?" Jo asked.

The sheriff looked at Nikki for the first time in his life and thought, *Oh, a light skinned girl with reddish brown hair and my daughter is following her for...* "Nikki," he said, "I'm sure you know who I am, but I'm here on a murder investigation."

"Murder investigation?" Nikki said.

"Yes," he answered. "A murder investigation."

Jo and Nikki looked at each other, wondering what the hell was going on. "Do you know Cedric Ralph Wilson? Better known as 'Dirty Red?'"

Nikki looked at Jo who gave no indication of what she was thinking. She knew she was alone. Nikki started laughing. "His name is Cedric?" She laughed.

Jo sensed that this was an act to throw the sheriff off guard. The sheriff smiled as Nikki finished laughing. "Yes," he said, "his name is Cedric. Do you know him?" the sheriff pressed on.

"Yes, I know Red," she said. "So what? Everybody knows Red."

"Well," the sheriff said, "it seems we have a cellphone record linking you and Red together."

"Me and Red? A cellphone?," Nikki asked then laughed. "Oh I get it, I get it! You're the father of that dumb bitch I fucked at school, right?"

Jo and Sheriff Johnson looked at each other. "Now Nikki!" Jo said, "The sheriff is here to ask you a few questions."

Nikki said, "Yeah, I fucked your daughter so now you want to try and tie Red and me together with that little murder investigation you have going on? Or is this the time when I remind you that I'm a minor and you really can't question me about shit?"

The sheriff looked at Nikki and saw he had seriously underestimated this girl. She knew the rules and she definitely either didn't respect him or whatever he had to say or the very system that he represented. Whatever it was, he knew that she was in control of this conversation, not him.

"You fucked my daughter?" the sheriff asked. "My daughter is sixteen years old and what you said is an admission of guilt to statutory rape, am I correct?"

Nikki looked at the sheriff and then at Jo and said, "It is what it is, Sheriff."

The sheriff got up to leave and took his hat from under his arm and put it on his head. He put his hat on his head smiled and then turned to leave, then suddenly turned back. "Jo, I shall be in touch with you and as far as this young lady is concerned," he said as he fixed his stare directly on her. "Let's just say she has become a person of interest in the murder investigation that we are conducting." With that, the sheriff turned and exited Jo's office. Nikki smiled as the sheriff left while Jo wondered what the hell she had gotten herself into.

RC and Blu sat on the bed, shaking their heads, thinking about all the money they had lost. Suddenly, Blu jumped up from the bed. "God damn it RC!" he said. "Why didn't you just pay that son-of-a-bitch?" He ran a hand thru his graying hair. "Now we don't have any money and you know them folks are already looking for us!"

RC, with that wide-eyed look of his, shook his head and said, "I know, I know Blu, but he was Asian and you know, I just didn't think he was gonna do anything."

Blu looked at RC and then at the envelope the gunman had left behind without looking at RC, who he was still contemplating killing. He picked the letter up and opened it. He frowned as his eyes focused on the note. It read, "Thanks, Dad," and Blu took it and huffed then threw it on the bed.

CHAPTER 19

"What you doing nigga? Slow down," Bang Bang said as Red hit fourth gear in his Camaro SS 1LE. Red looked at the speedometer and it said 120mph.

"I'm just getting started," Red said as he stepped hard on the accelerator.

"Oh shit," Bang Bang said. The car lurched forward even faster as the car's 426hp engine roared. *Hell,* Red thought, *I've been locked up for two days*, and he didn't know how long he would be out or truthfully with the meeting he was headed to be alive, so he was just going to live for the moment.

"Whoa, Red, slow down!" Bang shouted, "You gonna hit a deer and kill him and us."

Red smiled then began to ease off the accelerator. He loved to stretch out his baby, but Bang Bang was right. This was deer-hunting season and deer where running everywhere and contrary to popular belief, he didn't have a death wish, especially with so much money to be made. He laughed. "Chill out, nigga," he said, "I've got this…" Red looked in the rear view mirror and saw flashing blue lights. "Damn," he said.

"What's wrong, Red?" Bang Bang asked as Red eased off the accelerator.

"It's the god damn police!" Red said. "Just what the fuck we need."

Blue lights pulled closer as Red looked at Bang. Bang Bang had already pulled the Glock nine-millimeter from underneath the front passenger seat and was taking the safety off.

"What you want to do, Red?" Bang Bang asked. "You know, I'm down for whatever."

Red slowed the car down and said, "Put that shit up, Bang! We ain't got no reason to fuck up now."

The Camaro rolled to a stop as Bang Bang put the gun back under the front seat. Red and Bang Bang waited as the patrol car pulled to

a stop behind them. Red could see it was a county car. The officer emerged from the car and walked toward Red's car. "Shit," Red said, "it ain't nobody but Buster!"

Colonel Un lit up another one of the American cigarettes his men had bought for him. He was angry and anxious. Angry about his present state, and anxious about what was about to happen. His meeting with Red would, at the very least, clear up what was going on and hopefully lead to a way he could both clear his name and remain among the players or at the very least spare him from a very untimely exit from this earth. Colonel Un thought about his life, about how, as a boy, he used to sail boats and look at pictures of dinosaurs, how he used to imagine how the world was then. The dinosaurs eating something or being eaten by something, each one fighting for the right to life. That was exactly what he was doing today: fighting for his right to life.

Damn, he thought, *I must survive, because if I don't*... he heard the roar of an engine. He motioned to his men to check it out. Associate number one, the large one looked out the window with his gun in his hand. He saw a silver Jeep Wrangler pull into the parking space opposite their motel room. The vehicle sat there for a moment. "What's going on?" Colonel Un said.

"It's an old Jeep," the associate said as he looked away from the window blinds. "Good, Good," Colonel Un said. "It's somebody that I have been waiting for. Please escort them in."

The two associates looked at each other then opened the door and walked out to the sitting vehicle. They both waited patiently as they awaited the occupants exit from the vehicle. The vehicle, with its dark tinted windows and dirty exterior, looked rather nondescript, just your average country ride.

Suddenly, the door opened and out stepped this gorgeous white woman with long black hair dressed in a black business suit with a short skirt and black stockings. She was certainly a beautiful sight and more so compared to the vehicle she drove. "Colonel Un's men?" she asked and they nodded their heads yes as she got out of the vehicle and, carrying a black backpack, reached back and tossed it to the shorter of the two men. "Good," she said, "I didn't feel like carrying that heavy bag." The woman smiled and turned and started to walk.

Both of the men look at the woman in a bemused sort of way. They had heard about the arrogance of American women but this was their first encounter with one up close; they were both shocked and amused. She suddenly stopped and turned toward them. The woman turns around and then making a sort of courtesy toward the two men said, "Excuse me, maybe I should let you gentlemen lead the way." She giggled, showing her perfect white teeth. The men smiled at each other and shook their heads yes as they both tried to lead the way to the room.

"Buster," Red said, "what the hell you want?" He rolled down the window of his Camaro as Buster approached his car.

Buster took his time reaching Red's car and all along his hand was on his pistol. "Red, Red, Red, what the fuck do you think you're doing? Running down the road like you stole something?" Buster said as he looked at Red. He stood a couple of feet from Red's vehicle, just enough room to pull and fire his gun if he had to.

Red looked at Bang Bang and then back at Buster. He laughed. "You know how it is, Buster. I'm like a dog that's been caged up. When you get out, you just want to run and run, you know what I mean?"

Red and Bang Bang laughed.

Buster smiled and, never taking an eye off the two of them, said, "Well I guess I can see your point but you know..." Buster paused, "if a dog runs too much and too wild, sooner or later you got to put him down."

Red and Bang Bang stopped laughing. Buster, having known these two since grade schoo,l knew which buttons to push to get Red mad.

Red looked at Buster and thought, *I should smoke this fool, with his long head ass,* but he knew he had more important things to worry about, which all centered around money. Hustler's Class 101: no matter what the circumstances, get the money. It's always about the money. Red smiled and said, "That was a good one Buster. Now what do you want? Are you arresting me or is this a social visit?"

Buster looked at Red and thought about what to do next. He was under orders to keep an eye on him but that didn't include arresting

this man, a potential murderer or drug dealer, for speeding. He had to look at the big picture. "Just slow down, Red," Buster finally said. "You don't want to have no accident, now do you?"

Red and Bang Bang looked at each other and smiled. "Of course not, Officer Buster," Red said, "Now if you please, my boy and I had better get on home, you know all our babies' mamas are looking for us." Both Red and Bang Bang laughed.

Buster smiled and nodded. "Yep, I suppose so," he said. Red put the car into drive and floored the Camaro, leaving an eight-foot long tread mark on the pavement. Buster looked in disgust as the vehicle pulled away. *I'm gonna smoke that son-of-a-bitch one day*, he thought.

"Deandre," Colonel Un said, "how nice of you too come,"

"Where's Red?" Deandre asked.

"That's what I was about to ask you," the colonel said. "Here," he said, "please have a seat." The colonel pointed to a seat across from him at a small table beside the bed. Deandre smiled and sat down. *These people are staying in a po' dunk motel and looking for talking about money*, she thought. If these accommodations didn't bother them, she knew that she had better be on her guard because these people where desperate. "Where's Red?" she asked.

"I should be asking you that question," Colonel Un said.

There was a roar of an engine outside. Colonel Un's men rushed toward the window with their hands on their guns. "Who is it?" Colonel UN said. The shorter of his two associates took a look out the window of the small motel room. He saw a gray Camaro race into the parking lot. The car came to a sudden stop and out jumped two young black men. "I think it's them," he said as he looked at Colonel Un. Red and Bang Bang walked toward their meeting with the colonel. The big Korean stepped out the door and held up his hand. Red and Bang Bang stopped.

"I've got to search you," he said in an indifferent voice. Red and Bang Bang looked at each then Red shrugged his shoulders and then held up his hands.

"Sure," he said, "why not?"

The big Korean patted him down. "Okay," he said as he moved to Bang Bang and started to pat him down. He then looked at the both of them and nodded. "Okay," he said, "you can go in." Red and Bang Bang opened the door and entered the small motel room.

"Hey, bro," Red said as he looked at Deandre and then the Colonel.

"Mr. Red," the colonel said, "it's so good to see you safe and sound," He motioned for Red and Bang Bang to sit. "I'm sure you two would like a seat?" Red and Bang Bang nodded yes. "And me, you ask? The colonel said, "I would like to know where is my money and also why? You can't seem to wipe your ass when you shit?"

Red and Bang Bang jumped up from the table only to see Colonel Un's associates with their guns drawn and aimed at them.

"No, No," Colonel Un said, "I mean you no disrespect, no none at all," he said as he pulled a cigarette from his pack and lit it. "No, none at all."

Deandre smelled the cigarette and said, "You know in this country we really don't smoke in public."

The colonel laughed. "I know. I know," he said, "but it is I who run this ship," he said as he took a puff off the cigarette. "Not you, or Mr. Red, or Mr...? And your name is?" He pointed at Bang Bang.

"They call me Bang Bang," he said.

"Mr. Bang Bang here."

The colonel paced the room, drawing on his cigarette. "We have set you up in a profitable business and yet I don't see the profits, we were promised or any of the money at all and the astounding part of it, is not only is there no money but bodies are strewn around everywhere. Gentlemen," he said while exhaling the smoke through his nostrils, "I want to ask you the same question that I am being asked. Why should we continue with you, when we can go with somebody else?"

Suddenly, Red's cellphone went off. "May I?" Red said as he reached for his cellphone in his pocket. The colonel shook his head. *These Americans and their rush, rush, rush. Everything has to be now.* The colonel looked at his men then nodded at Red, yes.

Red pulled the cellphone from his pocket and pressed the answer button while putting the cellphone to his ear. "Yeah," he said. Red's face was non- committal; he was either mad, excited, or both. He just had a "whatever," look on his face. He nodded his head up and down and then took the phone from his ear and laid it on the table. He looked at the colonel and said, "Well as far as the money, I have that taken care of, now what's the other question?"

The colonel looked at Red and wondered what had happened? And why were these Americans so cocky and self-assured now?

Buster drove toward his mother's house still ticked off. He really didn't like Red. They had known each other all their lives but they were never friends. Red was the smart studious type that was quiet, never talking but always looking and observing. He never participated in athletics in which Buster excelled so they really never interacted except in the classroom. Buster was always struggling with his math problems while Red seemed to know the answer, almost immediately. That was why it really didn't surprise Buster when after they had both graduated, Red became a drug dealer. Maybe in some areas of the state or country, he would have gone to Harvard or Yale but in this world, a drug dealer was respected and was the master of his own fate, not stuck in some factory working seventy-hour weeks, supporting three baby mamas with just enough money left over to buy a bottle of cheap liquor or go to the creek casino or buffet night once a week.

That was if you were lucky. Other guys spent their time shuttling back and forth between jail and the streets, paying this lawyer, that fine, or drinking or drugging themselves to death, all the time plotting a way out of the mess they either created or fell into and all the time falling into a sea of hopelessness. Buster himself was lucky. Lucky his mother rode him hard not letting him make bad choices and because of his athletic ability, he was able to go to college and try and make something of himself. Yeah, he was lucky he thought and he was grateful his mother raised him up to be a man but know it was time for her to grow up and tell the truth about his father and quit telling the same lie she'd been telling all these years. *Yep*, he thought, *today is the moment of truth,* the day he learned who his father really was.

CHAPTER 20

A light rain fell as the Hearst pulled into the graveyard. Sheriff Johnson had put on his dress blues for the occasion, as he waited with the rest of the crowd for the young man's internment. The Hearst came to a stop as the pallbearers gathered around it. The door opened and the six young men waited as the driver instructed them were to go. The first two young men grabbed hold of the rails and started to pull as the casket slid out of the back or the Hearst. Then the next two came, as they carried the casket to the gurney, which then would lower the body into the ground. The sheriff looked around the crowd and saw the different women and children sobbing. He hated funerals, especially those of young black men. He felt that the future looked not brighter but dimmer because their lives had ended far too soon. Who would take care of their children? Who would take care of their wives? Nobody, he thought. Just another generation stuck in poverty and hopelessness.

The pallbearers lowered the casket onto the gurney as the crowd moved toward the minister standing next to the gurney. Sheriff Johnson scanned the crowd and seen who had been looking for. Representative Sam Jackson. He stood out because his was one of the few black faces in the crowd. Sheriff Johnson nodded his head at Sam who acknowledged it, with a nod of his own. "Family and friends," the Reverend John Poindexter says. "This is not a joyous occasion, as we lay to rest the body of James Wyatt III," the preacher began. "He was in the early stage of fatherhood and adulthood as he provided for his family and helped his friends become part of community in which he both lived and worked."

The sheriff made his way over toward Sam, who, likewise, did the same as they both moved to the back of the crowd. Sheriff Johnson thrust his right hand out as they met and the two men shook hands. "Glad you could come, Sam," the sheriff said. "I didn't know if you would make it or not."

Sam, turning and looking at the crowd, said, "Well these are my people as well as yours, it lets them know that there's at least one politician that cares." Sam looked back at the sheriff who smiled.

"You know?" the sheriff began, "That's one thing I sensed about you when we first met, that you do care. Now what have you got for me?"

Sam looked around making sure no one could hear what he was about to say. "I checked with a friend of mine in the in the DEA and he said that they had been hearing rumors involving drug smuggling through the auto parts suppliers in Korea to here."

The sheriff raised his right hand to his chin as his eyes narrowed. "Oh yeah?" the sheriff said.

"Yes," Sam says.

"How could that be? Don't the parts go through U.S. Customs?"

"No," Sam said. "The auto plants are part of a foreign trade zone, so there not subject to U.S. laws or U.S. Customs."

"You mean they just come right on into the U.S.?" the Sheriff said.

"Right," Sam said, "And get this?" Sam moved closer. "The reason you and I have been getting so much pressure is that the chairman of the whole thing has taken notice and is here himself personally to fix the problem."

Sheriff Johnson nodded his head up and down.

"Lord Jesus!" a woman in the front of the crowd shrieked. "Why did they have to kill my baby? Why!."

"I know what you're saying, Sam," the sheriff said. "But what I don't know is how in the hell is Red and his gang involved and what in the hell role did this girl Nikki play in these boys' murders?"

Sam said, "I don't know."

"Well," the sheriff began and the preacher finished his eulogy and the gunnery started to lower the casket in the ground. "You've supplied me with the why. I guess I've got to figure out the how."

Nikki's arm was burning with pain. The tattoo that she'd gotten was hurting as she walked down the street toward home. She had skipped school today. She was not trying to run into them Koreans again. She figured she better lay low for a while and besides she heard Red was getting out and she definitely needed to see him. "Hey girl!" a voice

said. Nikki looked around and saw a white Ford F150 pickup truck following here. *Oh god*, she thought. It was Mayor Heard leaning out the truck's driver window smiling that gap toothed smile of his.

"Where you going?" he asked. "You need a ride?"

Nikki smiled and said, "No. I'm just going up the street."

The mayor pulled the truck over to the side of the road that Nikki was walking on and came to a stop next to her. "Well," he said. "I'm just riding and I thought you and I could converse a little since were on that Wi-Fi!"

Nikki looked at the mayor, puzzled by what he said. "You said Wi-Fi?,"

"Yeah," he said, "'cause you and me are certainly connected." *What a fool*, Nikki thought, *this old man is out here trying to holler at her using old movie lines.*

"Well the connection is down," she said and laughed.

The mayor, unperturbed, pressed on. "Aw, come on," he said. "I know what's up." He licked his lips, looking Nikki up and down. "A man like me could help a young girl like you. Know what I mean?"

Nikki knew she had to get this old asshole away from her as soon as possible. She had seen him and talked to him at the club before but that was just play. She didn't have time for him now so she looked around and turned and started walking down Jo's street.

The mayor, looking at her as she turned and walked away, said, "You can run but you can't hide." He laughed and pulled away, saying, "You come see daddy when you need something, okay?"

Nikki didn't turn her head but just kept walking away. *Yeah right*, she thought to herself. What did she need an old man like that for? She was young and pretty and was hooked up with Red. She didn't need nobody else. She was just passing Jo's house when she finally came out her thoughts to notice that Jo's car was in the driveway. *What's she doing home*? she thought. *She should be at school*. Nikki smiled a mischievous smile. What about a little play play with Jo? She had a couple of hours before she would met up with Red, so why not? *Yeah*, she thought, *why not? This could be fun*. She turned right and headed up Jo's driveway.

RC and Blu didn't speak as Blu headed down I-10 toward home. Blu was still mad at RC and all the mess that he had caused. All that money gone because this fool wouldn't pay a drug dealer twenty dollars? *What a fool*, Blu thought and he was a bigger fool for bringing him with him. Blu didn't know what made him madder: that he brought the fool or the fool himself so he just watched the road trying to let the road calm him down before he killed this nigga. Suddenly, RC snapped his fingers. "Damn," he said. "I almost forgot about this." RC reached under the passenger seat and pulled out a paper bag.

Blu looked over and said. "What's that?" RC opened the bag and pulls out the thirty-eight-caliber revolver that was in the backpack and about ten stacks of one hundred dollar bills. "What the hell you doing with that?" Blu asked. He was happy to see the money but he sure didn't want to hear RC's explanation. He really wasn't in the mood to separate fact from fantasy, and RC did a lot of both.

"Well I was placing side bets while you was gambling and I won a little bit and let me tell you Blu, this is a blessing from God," the reverend said as he smiled that gapped-toothed smile of his. "And I know the Lord wanted me to keep this and he also wanted me to keep the gun, in case we needed it," he said.

"Well I guess you was right RC," Blu said. "That is you and the Lord 'cause we sure could have used it when we was up in the hotel room getting robbed!."

"But Blu," RC said as Blu grabbed the money out of his hand. "We still got some money left! Let's stop at the casino in Wetumpka on the way back and see what we can do?" RC said. "It's a blessing."

Blu almost stopped the car as he shot a mean look at RC. "After all this shit, you still want to gamble?" Blu asked.

"Yeah, why not?" RC asked, smiling. "We still ain't playing with none of our money."

Damn, Blu thought, *for once this fool made sense in a way*. Blu shook his head from side to side and then said, "Well I guess you do have a point, but we need to get rid of that gun. We don't know anything about it or where it came from or nothing." Blu frowned up his face as he thought. "When we get to Mobile, we'll dump it there."

"Yeah, Blu, yeah," RC said. "That's what we'll do. Dump the gun, then go to the casino."

Blu nodded his head in agreement and at same time he wondered what in the hell he was doing.

The colonel looked at Red trying to see if he was joking or not. He then looked at Deandre and Bang Bang. No reaction. They were neither exited nor surprised at Red and his saying that he had the money. "You Americans are always joking around," the colonel said.

"This ain't no joke," Red said, "My associates down in Biloxi tell me that they have the money and want to know when they can bring it up."

The colonel pulled out another cigarette and lit it. "You see?" Red continued, "We had to get the money out of here with that sheriff conducting his murder investigation, so we had somebody take it away," Red looked at Bang Bang who nodded his head up and down. "You see, Colonel," Red continued, "I can handle my business on this end."

Red then looked at Deandre and Bang Bang before adding, "What about you on your end colonel? Why did you kill those boys who were bringing the meth out of the plant?"

The colonel, who hand been puffing away on his cigarette, suddenly stamped it out in the ash tray joining the already overflowing half-smoked cigarettes already there. "I assure you gentlemen and lady," the colonel said, "that I had nothing to do with that."

"Well somebody Korean did," Red said. "One of my lookouts told me they saw four Korean dudes drive up with guns before them boys was killed." The colonel smiled, trying not to let Red know what he suspected, that his rival was sticking his nose in his business. "Look, Colonel," Red said, "the plan was for you to get the drugs here and I was to take care of the distribution, was it not?"

The colonel nodded his head yes. "Then what's with all these killings? You're making the situation worse!" Red slapped his hand down on the table. The colonel's men moved their hands toward their weapons. The colonel looked at them and raised his hand to stop them. The colonel knew he needed Red and the service he provided

them. If he got rid of him, it would mean months of work would go down the drain and they were too far along in the game to start over. The colonel again reached into his pocket and pulled out his pack of cigarettes and took one from the pack. Instead of lighting it he held it between his first two fingers. "I know," the colonel began, "that we have hit a rocky place in our relationship but rest assured that the people that have been eliminated had to be, for we cannot risk exposure." The colonel then put the cigarette up to his lips but still did not light it. "I, myself," the colonel continues, "am under constant scrutiny from my superiors and perhaps it was they who killed the young men, but it was not me." The colonel lit his cigarette and took a short puff.

"Then who am I dealing with?" Red asked. "You're telling me one thing and you've got people running around who you don't know killing folks and making decisions—decisions you know nothing about?" Red looked at Deandre, as he stood up from the table. "I think you better clean up your own house before you decide to clean up mine," Red said as he turned and headed toward the door. "Until then, I'm out."

Red nodded his head at the Korean by the door as he reached for the door handle. The small Korean looked at the colonel, who said, "That's all right. Let him go, but before you leave," the colonel said before taking another puff of his cigarette. "When can I expect the money?"

Red turned and flashing the gold grill in his mouth, smiled and said, "Colonel, like I said I got you, what you need to do is clean up your house, I got mine." With that, Red walked out the door followed by Bang Bang.

The colonel watched Red go, knowing that what he said was true. He was not fully aware of exactly what was going on and the one thing he knew now was that most of it was coming from his camp not Red's.

Nikki walked back up the drive having knocked on Jo's door for about five minutes. No answer. *Maybe she rode to work with her son or something,* Nikki thought. Nikki reached the end of the drive and turned and headed toward the house. The rain was falling a little heavier now so she sped up trying to get home before the rain really fell. Nikki put her hoodie and walked quickly, determined to beat the rain. She was so absorbed in what she was doing that she didn't notice the Black SUV behind her. The SUV pulled in front of her and suddenly stopped.

Nikki looked up and saw a tinted window roll down and yellow envelope come flying out the window onto the sidewalk in front of her.

The SUV pulled off. Nikki stopped and looked at the package lying on the ground. She looked around and seeing no one stopped and picked the package up. She looked at the package and seeing no markings on it decided to open it. "What the hell is…?" Nikki opened the package and inside is about ten thousand dollars in cash and a note. "What?" Nikki said as she opened the note. The note said, "Good job!"

Nikki looked up and saw the SUV turning the corner and accelerating. "Good job?" she repeated to herself as she continued to look at the note. She closed the note and stuffed it back in the envelope. She looked around again and wondered, *I wonder if they know*, she thought.

CHAPTER 21

Sheriff Johnson walked through the door of the jail and looked around the office. He smiled at the 911 operators as they took calls and dispatch officers around the county. Tallapoosa County was seven hundred sixty-seven square miles of real estate with a population of forty-one thousand people. His office had a lot of space to cover. There were roaming dogs to cattle loose to gang activity in the few projects in the area. No matter what the problem, however, people wanted the sheriff and with every resource at his disposal he was going to give the people what they wanted. What he promised them when he was elected and nothing less?

He quickly hurried to office and opened the door only to see Deputy Oliver sitting at his desk looking at the computer screen. "Playing Candy Crush again?" the sheriff asked as he moved toward his desk. He waved Oliver out of his chair. Oliver hesitated. "Sheriff, I'm about to…."

"Oliver, get out of that chair!" the sheriff commanded. Deputy Oliver scurried out of the chair and the sheriff flopped down in the chair and put his feet up on the desk. He ran his hand over his mostly bald head and said, "You know Oliver, I think I figured out what was going on in the murder case." Deputy Oliver looked at the sheriff and said, "What you got, Sheriff?"

"I think," the sheriff said, "that our victims were mules, taking drugs to Red and his boys to sell," the sheriff paused, "I also think that the boys and their sponsor the Korean killed in the other county got greedy and were killed because of it."

Deputy Oliver nodded his head and then said, "Why is that, Sheriff?"

"Well," the sheriff said as he dropped his feet off of his desk and leaned forward, placing his hands on it, "I've come across some information that that is—let's say—confidential and those folks told me that the plant those boys were working at, what? Kwansung is a

foreign trade zone and they can bring parts in oversees and are not subject to inspection by U.S. Customs."

"You tell me," Deputy Oliver said, "that Red planned all this?"

The Sheriff laughed. "I said Red was smart but not that smart. No, he had help."

"From whom?," Deputy Oliver asked, "You think the company was involved?"

The sheriff shook his head. "Maybe," he said, "Maybe not. That's for us to figure out," the sheriff said. "What we need, Oliver, is for that greedy son-of-a-bitch, whoever it is, to make a mistake."

"Make a mistake?" Oliver said.

"Oh yeah," the sheriff said. "The one thing about a greedy or needy son-of-a-bitch is that they always saw the money and their only motivation. You put a little pressure on 'em and depending on how needy or greedy they are, they always forget to do something or make a mistake, and when they do…,"

"We got em," Deputy Oliver said.

"Yeah Oliver," the sheriff said, "We got em."

Jo looked out the window. She saw Nikki walking up the drive. She heard someone knock but she really wasn't in the mood for any company. She had taken the day off to clear her mind. She looked at Nikki and wondered if she should call her back but decides against it. *Hell yeah*, she thought, *let that bitch walk on*! Ever since she came around stuff that was already shaky, it got blown up. She was young. She didn't care or know whatever she did could ruin careers or relationships. Jo did. She knew that the wrong move or saying the wrong thing could lead to disaster. Her life ruined because of some sixteen-year-old. *Fuck that*! she thought.

She saw a police cruiser pull up in the yard and it was Buster. *Well*, she thought, *it is time. Time to let him know*. Let him know the secret she had kept for years about who his father was.

The black SUV accelerated as it sped down the state highway headed up Highway 280. The company's headquarters were less than two miles away but the chairman wanted to be seen in public as less as possible. The chairman looked out the window. There was so much space and greenery. It was no doubt a beautiful place. The chairman

would have preferred to have been back in Korea but he knew if his family was going to carry on, sacrifices had to be made. If his time was one of them so be it.

His men had discovered the disease running through his company and he was there to solve it. Granted most of it had been solved for him but he was here to make sure that it never happened again. The car slowed down and made a right hand turn onto the long drive to the security gate. The chairman turned his head and looked at the brand new building and the parking lots full of cars ready to be sold. *Yes*, he thought to himself, *I have to protect not only my family, but also the legacy I will leave behind and if some people had to die along the way, so be it.*

Buster unlocked the door to the house and walks in. He looked around the house and saw no one. *Just like her*, he thought, *avoiding the problem.* "Buster, is that you?" a voice came from the kitchen. "Yeah Mom," Buster answered.

"Well, dinner's ready come on in," Jo said from the kitchen. Buster threw his head back and shakes his head. He wondered what kind of production this was going be as he walked into the kitchen. Buster walked through the kitchen door and looked at the kitchen table. On it was his baby pictures along with his football and basketball trophies.

Buster looked at his mother and wondered what was going on. "What's this, Mom?" Buster asked.

"It's your life," Jo began. "A life filled with hope and accomplishment," Jo said as she sat at the kitchen table. "Is this your way of not answering what I asked you, Mom? By bringing up my childhood?"

Jo, sitting at the table with her legs crossed and sipping a cup of tea, smiled. "No son," she said, "I'm not avoiding the question or trying to hide from it. I'm just trying to show you the life that you've had. The life in front of you!" Buster looked at his sixth grade picture with his closely cut head and the round circle drawn into his head by his then barber.

He remembered him asking his mother then who his father was, and her saying that he died in Iraq during the war. Oh, what a brave soldier he thought his father was. How he died for his country. At least that was what he told all the kids at school when they asked him

who his daddy was. He was a war hero he told them. Never mind that he had never seen or spoken to him. He was trusting that what his mother told him was the truth. Why wouldn't he be? She was, after all, his mother.

"Mom, you know I love you and I always will," Buster said. "I just want you to tell me…" Buster looked at Jo and deep into her eyes, "…the truth."

Jo looked at her son and felt the pain he must have endured, the pain she had endured. It was time for it to end, time for the truth. "When I was young, Buster," she began. "I was raped by my uncle and from that you were born."

Jo said it and waited for Buster's response. Buster heard what his mother said and digested it. At first, anger fills him. He was angry that a relative of his would rape his mother and also angry that his mother had kept this secret for so many years. "What uncle?" Buster said.

"He wasn't a blood uncle if that's what you're asking and yes you do know him," Jo answered.

"Who is it, Mom?" Buster asked. "Just tell it, tell it all and don't hold back nothing!"

Jo's throat was suddenly dry as though she couldn't speak or say anything. She cleared her throat and then said, "I was young and…" Jo began to tell the story she had so buried in her consciousness that it surprised her that she knew and could recite the events that transpired that day, she just hoped it was enough that not only would it save her relationship with her son but put to rest the past that had haunted her.

"I'm sorry, Sheriff," the security guard said, "but unless you make an appointment I can't let you in."

The sheriff smiled as he looked at the young security guard. "Well I'm trying to be polite, but I see I'm going to have to be a little bit plainer in my English. Maybe it's the southern boy in me but I'm not asking to see nobody. I'm in the middle of a murder investigation involving this company and I'm going to see the plant manager," the sheriff said. "This is not a request." The sheriff looked out his car window as he sat in his police cruiser at the visitor's entrance of the Kwansung manufacturing plant.

The young security officer looked at him then retreated to the guard post. The sheriff waited patiently for the dominos to start to fall. He reached for the car radio and pressed the on button for the radio. *"Walking with my forty I might catch a body/ Rruum rrum rra/ I might catch a body/ Rolling off a molly/ I might catch a body/ Rolly cost 'bout forty/ I might catch a body."* The sheriff quickly reached for the selector button and switched the station. *"With all my heart I love you baby/ stay with me and you will see/ My arms will hold you/ baby never leave/ 'cause I believe/ I'm in love, sweet love..."* That's more like it, the sheriff thought. *When did we go from the love everybody years, to the kill everybody years?* He wondered.

The security officer hurried back to the sheriff's car. "I'm sorry sir...." he began.

Sheriff Johnson held his hand and said, "Don't worry about it son. All right, Ollie roll!" the sheriff said in his radio. Two sheriffs' cars and four state trooper cars pulled into the entrance, blocking it. The sheriff exited his vehicle and looking at the security officer said, "The ball's, as they say, is in your court."

The young security officer looked at all the police cruisers and the flashing lights and his mouth dropped open. He stammered, "Yes sir!," as he turned and headed back to the entrance way. The sheriff smiled and thought to himself, *Yeah, game on!* as the deputies and state troopers open their car doors and exited there vehicles.

"But why," Buster said as he looked at his mother, "couldn't you have told me about this sooner?" Jo turned from him, not having an answer. How could she tell him that she had buried the truth for so long that now it seemed to her to be a dream? Something so long ago that the people and the facts were long ago pushed back into the recesses of her mind. She hadn't seen or heard from her aunt in over twenty years or even thought about her.

She didn't even remember if she had a baby shower or not. She didn't even remember who took her to the hospital. She just remembered when the nurse brought her Buster and she looked at him for the first time and she saw that curly black hair and that pushed up nose and how bright skinned he was, she knew right then that she would love him like she had never loved anything. That she would die to protect him and that god had indeed blessed her with the responsibility to raise this child and protect him. "I just couldn't," Jo started, "I didn't know what to do!" Jo wrung her hands as she looked down. "For the longest time Buster, I felt guilty, responsible for what happened."

"But why? Mama," Buster said, "you didn't do anything wrong."

"I know, I know," Jo began, "but when you're young, you see everything that your mother and father says as being the law of the world. Well at least I did."

Buster, who had been standing with his arm resting on the fireplace, didn't move. He didn't know what to make of her story or of her. The story she told him had been so incredible that he knew it had to be true but there were still questions to be answered, he thought and tonight he was going to find out. "What about your parents?" he asked. "Why haven't you ever mentioned them or spoke of them?"

Jo laughed as she thought of her parents. "Oh them," she said. "Of course they kicked me out of the house, told me they weren't going to have a whore living in their house."

"Why didn't you tell them?" Buster asked.

"I tried," Jo said as tears streamed down her face. "I tried. My father, the preacher, didn't want to hear it and my mother, being the good wife she was, fully supported him. They let me stay until you were born but two weeks after I was gone and I haven't been back or heard from them since."

Buster shook his head and thought how good people could be so cruel, so unfeeling. How they would reject their own flesh and blood because of what other people thought. He wouldn't, though. No matter what his mother had done and what they both continued to do, he knew one thing: she loved him and would never abandon him or turn him out in the world with no place to go and he decided right then, that neither would he. "Come here," he said.

Jo moved slowly across the room and they locked eyes. He opened his arms as his mother moved toward him and they hugged, knowing that they were the only thing that they both had in the world.

Sheriff Johnson walked through the entrance of the manufacturing facility. The office was brightly lit as the facility operated night and day twenty-four hours a day. The young scruffy bearded white security officer at the front gate had given way to a fiftyish, almost totally gray-headed white security officer. The security officer said, "Jump in," as he stepped into an electric golf cart.

The sheriff took a seat next to the security officer in the golf cart and said, "Let's go." With that, the security officer floored the golf cart as they sped away from the gate toward the entrance of the building.

Sheriff Johnson looked around at the wide open spaces that the company sat on. There was a water fountain that continuously ran along with the freshly planted trees. It was nice the sheriff thought. The golf cart raced across the lot and the sheriff thought *Yeah, now we will see what's going on*. The security guard was silent. He said nothing as they reached their destination. The vehicle slowed as they reached the front building entrance. The vehicle finally came to a stop and the security officer hopped out of the vehicle smiled as he looked at the sheriff and said, "Follow me."

The sheriff got out of his seat and followed the security officer into the building. The security officer stopped as he was entering the building. In front of him was a Korean man in black glasses along with two white men. He recognized one of the men. It was Sam Jackson. The sheriff, though surprised, didn't let on that he knew Sam. Instead he said, "Gentlemen, so good to see you," and smiled.

The Korean and the other white men nodded their heads as Sam Jackson said, "Sheriff Johnson, I believe we met a couple of days ago."

CHAPTER 22

Nikki counted the money again. Ten thousand dollars was more money than she had ever seen, well except for the money she'd seen Red count out. It shocked her, that she had this much money and it puzzled her how she got it. *Crisp one hundred dollar bills, yes*! she thought. She was happy she had the money but she thought about how did she get it? The note said, "Good Job." *What did that mean*? she wondered. *Good job for what*? Nikki thought and looked at the money, then looked at the money and thought, *Fuck, this money was sent to me as a blessing and it's mine to do what I please* and right now she wanted those new pair of Jordan One Flight Two's. Then she would...

Honk, honk! a horn honked outside Nikki's house. Nikki jumped up and ran to the window. She raised part of the Venetian blind and saw Red and his crew. She had forgotten about him. Since she had gotten the money, it was all she thought about or cared about. She didn't care at the moment but Red was Red and she needed him though at the moment less so than she did two hours ago. She quickly hurried back to money she had been counting on the table and scooped it up and took it to her room. *Honk, honk*! the horn sounded again. Nikki scanned the room.

She'd put it under the bed, she thought. *No, bad idea.* She'd put it in her closet, she thought. *No*, again, *bad idea.* She looked and finally thought yeah. Yeah, she'd put it her old Jordan boxes with the other athletic shoes. Her mother and certainly RC would never look there. She quickly opened one of the boxes and stashed it there, quickly closing the box and hurrying back out the room. She ran to the door, opened it, and stepped out as she saw Bang Bang exit the car. She waved and smiled at Bang Bang and Red as she slammed the door shut. She ran down the walkway and smiled and said, "My niggas!"

Blu, tired of listening to rap, pushed the tune button, surfing the radio waves. He didn't know the radio stations in Mobile so he kept

mashing the button on the radio until he heard, "*I need a backup lover/ I need a girlfriend/ A backup lover/ Oh, baby, I need a spare.*" Yeah, Blu thought, *some O.B. Buchanan*. Blu then looked at RC who was sleeping peacefully in the passenger seat. He decided to have some fun and floored the gas pedal on his big block engine. The car roared and RC arose from his sleep.

"What, what?" RC asked. "Blu, what the hell's going on?" RC's eyes went from half open to wide open as he looked over at the speedometer and saw it inching toward a hundred and ten miles per hour. "What's wrong, Blu? The police after us?" RC turned around and looked out the rear window.

Blu, unable to control himself any longer, laughed as he eased off the gas pedal. "No, noooo." Blu laughed. "Ain't nothin' happening! I'm just messing with you a bit." Blu laughed again before saying, "We only about twenty miles from Mobile. We can get rid of that gun then keep on going to Wetumpka."

RC looked at Blu and shook his head. "You always playin', Blu," RC said, "I ain't never seen no grown man play as much as you!"

"Oh yeah," Blu said. "What about you and that crack dealer?"

RC looked at Blu and said, "Let's leave that alone, okay? It was my fault, but at least we're alive and got some money to do something with." RC huffed and looks out the window. Blu thought maybe he should just let it go. RC was right; they did have some money and besides it wasn't any of it their money, so… "I'll be glad to get rid of that pistol," RC said. "It ain't nothing but bad luck, I tell you. Bad Luck." Of all the things RC had said during this trip, Blu feared that what he just said about the pistol was about as close to the truth as you could get.

Nikki hugged Bang Bang and then Red. "I'm glad you two are out," Nikki said, "I knew that couldn't no jail cell hold y'all two." Nikki giggled as Red and Bang Bang looked at each other.

"Bang," Red said, "why don't you go check on that package?" Bang Bang nodded his head and exited the room while Red looked at Nikki and said, "Come on, take a seat." Red motioned toward the living room of his house. Red's house was nothing like the "spot" as he liked to call it. No, he had a big black leather sectional sofa and a sixty-five-inch curved screen TV in front of it. The room was painted red and white, with a white ceiling and red walls as an homage to his favorite team. Nikki sat in the middle of the sofa while Red sat down next to her. "I'm glad to see you Nikki since the last time I saw you, you were kind of in a rush," Red said.

"Oh no Red, I was just trying to get home that's all." Nikki smiled as she says this while Red shook his head up and down.

"That was the same night them two niggas came up dead wasn't it?" Red said as Nikki shrugged her shoulders.

"I don't remember," she finally said.

"In fact, I think you and your boyfriend, that Korean dude, was at the spot about a half hour before them boys arrived?"

"I don't know," Nikki said, "I wasn't here, besides what's with all these questions? You know me and you always done each other right,"

Nikki got up off the couch and put her hands on her hips. "That's why I'm over here."

"Oh yeah," Red said.

"Yeah, you know them boys at the plant are gone and so is Jung-Hoon. You gonna need somebody to get them drugs out of there and bring it to you."

Red studied Nikki as he reached toward a black wooden box laying on his table. He opened the box and pulled out a blunt, lights it and inhaling the smoke deeply. He coughed slightly and tried to pass it to Nikki.

"No thanks," Nikki said, "I get real silly when I smoke and this ain't the time."

Red laughed and said, "No, it's not the time."

"Well?" Nikki said as Red continued to toke on the blunt.

"Yeah you're right," Red finally said, "I'm gonna need someone to bring them drugs out of there, what do you suggest?" Red asked as he took another hit off the blunt.

"Let me handle it, Red," Nikki said as she moved closer to Red on the couch. She moved close enough that their legs were touching and she could touch him. She reached her hand over between Red's legs and started massaging his penis. Red slumped back in the

couch and, putting one hand behind his head, sat back and took another puff off his blunt. "You know," Red began, "it don't make no difference what you do, I'm still goanna do things like I want, where I make money."

Nikki, looking at the bulge in Red's pants and then looking at him, said, "I wouldn't have it any other way. I also got to be paid. This," Nikki said, "is just play play." Nikki unbuttoned Red's jeans and squeezed his dick hard. Red lay his head back and blows the smoke out from his blunt. Bang Bang, looking at the entire scene unfolding behind a partially closed door in the kitchen, shook his head and said, "Yeah, play, play."

"Well Sam, how you doing?" Sheriff Johnson asked.

"Just fine, Sheriff," Sam Jackson said. "In fact, I'm doing mighty fine."

Sheriff Johnson smiled at Sam while he scanned the crowd of company officials and security personnel. "Hello Sheriff Johnson, I'm Ye-Jun Sung," A Korean stepped forward and thrust out his hand. Sheriff Johnson gripped his hand and the Korean shook it vigorously. "I understand that you are conducting a murder investigation and we are here to help." This Korean guy was around six feet and had black hair and a bad case of acne. He wore wire-rimmed glasses and smiled as he spoke to the sheriff.

Pleasant enough fellow, the sheriff thought, *time to begin round one*. "Well, as you know, three of your employees have been murdered with in the past few days. We have reason to believe," the sheriff began, "that contraband, that is illegal drugs, have been or are being shipped to your company and being distributed outside into various communities in Alabama."

Mr. Sung looked at Sheriff Johnson then at Sam Jackson. He then looked at the small army of company officials and waved them over to him. "Please excuse me," he said. The Koreans huddled together as Sheriff Johnson and Sam Jackson watched. Sam, who had been on the Korean side of the room, moved toward the sheriff.

Sheriff Johnson looked at him and said under his breath and out of earshot of the Koreans, "Up jumped the devil!"

Sam smiled and laughed. "Whoa, wait a minute, Sheriff," Sam Jackson began, "I've been trying to get in and see these guys for two days and what about you? You just happened to stop by?"

The sheriff turned and looked around at the clean and neatly kept office. He wondered what it must be like for the workers, for them to spend their whole life coming to the same place at the same time every day, doing the same thing over and over again. He could never do it, he thought. Though in many respects, wasn't his job the same thing, day after day? "Well," the sheriff said, "you've got to shake the tree to get some fruit."

The Koreans broke from the huddle and Mr. Sung walked up to Sheriff Johnson. "If you will, follow me please." Mr. Sung started walking through the offices at a brisk pace. He headed toward a stairwell leading to the top floor of the building. Sam and Sheriff Johnson both began to follow. In the middle of the staircase,

Mr. Jung stopped and turned. "Not you, just him," he said as he pointed at Sam.

Sam and Sheriff Johnson looked at each other. Sam nodded his head up and down as he looked at Sheriff Johnson. Mr. Sung continued up the staircase with the sheriff close behind. *Round two*, he thought as he climbed the staircase.

"Throw it in, throw it in," RC said as he and Blu stood on the beach in Mobile Bay. Blu looked at the murky green waters and hesitated. "What if somebody shot somebody with this gun and two years later they traced it back to us?" Blu asked as he held the pistol in his right hand.

"Blu, what are you taking about? You're throwing the gun in to saltwater, the most corrosive element known to mankind. If somebody does find it, it will have corroded so much that the finger prints will be long gone."

Blu looked at RC. He didn't know if what Blu was saying was right, but eh, it sounded good. Blu took the pistol and flung it as far as he could. He heard the sound of the pistol hitting the water. Blu and RC looked around and not seeing anybody, turned and headed back to the car.

"Blu," RC began, "I don't know about you but I'm glad to get rid of that pistol."

Blu stuck his hands into his pockets. "I know, right?" Blu said. "I don't like having no gun around that I don't know where it came from."

Suddenly some lights flashed as both RC and Blu ducked behind the car. RC, whispering, asked, "What the hell is that, Blu?"

Blu looked at RC and said, "I don't know." They both looked up and saw a car pull up about one hundred yards from them. A man exited the car followed by another man. RC and Blu both peeped over the car hood, making sure that no one saw them. "Why are we hiding?" RC finally asked.

Blu, with a disgusted look on his face, looked at RC and shook his head. "Because we just got rid of that pistol and we don't want anyone to know that we're here," Blu said.

"Well," RC began, "nobody does!"

Blu did not explode and tell RC that that was the way he wanted to keep it as they both hear voices. They listened and all they can hear is, what sounds like to them gibberish. "What they saying, Blu?" RC asked.

Blu listened while waving to RC to shut up. It was some kind of foreign language that he didn't know. "I don't know?" Blu answered. The two men at the car walked toward the water just to the right of them. The two men looked at the water and continued to talk.

"What we goanna do Blu?" RC asked.

"Just shut up!" Blu snapped back. "We'll lay low here and wait for them to leave." Blu slumped to the ground with his back up against the car. RC did the same.

"How long you think?" RC barely got his sentence out before both of them heard an engine in the distance. "What's that?" RC asked softly. Blu shook his head back and forth, indicating he didn't know. The engine noise grew louder as Blu and RC sat there.

Finally, Blu got to his knees and slowly peeked back over the hood. Blu saw the two men waving at a small boat. The boat cut its engine as it neared the shoreline. A big spotlight suddenly turned on in the boat and both of the men on the shore were illuminated. Blu looked then ducked down. "RC," he said, "that's the same dude that robbed us!"

"What?" RC said as he peeked over the car. The two men on shore waded out in the water until their pant legs were soaked up to their knees.

Both RC and Blu looked at the two men in the spotlights. "Now, tell me RC ain't them one of the dudes?" Blu said. "The drug dealer who robbed us?"

RC looked the turned back toward Blu. "I don't know, I can't see too good," RC said. Someone from the boat threw out an anchor into the water off the shore. The two men on shore rushed toward the boat. The man on the boat who had dumped the anchor pulled a black bag off the deck of the boat and tossed it to the men on shore. The two men moved toward it and opened it. They both looked at each other then back at the man on the boat. The man Blu thought was the drug dealer that robbed them threw his right hand up with his thumb pointed upward. The man on the boat said something and then pulled the anchor up and waved at the two men on shore. The boat's engine roared as the boat moved away from the shoreline. Blu and RC looked at each other as the two men zipped up the bag and carried it to their car, a nondescript rental car—probably a Hyundai or Honda. The other man, who was with the man that Blu thought robbed them, opened the trunk and threw the bag inside. The two men laughed as they entered the car. The engine started and the two men pulled away. Blu looked at RC and said, "Come on, let's go!" as he jumped up from his crouching position and raced around to the driver side of the car.

RC stood up and said, "Go? Go where?."

"Just shut up and get in the car RC!" Blu said. "Maybe we can get that money back!"

RC opened the passenger door as Blu started the engine. RC barely closed the door as Blu floors the car, throwing sand everywhere. "Damn, Blu," RC said as Blu headed off toward the car that just pulled off.

Sheriff Johnson walked through the double doors and was immediately met with the sounds of the plant: hoses hissing, motors running, people scurrying about. Mr. Sung led the way. Three or four assistants followed closely as they walked toward the far end of the

building. The sheriff estimated that they had already walked a mile when they went through another door that led to the outside of the plant. Mr. Sung pointed at the various trucks moving about the huge yard. "This," he said, "is where our inventory is both processed and stored." Mr. Sung pushed up on his glasses that had fallen a bit on the long walk here. "It goes from there," Mr. Sung pointed at the truck entrance and unloading area, "to here, where it is stored and held until it's processed and assembled into the final product," Sung motioned for the sheriff to come back in and the sheriff complied. The door shut as Mr. Sung again led the sheriff through the noise and the people hurrying about doing their jobs.

They headed across the plant to another door. This room was a row of computers and monitors where people sat at their desks and watched the computer monitors. Mr. Jung stopped and turned toward the sheriff. "This is our central dispatch, where we monitor each and every part that is received and assembled." The sheriff nodded his head yes. "As you can see, Sheriff, there is no way that any drugs or any illegal activity could enter without us seeing it or knowing about it."

"That," the sheriff began, "is exactly my point, three of your employees have been killed during the last week and the only thing any of them have in common is that they worked here."

Mr. Sung nodded his head in agreement, then smiled at the sheriff and said, "That, as they say, is merely a coincidence."

Sheriff Johnson looked at this smug son-of-a-bitch and the smile disappeared from his face. "You see, Mr. Sung. I know that you're protected by all the trade laws but I have the right to inspect everything that is brought into this plant, from Singapore, from Korea or from where ever you bring the materials you bring in here and unless I hear some kind of change in attitude, I will shut this plant down and make a full inspection of the whole facility."

The chairman looked at the row of monitors and cameras at his disposal. He followed every bit of the action between the sheriff and one of his lieutenants from the time the sheriff stepped onto the property. *Strange place, this Alabama,* he thought, *no matter who you paid, things didn't always go as planned.* This Sheriff? He really

didn't know what to make of him. Money didn't seem to matter to him or power, the two sins that turned most men's heads. Nor was it something else, a sense of control, a sense of order that he craved? Women or drugs maybe? The chairman thought hard about how to deal with this sheriff. This sheriff, he was impressive, very impressive.

The colonel looked at the television playing. "Nee Nee, you're just a bitch, you're not a real friend, you're just interested in what you got or can get!" Deandre said as the colonel looked on.

What? he thought. *Is this society so decadent that the women openly fight against each other while buying what they want, saying what they want with no real consequences? Were greed and selfishness so prevalent?* The colonel grabbed the remote control and turned down the volume. He was thinking about his mission, his responsibility to both his family and to his country. His contacts had confirmed what he thought. Even though his chief rival was indeed active it wasn't him that was the source of his problems.

His contacts had informed him about Red, how he was in business with the Vietnamese gangs in the area. The Vietnamese had the pipeline for distributing the methamphetamine that they imported into the U.S., so it was no surprise to him that Red was in business with them. What he didn't know was who the other players were, who was he competing against, but did that matter? As long as the product was being distributed and he was receiving the expected return on investment, shouldn't he be satisfied?

Yes, but no, he thought. He could be happy in the fact that his partner in this endeavor had as much or more to lose than him but the fact that there were three dead bodies didn't escape his notice. Two dead bodies and he didn't know who killed them, and the one he did kill was his primary contact inside of the company, yes, those where major concerns. Now he had to replace three major pieces in this chest match. There were far too many questions and players in this game to his liking, yes far too many, indeed. He knew he had to make a move now. Good or bad or indifferent, he had to make a move just like in chest to try and reestablish control of the situation. He knew exactly what to do. He reached over to the side table and took a cigarette from his pack and lit it. Taking a puff, he called out, "Chang-Bok." The skinny associate who was across the room with the fat associate playing cards looked up. He nodded his head yes. "That young girl who escaped us?" the colonel asked, drawing on his cigarette. "See if you can find her again."

Chang-Bok nodded his head yes while returning to the card game that he and the other associate were playing. The colonel, seeing this, raised his voice only slightly. "Now, Chang-Bok," he said, "lives hang in the balance, especially ours."

Chang-Bok turned his head back to the colonel and stares for a moment then nodded his head yes and got up from the table and headed toward the door. "And take Ji-Hu with you," The colonel said as an afterthought. Ji-Hu was a good man to have when things got physical but when it came to thinking, he was a bit slow. Both men got up from the table and exited the room, leaving the colonel in a smoky haze as he puffed away as the door closes.

"Blu, don't get too close!" RC said as they followed the maroon and red F-150 truck. Blu shot a look at RC. "Will you calm down?," Blu said, "I got this."

Blu hung back about two hundred feet, just enough to see the tail lights. It was dark, about seven o'clock. They had passed into Alabama and were headed of all places home. "Where you think these boys are headed, Blu?" RC asked as they headed down Highway 280.

"Wherever it is?" Blu began, "it's not too far from home." Blu clicked on his satellite radio. Even though he drove a classic, everything in his car was up to date. From the CD player and GPS, to the satellite radio, this was as modern a ride as was possible. Blu, country as he was, wasn't going to be out-technologied by anyone. "*Rollin down the street/ smoking indo/ sipping on gin and juice/ Laid back (with my mind on my money and my money on my mind).*" Blu started bobbing his head as he looked at R.C. "Yeah RC, that's some real music there!" The F-150 truck ahead of him slowed down on Highway 280 and prepared to make a turn.

"Where is he going, Blu?" RC asked. "You think to..." The F-150 made a left into a gas station. "They stopping at the Bottle, Blu ," RC said as Blu kept driving straight ahead on the highway.

"What you doing Blu!" RC shouted out.

"They are going to the Bottle."

"Shut the fuck up!" Blu said finally. "I know where they're going. I'm gonna go to the next exit and turn around and come back in case they spotted us."

RC sat back in his seat and shook his head yes, acknowledging what Blu said. "Yeah, yeah, I see what you're doing. Yeah," RC said. "*Sipping on gin and juice*," the song played as Blu headed to the next exit.

Sheriff Johnson had taken the ten-cent tour of the facility and they had even let him look in a couple of bags and they found exactly what he thought: nothing. Mr. Sung, smiling the whole time, told him bullshit, hoping he'd get tired of the runaround and just leave. He had news for him: this wasn't over. No, this wasn't over by a long shot.

"Are you satisfied, Sheriff?" Mr. Sung asked. "As you can see, the company is in no way knowledgeable in this murder investigation of yours." Mr. Sung turned and looked at his crowd of underlings. They all nodded their heads yes as the sheriff looked at Sam Jackson.

"Well," the sheriff began, "I know that on the surface that everything seems normal, but at the same time I have three dead bodies and all three of them came from this plant."

The sheriff paused and looked out the window of the small conference room they were in. He looked at the neatly cut grass, the trees that were just starting to shed their leaves and he nodded his head up and down. "You know," the sheriff began, "the one thing I find really strange about this case, besides the three dead bodies is that there is absolutely little to no news coverage. It's like we're in a media dead zone. There's no breaking news. No eyewitness news reports. Nothing, I mean, I wonder about that." The smile on Mr. Sung face faded as the sheriff continued, "I just wonder if a couple of my friends in the media—"

"Now you just hold on a minute, Sheriff," Sam Jackson interjected, "Kwansung is a good employer here in the state of Alabama and is under the protection of the federal trade agreement between our two countries. We, that is the company and the state, have cooperated and assisted in your investigation, so why do you persist in this investigation of the company?"

The sheriff looked at Sam, then smiled. "Sam," he said, "the reason I persist and question you and this company is because I have three dead bodies and no suspects. Oh I have could be, should be, and might be, but I don't have who did and why?"

Everyone was silent, each interested party waiting for the other to make a move. The sheriff again looked out at the picturesque scenery out the second floor window. Finally there was movement, Mr. Sung is called to the side. There he conferred with his platoon of associates and finally he broke the huddle and stepped forward to the sheriff. "Sheriff," he began, "I would like you to come to a meeting with the chairman in the morning." The sheriff nodded his head yes and Mr. Sung asked, "What time can you be available?"

The sheriff looked at Sam. *Well played Sam*, the sheriff thought. *Well played. Round three.*

Blu was more confused than ever. He had been following this truck for more than three hours and for some reason the truck was leading him home. His plan, which was to steal the money back, was losing more and more steam. Here he was back in the woods where they had come from. No casino, no money? What the fuck was going on?

The F-150 was headed down the highway toward Red's place. *Red's place*, he thought. *No, this couldn't be happening. Why in the fuck would the Vietnamese Mafia be headed toward Reds*? The F-150 turned slowly into Red's driveway. Blu slowed down, he and RC were about one hundred fifty to two hundred yards away. Blu turned off the lights but kept rolling. The F-150 stopped in the yard and kept their lights on. Blu looked hard. It was a full moon. It wasn't hard to see what was going on. The gang members exited the vehicle, carrying their backpack. He saw Red and Bang Bang open the door and after all the greetings let them in. *What the hell*? Blu thought. "RC," Blu said, "we've been played." Blu looked at RC and RC looked at Blu. They were both too stunned to say anything.

CHAPTER 23

It was six o'clock in the morning and the store wasn't open yet. Men who had spent their entire lives getting up at 4.30 really couldn't understand why Patel couldn't get here and open up any sooner, so the early birds sat in their cars waiting for the store to open. Rooter, the town hustler, was there with freshly shelled pecans ready for sale, so were the Woody brothers from one of the few black families that still made a living from farming. They raised cows, pigs and grew whatever was in season. This being fall, they had collards for sale. Finally the lights came on in the store and the men slowly exited their cars.

"Y'all need to get some of these pecans!" Rooter called out as the men looked at each other and filed into the store. The coffee was good and cheap and along with a breakfast of grits, eggs, sausage or bacon, and a biscuit cost you less than five dollars. Not bad in this economy. The men got their breakfast, got their coffee then the best part of their day began: the day's gossip. Ruford Heard, one of the Heard boys, started it off. "Anybody seen Blu and RC? They've been missing for two days."

Nobody said anything as they ate and drank. "Shit," Rooter said, "you know them boys like to gamble, they probably out at the casino, losing money to them Indians." A couple of the men nodded their heads in agreement. "I got this board," Rooter says. "Every quarter pays and you can win that Yukon truck over at Possum's house. Hundred dollars a square!" Rooter shouted out.

The men ignored him and continued on with their conversations. "Alabama going to kick Auburns ass again," Shorty said as Bob Heard shot back.

"You always say that, Shorty, and then when Auburn wins, you want to poison a tree or kill your neighbor's dog. You Alabama fans are the most spoiled fans in America." With that, all the guys laughed as more cars pulled into the large, maybe two-acre, parking lot, some on their way to work, some passing through and the ones walking or

getting rides there to get a beer. Yep, nothing like a 211 in the morning to get you started." Dez ,Dez," a man in a car says as he exit's one of the cars in the drive. There is a young man with medium dreads standing on the opposite corner of the store

This part of the corner was the Dead Beat Lounge. Named so because of all the drunks and druggies that hung around there. "Dez," the young man persisted in calling the other man's name. The man he to whom he appeared to be talking ignored him and kept drinking his just-purchased beer. Finally, the man calling Dez's name walked up to him and slapped the beer out of his hands. "Nigga, you hear me talking to you? Where's my mutherfucking money?"

Dez looked at the other man and said, "Look Rock, I ain't got no money. You know I don't get no money until the first of the month."

"Nigga, that's what you said last month," Rock said, "I tell you what?" Rock pulled out his nine-millimeter pistol and put it to Dez's head. "At your funeral, your bitch can talk about how you was gonna get that money." Rock cocked back the trigger.

The old men on DDC looked at the proceedings and shook their head. Finally, Ray Heard said, "Doodlebug, what the hell you doing?"

Rock looked over at Ray. "Stay out of this, Uncle Ray. This don't concern you."

"The hell it doesn't, Doodlebug. What I'm goanna tell my sister? That I stood by and let you kill a man over what? How much he owe you?"

"That ain't the point, Uncle Ray, you can't let these niggas disrespect you and not pay you! If he does it, the next nigga goanna do it and the next."

"And your ass is goanna end up dead or in jail, with your family left to pick up the pieces, take care of your kids, tell them their daddy's out of the country, on vacation, out of town saying anything 'cept to say your daddy was a damn fool that didn't give a damn about nobody but himself."

Rock looked at Ray then at Dez. He eased the trigger back on his nine and looked at Dez and said, "Nigga, God is smiling on you today. You better have my money next month or God or Uncle Ray gonna save your ass." Rock put his nine back in his pants waist and turned and walked toward his car.

Dez, sweating the whole time, breathed a sigh of relief as he pulled out an old thirty-two caliber revolver from his sock and fired a single shot at Rock, hitting him in the back of his head. Blood and bone spew as Rock falls to the ground. "Who you think you is, nigga?" Dez asked. "Don't nobody threaten me and live." The corner erupted with people screaming and shouting as Ray heard looks at his nephew laying, dying on the ground.

Deandre's cellphone went off with its soft clanging chime. She had picked a soft Chinese gong chime tone to wake her in the morning. She had a fascination with Chinese culture. Everything in her home reinforced this, her Feng Shui dragon statue facing toward the east symbolizing the spring, her Vermilion bird painting facing toward the south symbolizing the summer, the porcelain white tiger on her mantle facing the west symbolizing autumn and lastly the figurine of the black tortes on her table symbolizing the winter all, to reinforce her positive Qi or life force. The time on her smart phone read eight o'clock. *Good,* she thought, *I can get a good run in.*

Deandre got out of her bed naked. She rarely wore any clothes to bed, this as a result of her three-year boyfriend in college. He wanted to pound her and her him three to four times a day, so the less clothes the better. That was a long time ago, what ten years? Yet she still slept naked waiting for that right man to come along and take advantage of the situation.

Deandre slipped a night robe on and headed to the kitchen.

She had to have her morning coffee, black with sugar and cream, just sweet enough to get her going. Deandre grabbed the coffee pot and filled it with water. She opened the cabinet to get a coffee filter and the coffee and suddenly, if on cue, there was a knock on her door. "Fuck," she said, "who in the hell is that?"

She closed up her nightgown and headed to the door. She looked out the peephole and said, "Damn." She turned the dead bolt lock and opened the door. "Could you have come any earlier?" Deandre asked sarcastically as she grabbed Nikki and pulls her through the door.

"Who did you fuck last night?" Nikki asked. "It wasn't me so could you be a little nicer?" Nikki pulled away as Deandre put her hands on her hips.

"Did anybody see you?" Deandre asked. Nikki turned away from Deandre and headed toward the refrigerator.

"Yeah," Nikki said, "the whole town." Nikki opened the refrigerator door and said, "Let's see, some eggs, turkey bacon, and milk and…" Nikki popped her head up out of the refrigerator and looks on the kitchen counter. "Ow," she said as she closed the refrigerator door and heads toward the kitchen counter.

Deandre looked at this calamity in motion and shook her head and couldn't help but smile. Her half-sister was a mess, and she knew it, but she was her sister, though very few people knew it, and she loved her to death. "What are you here for? To eat me out of house and home?" Deandre asked.

Nikki looked at Deandre and smiled as she looks around the kitchen counter. "Let's see, wheat bread, yuck! And what's this? Cinnabon? Yeah!" Nikki cheered as she turned toward Deandre. "I went over to Red's yesterday," Nikki said, not caring one way or the other.

Deandre's eyes narrowed. She knew this was coming; whenever her sister showed up, trouble was sure to follow. Deandre headed toward the kitchen cabinet and reached down and opened up the bottom cabinet and pulled out a cast iron skillet. She held it up in the air and said, "Before I hit you upside your head with it, please tell me you didn't screw nothing up?,"

"Whoa, sis," Nikki said, "You know I didn't, I mean I did screw—" "Nikki!" Deandre shouted.

"Okay, okay! Nikki said. "I know where Red's got the money stashed." Deandre lowered the skillet and put it on the kitchen stove.

"Bring me those eggs and bacon from the refrigerator while you tell me what's going on," Deandre said as Nikki began her tale. Outside the house the two Korean associates waited and watched, having followed Nikki from her house, observing everything she did and waiting for the colonel's next command.

Sheriff Johnson jumped from his vehicle as the emergency vehicles screeched to a stop at the corner store. He had heard about the shooting on his way to work and was among the first to arrive. "Get back, get back, and let these folks do their job!" the sheriff shouted as

emergency workers rushed to the victim lying on cold asphalt. The sheriff surveyed the crowd and saw Ray Heard standing by himself as if in a trance. He walked toward him. "Ray," the sheriff said. No answer. "Ray," the sheriff said again. Ray Heard looked at the sheriff with tears streaming down his eyes. "What happened, Ray?" the sheriff asked.

The emergency workers huddle over the body. Ray Heard looks at the sheriff and said, "My nephew has been killed sheriff."

"Well what happened?" The sheriff said. "Who did it?"

Ray Heard looked at the sheriff and said, with tears still streaming down his eyes, "We killed him, Sheriff, each and every one of us who said, 'He's just going through a phase, he'll be all right. It's the white man's fault that everything's messed up.'" Ray took his right arm and wiped the tears from his face on the back of his sleeve. "Each one of us that failed to see about our children, failed to make that child support payment, or even care to see if the child we fathered was even alive, we did this."

The sheriff looked at Ray and shook his head. He knew what he was saying was true but this was a murder and he had to get to the bottom of it. "Well Ray," the sheriff said, "who did it? What happened?"

Ray looked at the sheriff and smiled. "I don't know, Sheriff," he said, "I didn't see nothing." The sheriff stared at Ray as the emergency workers draped Rock's dead body with a white cloth.

Buster ran toward the front door closet. "I've got to go, Mom. There's been a shooting at the store."

Jo, standing in the entrance to the kitchen, looked at Buster rushing to the door. "I know, baby. Be careful," she said.

Buster opened the door and was out in a flash. Buster had gotten the call about seven o'clock, and fifteen minutes later was walking out the door. *The life of a police officer,* Jo thought. Everything was going fine one day and the next total disaster. It was an insecure life, never knowing if your loved one was coming home or not, never knowing how long they would be at work that day. It wasn't for the average person, a nine to five or whatever shift you worked at the plant. No it was a way of life, trying to protect the innocent, prosecute the guilty, and the results always fell somewhere in between.

No it wasn't an easy life and one Jo couldn't understand why her son had chosen, but one that she wholeheartedly supported. It was a life he had chosen and she could attest for one, that the world was a much better place for him having done so. She looked at the door and turned into the kitchen. She poured a cup of coffee and sat at the kitchen table slowly sipping it. *Aw*, she thought. *This should be an easy day, no school, no problems, and especially no Nikki. Yes, this should be an easy day*, or so she thought, as she sipped on her coffee.

The reverend entered the home of the deceased, Theodore Heard, Jr., better known as Rock, and nodded his head. "God bless you, sister," he said to one of Rock's relatives. "I'm so sorry to hear of your loss," the reverend said and made his way into the main living room. It was a double-wide trailer home and the living room was packed with relatives grieving the loss of a loved one. "Simply tragic, simply tragic," he said to the weeping family, some holding each other.

He looked and saw Rock's mother, Nettie Heard, who was sitting in a red recliner staring and rocking, oblivious to the surrounding world. Reverend Clark proceeded through the room until he was standing directly in front of her. He knelt downs in front of her and reached out with his hand and grasped her hand. He looked right in her eyes and said, "I know this might sound strange but you know, he has a better plan for us, sister Heard. Even though mortal man might not know the workings of the Lord, believe me it will all work out for the best."

Nettie Heard continued to stare straight ahead as a tear rolled from her eyes. The reverend Clark shook her hand then rose from the floor until he was standing in front of Nettie. He smiled and turned to walk away as she said, "I hope the Lord has a plan to feed his three children that he left behind, because I sure don't." Nettie continued to stare straight ahead.

The reverend shook his head and said, "Please, can I get you to bow your heads as I lead you in a moment of prayer?" The people in the room and Nettie bowed their heads as the reverend began, "Our Father," and Nettie continued to stare straight ahead, lost in her own thoughts.

Blu had heard about the shooting and he hated that every argument, it seemed, every disagreement in town always ended up with someone being shot. Not stabbed or beat up, but someone shot and killed. *Just absolutely mindless*, he thought, *and so unnecessary*. Blu hated it but he had other thoughts on his mind. The way he and RC were manipulated, played into a trip that could only lead to failure and all of it orchestrated by his son and Red. That was what concerned him most.

Blu, having been gone from his business for the past few days, knew he had to check in with his people. It was still early and if they did things the way he taught them they wouldn't be up for another couple of hours. Blu decided he'd make himself a cup of coffee. He reached for the coffee can and opened it. What? Maybe a half a spoon left? Blu took the coffee pot and took out the old filter and threw it away. He reached in the cabinet and got a fresh filter and put it in the coffee pot and then put in the last of his coffee. He then poured some water into the coffee pot. He didn't heed the whole pot full of water since he only had a little coffee so he filled it halfway and poured the water into his coffee container. He closed the lid and plugged the coffee pot in. After a few seconds, the coffee started to drip. *Good*, Blu thought, *there's nothing like a fresh cup of coffee in the morning.*

Knock, knock, knock, Blu heard the as someone knocked at the door. Blu, always conscious, moved to the middle drawer of his kitchen counter. That was where he kept his "Snake Killer," a forty-five caliber over and under derringer that he kept in the drawer. "Who is it?" Blu asked.

"Bang," the reply came. Blu closed the kitchen drawer and walked to his kitchen door. Blu unlocked the deadbolt lock and opened the door. Bang Bang, dressed in saggy jeans and a blue-striped shirt that perfectly matched his fresh pair of Jordans, stood at the door.

"Hey, Pops," Bang Bang said as he smiled at the door. "Can I come in?" he said.

Blu said, "Yeah, come on in."

Bang Bang opened the screen door and walks in. The screen door closed hard as Bang made his way into the kitchen. Blu, replaying the past two days in his head and knowing he should be cautious, said, "So what brings you here? Amongst the poor people."

Bang Bang laughed and said, "No, no, that's not you, Dad! That's not you!" Both of them laughed as Bang made his way to the kitchen table. He pulled out a chair and turned it around and sat down in it. "You ain't never asked me what brings me here," Bang said. "What's up?" Bang Bang said straightforwardly.

Blu looked at Bang and his eyes furrowed as he looks at him. He thought to himself, *What in the hell this nigga fixing to come up with*? He was looking to see what answers he could get to solve this puzzle he found himself in.

Blu headed for his kitchen cabinet and opened it. He rumbled around the cabinet and pulled out a box of Honey Nut Cheerios. He put it on his kitchen table and said, "Remember this?"

Blu remembered whenever he and his son had a disagreement or when he had made promises to him that he couldn't keep, everything seemed to disappear with a bowl of Honey Nut Cheerios. Bang Bang looked at the box of Honey Nut Cheerios and his face lit up. "Where's the bowl and the milk?" he asked.

Blu said, "This ain't the first time you been here, you know where they at."

Bang Bang jumped up from the table and rushed toward the cabinet and then the refrigerator. He smiled as he said, "Dad, you remember when I wanted to quit school and take my rap group to Atlanta?"

Blu smiled then laughed. "Yeah, I remember," he said. "What was the name of that group?"

"The Hustle Continues," Bang Bang answered.

Blu laughed. "Yeah, yeah, I remember that." Both men took turns pouring the cereal and milk and immediately dug in. "Didn't T. I. have a patent on that?" Blu looked at his son and smiles. He loved what happened this day, that he and his son tried to reconnect, but he knew that the day wasn't over yet, not over yet by a long shot.

CHAPTER 24

The chairman thought about all the events that had occurred and the reason he was really there. He thought about all the murders, about the threat to his business, with all the drugs being run through his company. But no, his thoughts were focused mainly on not his business, but his family and by doing so also to foster the hope of reunification between the north and south. Reuniting both countries would cause an economic behemoth that could not be matched by any country in the world he believed, so it was of upmost importance for him to make contact with his son, who was here in this country, employed by the rival north and to let them know that there was indeed a path to reunification and not by the politicians who had a little or lot to gain by the move but through family. The only true and lasting relationship any man or women has on this planet.

Now, however, he had to deal with the mess the company found itself in. He was aware of the drugs being run through his company months ago, having been alerted by subordinates, as they tracked the origin of the drugs, and their destination. This in when he became aware that his son was involved. Through his contacts in the north he had kept up with his long-ago love and their love child, watching from afar as he ran the family business, and pressed on with his own prearranged marriage and family, wondering what might have been. He kept his distance but now when fate dealt him this hand, he had to make contact, to try and force the issue. He first must deal with this situation and the rest would fall into place. He looked at his watch. It was exactly nine o'clock in the morning. He looked at his lead subordinate in this country and asked, "Is he here yet?"

The subordinate shook his head no. "There has been a murder in the town."

The chairman raised an eyebrow as he thinks what this means. "Any of our people involved?" he asked.

The subordinate cleared his throat before he said, "We don't know yet."

The chairman shook his head as he said, "Then what are you here for?" The subordinate bowed his head and quickly turned and left the room as the chairman sat alone in his thoughts.

The bodies were starting to pile up, Sheriff Johnson thought. It was election year and he didn't want people to think that he didn't have a handle on things, that this was a lawless community and that every time you stepped out the door, only the Lord knew if you were coming back home. No, this wasn't that type of town at least in his mind. Three murders directly in this community in less than a week and one murder not committed here but close enough. He knew that he had to do something fast to let the community know that this sheriff wouldn't tolerate it, no, not in the least.

The sheriff picked up his radio receiver and mashed the button. "Come on, Buster?" the sheriff said.

"Yes, Sheriff?" came the reply.

"We gonna set up a roadblock up on fourteen and forty-two," Sheriff Johnson said.

"But Sheriff, it's the end of the month. Ain't nobody—"

The sheriff interrupted, "You let me worry about that, Buster. You just set up the roadblock and I don't care if they got an expired tag, or if you knew these folks from the time they were born, you write them up, understand?"

There was a pause on the other end until Buster replied, "Got you, Sheriff," he said.

The sheriff nodded his head up and down as he thought, *Good, I've got to show these people that we're in control.* Suddenly, he remembered about his appointment with the chairman. "Shit," he said out loud, "I almost forgot." He gunned his Charger and headed for the turnoff to the factory. *Yeah*, he thought. *This here should be good.*

Nikki exited her sister's house and headed down the street. Everything was going fine, or so she thought. Nobody suspected her of anything, except that sheriff and he didn't have anything, or

he would have brought her in. She had run this game to perfection with not a thing connected to her. The money tossed out of the SUV puzzled her, but not really. Whoever it was probably was just seeing how she would react, what she'd do, and since she didn't do anything or wouldn't do anything, that should throw them off. Yeah, life was just rolling along, going well.

Nikki turned down MLK Boulevard and continued walking. Martin Luther King was a revered leader, a game changer in the black community, if not the world. His ideology of nonviolence not only changed the United States, but the world. Nikki didn't care. She had heard of him and what he did but he died long before she was born and all that she knew was that niggas killed niggas and white folks decided what the consequences would be.

She turned left and headed down George Wallace Street, toward Jo's house. She hadn't seen her boo in a couple of days and she knew once you had sex with someone anyone if you didn't see them within two days, it meant you lost the bond, the physical bond you both had created. She felt something for Jo. She didn't know what it was. But something. She was dropping by to genuinely see she how she was. She continued walking's down MLK, not thinking about history, but thinking about her problems, her life. Nikki continued walking until she finally reached Jo's house.

Nikki looked at the house and not knowing what to expect, walked cautiously down the drive. Dogs barking in the neighborhood announced her arrival as she walked to the front door. She stopped and instead of knocking on the door, immediately hesitated, listening for voices inside. Hearing nothing, she proceeded to knock on the door. The door suddenly flew open and Jo stood there with her hands on her hips. "Oh look who's here," Jo said sarcastically. "Miss Nikki Flowers, the countrified queen for a day." With that, Jo turned and opened the door, allowing Nikki access to her home. "What is it today, Nikki?" Jo continued, "Miss Light Skin queen for a day. What light skin shit you got going on today?"

Nikki looked at Jo as she walked away from her. *Damn*, she thought, *if I have ass like that when I'm thirty plus...* but this was about business. "What's up my nigga?" Nikki asked. "I'm not in the door five

minutes and you attack me?" Nikki said, "I thought we were friends." Nikki brushed past Jo and entered the house.

Jo was through with this bitch; she was young and thought she was entitled to everything. The world was her oyster and damn what anybody said or did everything was the way she saw it. Damn everybody else. "This is my house," Jo said, "and I let into it, whoever I please."

Nikki looked back at Jo and took a seat in the dining area. "Damn Jo," Nikki said. "I came over here because I thought we had a connection."

"Connection?" Jo said as her eyes widened and her nostrils flared. "Because we fucked one day? Girl, I…,"

There was a knock at the door. Jo and Nikki looked at each other, immediately stopping their conversation. Jo looked at Nikki, still angry, and said, "You just wait a minute," as she turned and headed toward the door. She turned the doorknob and opened the door only to find…

"Good morning, ladies," the colonel said, smoking a cigarette and flanked by his two associates. "It's been some time since I last talked to you?" He smiled as he and his two associates entered the house.

Blu and Bang Bang's breakfast had morphed into a video game challenge. Old school versus new school. "Man, this shit you're playing," Blu began, "is all computer graphics and who's right and wrong. Classic way you guys play these games, everything a life and death situation that you're able to come back from. Game over. Reset the game. If you get killed or beaten you just reset the game. It's an illusion of life. You think life goes on and on instead of seeing life as it is. You have moments you enjoy; you have moments you hate but no matter what your situation you just got to keep moving on."

Bang Bang looked at his father and thought about what he said. "Yeah, Dad," he said, "You got to just keep moving forward."

Blu, having finished the last of his breakfast, sat back in his chair and said, "That's why it important for me to know why you played me!"

Bang Bang looked at his father and laughs. "That's because you wanted to be played… You're the righteous father, even though nobody

has seen you in ten years and now that you're old, it's time for you to cash in, for your family to forgive and forget and elevate you to this all-knowing and generous father. Do you know how many times we went to sleep hungry when you weren't there? You looked at that money that you got as a justification for all the wrongs and rights in your life, didn't you?"

Blu looked at his son and anger built up in him. "What the hell do you mean," Blu asked. "I took you to school and picked you up. I was an active father. You never went hungry!" Blu was so angry he could literally turn red, but he took a deep breath and exhaled then thought what his son was doing: trying to bait him. "You know these hos you and your boys are fucking and not caring what they think and what they do?" Blu asked. "That's the relationship I had with your mother. I had plenty of girls but she was the one who turned up pregnant, and who I had to deal with. I didn't think no more of her then as I do today, just another ho."

The blood rushed through Bang Bang's temples "What the fuck are you saying?" Bang Bang asked. "That my mother is just another ho?,"

"No, no, no, I'm not saying that," Blu said and paused. "I'm just saying that the same way you feel about your female friends is the same way I felt about the women of my time. Y'all have just talked about it more, twittered it, Facebooked it and told everybody in God's creation. The only thing that separates us is time."

Bang Bang looked at his father and understood what he was talking about. "How do we break the circle?" he asked. "I don't want my kids to grow up and do me. I want them to do better," Bang said.

"It's God's will, son. That's all I can say. The plans that I thought would work didn't, and the ones I've never thought would work came to be. Faith," Blu said. "That is the only thing that can sustain a man or woman through this this thing called life." Blu looked at Bang Bang to see if his message hit home.

"I mean," Bang Bang said, "if you think I'm goanna go soft on you, no it doesn't." Bang Bang fired up the video game and said, "Bam, yeah you know I'm a winner."

Blu smiled as he pressed his controller and said, "I bet you didn't see that coming?" They both laughed as they continued to play the

video game, each silently accepting the fact their lives mirrored the video game—just one battle after another.

Sheriff Johnson pulled into the parking lot of Kwansung. He was late, but hell with the way stuff was happening, he was sure the chairman understood. Hell, the sheriff thought, even if he didn't, he was the man. Kwa sung had a lot to answer for and perhaps it was the root of all that had ensued. The drugs coming through their ports and passageways were the problem and in the sheriff's mind, somebody higher up had to know something. That was why he was here: to find out who knew what. The sheriff parked his Dodge Charger in the handicapped zone in front of the building.

He cut the engine off and just sat there for a moment. He thought about how just five years ago, this was nothing but cow pastures and now thousands of people from as far away as Montgomery worked here. He didn't want to create any controversy but he had a murder investigation underway and he didn't want anyone to lose their jobs, but he had a case to solve.

He exited the car and headed toward the guard shack. It was game day in Alabama, the big one Auburn versus the University of Alabama and for those of you not aware of this yearlong ritual, this was it, the big one, the one thing in Alabama more important than Grandma's biscuits on Saturday morning. The right to talk shit to your neighbor every morning for the rest of the year, so the sheriff was anxious to do something today positive and if not head back to his house for kick off. Yeah, he thought, he'd better hurry up.

The chairman watched as the sheriff came through the turnstiles at the company's entrance. The sheriff was two hours late and time was something a man in his position had little of. He still had to make contact with his son, something that had laid on his mind for the past thirty years. Family, no matter what the circumstances, was always the most important thing in life. This, however, had to take a back seat to what was happening right now. The company's name was at stake. He had shareholders to consider and profits to be made and not only

that, all the employees looking for paychecks were always upmost in his mind.

Sheriff Johnson walked through the turnstile as the escorts watched his every move. He noticed all the cameras looking at him and wondered if the chairman himself was watching. He paused for a moment, as a security guard handed him a sign-in sheet. One of his escorts approached him. "Aw, Sheriff," he began, "I see that you finally made it." The escort smiled that wide smile and the dark rimmed glasses made him look every bit of The Joker in *Batman*, minus the glasses. He wondered what kind of joke the chairman had cooked up for him. "Right this way please," the escort said and bowed, something the sheriff didn't expect.

The sheriff looked at him with a bewildered look on his face and headed to the gate as another escort sat in a golf cart, smiling at him. "This way sheriff," the man in the golf cart said. The sheriff noticed that all the subordinates were Korean, not one American. *I don't know what is going on*, the sheriff thought, *but it's obvious the Koreans are in charge of everything here*. The sheriff climbed into the golf cart and the Korean associate gunned the golf cart and away they went. The sheriff looked at the vast plant and all the warehouses as they passed by. All these cars, all these jobs, all this money; he knew the line of questioning that he would bring and all that he thought will be brought into question, but what of the people that were dead and their families? Didn't they deserve some kind of justice? The golf cart turned and they pulled up to the shipping and receiving building.

It was just another building in this vast complex. He noticed nothing special about it as the golf cart came to a stop. There stood another Korean but without the eyeglasses. The sheriff got out of the golf cart and the Korean standing there said, "Follow me," as he began walking toward the building. The sheriff followed the Korean as they entered the building. There were three to four guards waiting for them, all Korean. They entered the building. It was a narrow corridor with guards every five feet. It was around fifteen feet long, leading to a huge black door. The Koreans led the way as they walked down the long corridor. The sheriff thought, *I know this this guy doesn't shit in the same toilet as I do, but he's just a man with a lot to answer to for.*

The men marched toward the huge black door and then stop. The lead Korean, the one that drove him to the building, stopped and turned toward the sheriff. "Could you please remove the weapon from your gun belt, Sheriff," he said.

The sheriff looked at him then laughed. "The only way that will happen," the sheriff began, "is over my dead body." There was a pause as the sheriff looked at the Korean and he at him.

Finally, the Korean laughed and said, "Of course, Sheriff, of course. After all, this is your country." *Yes it is*, the sheriff thought, *yes it is, no matter all the problems this is his country.* "Well if you will follow me," the lead Korean said.

They moved to the door and it automatically opened and the two of them walked through the door. In the room there was a singular desk with the chairman seated behind it. There was no side chair, no couch, nothing. Just a desk with the chairman seated at it. The sheriff and the Korean associate moved toward the desk and stopped in front of it. The chairman and the Korean associate looked at each other and nodded. The Korean associate nodded and turned and made his way toward the black doors and exited. The sheriff stood there motionless, looking at the proceedings. He looked at the chairman and he at him. The chairman started the conversation. "Sheriff Johnson," he said, "I understand that there's some question's that you would like to ask me."

The sheriff looked at the chairman. He was a small man sitting behind a huge desk. His closely cropped hair and the blackness of it totally bellied his age. The chairman studied the sheriff and thought to offer him a seat, but no, this would mean that he was in a compromising position. It was best to let him stand and wonder what was coming next.

"As you know," the sheriff began, "there have been a few murders in our town linked to your company. We know about the drug link between your company and the murders and what I'm trying to ascertain is what involvement your company had in this?"

The chairman looked at the sheriff and smiled. "As you know Sheriff, I cannot answer that question because of the legal ramifications

of it and potential litigation of these open-ended questions." The chairman stated, "What I can tell you are is that the company will openly cooperate with your investigation."

The sheriff took his hat, removed it from his head, and started twirling it in his hands. The sheriff thought about the three dead bodies connected to this company and the cooperation they were now willing to give and said, "Well that's all nice and good, but with the help of the federal government agencies that I've contacted, there's no doubt that whatever your companies involvement, the truth will soon be uncovered." The sheriff was bluffing. He hadn't contacted any federal agencies and none of them but he knew the threat of any federal involvement in the state of Alabama was enough to scare any state lobbyist, legislature, or bureaucrat, or business into action, hence his protection.

The chairman looked at the sheriff and said, "I'm sorry, Sheriff," he began, "but will you please take a seat?" The chairman motioned to the sheriff to take a seat. The sheriff nodded his head and took a seat at the table. "Excuse me, Sheriff," the chairman said. "But it is bad manners and business to not offer my quest any kind of refreshments. What would you like?" The chairman clapped his hands together and suddenly the double doors to his office opened. In walked a small army of servants. They rolled carts of food and drink into the room followed by musicians and dancers. Then come the women, scantily clad of all shapes, colors, and hues. The food servants parked the food by the chairman's desk, while the musicians took a space next to the chairman's desk and gently started playing a Western song, "Don't Let Me Be Lonely Tonight," on Eastern interments.

The women gather around the chairman as he smiled and said, "What would be your pleasure, Sheriff?" The sheriff was impressed with the dog-and-pony show the chairman had just put on. He stood and walked to the food cart. He surveyed the offerings and then looked at the girls and smilesd "I'm impressed," the sheriff said. "Only one thing wrong though."

"What?" the chairman asked as he looked around the room as the sheriff returned to his seat.

The sheriff sat down and said, "No fried chicken."

The chairman clapped his hands together angrily and the girls, the food, and the musicians almost ran from the room. One of the servants remained behind as the others quickly exited the room. The chairman called him over and addressed him harshly as the sheriff thought to himself, *Round three, knockout round.*

CHAPTER 25

The colonel smiled at Nikki and Jo. After all, they were two attractive women and he knew this was business, but two lovely women softened him just a bit. "Ladies, if I might," the colonel began. "I have a few problems that I would like for you to help me solve."

"But we don't know nothing," Nikki said.

The colonel crossed his arms then shook his head. "I know what you say," he began, "but from my simple observations you two are involved in everything, especially this young lady right here," the colonel said, pointing a finger at Nikki. Nikki and Jo looked at each other, considering the colonel's words. Jo thought the same thing and wanted the colonel to keep this line of questioning going. Nikki, on the other hand, wanted to keep her game intact. Fuck what anybody else thought, especially if they didn't know anything. "You know that I've lost a significant amount of money here," the colonel said, "and that we have a significant investment here." The colonel reached into his pocket and pulled out his ever-present pack of cigarettes. The two women listened as the colonel lit up a cigarette and started smoking. "What you two women don't know," the colonel continued, "is that we need—I need—help because of a couple of recent setbacks," the colonel said as he exhaled the smoke. "I need, no, we need a couple of partners to help us achieve our goals." The colonel dropped ashes on Jo's clean floor.

Jo and Nikki looked at each other and Nikki spoke, "So what does that mean? You what me and Jo to move your stuff for you?," Nikki looked at Jo who shook her head no.

"No, No, No," the colonel said, "I already have someone for that. What we need," the colonel continued, "is for someone to make friends with one or so of the gentlemen at Kwansung so that we may be assured of receiving our shipments and then for to deliver it the designated area."

"What? Jo asked. "You're looking for a couple of mules to transport drugs?" Jo shook her head no. "What if we get caught, what about my job? My family? I won't do it." Jo folded her hands and poked her lips out in defiance.

Nikki looked at Jo and said, "Wait a minute Jo, wait a minute. We both know a lot of people over at the plant; this could be easy money for us. How much money we talking?" Nikki asked.

The colonel smiled before he said, "Ten thousand per drop."

Nikki smiled and looked at Jo. "That could go to my college fund," Nikki began. "That's about the only way I'll go, if I pay for it myself."

Jo still shook her head no. "That will barely be enough to get you out of jail if you're caught," Jo said.

Nikki nodded her head up and down and then said, "What about ten thousand a drop and we handle the time that it happens?" Nikki countered.

"No," the colonel said. "It is our operation, our money," the colonel said as he continued to smoke on his cigarette.

"But it's our lives" Jo said, "if it doesn't work, you just pack up and go." Jo looked at Nikki. "We have to live with all the fallout, all the consequences."

The colonel looked at Jo and considered what she was saying. He knew that what she was saying was right and he wouldn't consider what she was saying excepting that. He needed her, needed them. "I understand what you're saying," the colonel said, "and that is acceptable."

Jo and Nikki looked at each other, trying to contain their excitement. "Girl power!" Nikki said. "We gonna run this mutherfucker, Jo!"

Jo and the colonel looked at each other. The colonel didn't need to say what needed to be said. "Now look, Nikki," Jo said, "this is about business; we don't need nobody but us, the people in this room, knowing about it. Understand?"

Nikki looked at the colonel then at Jo. "Yeah, I understand."

Jo looked at Nikki and knows she heard her but knows deep down in her soul, that there was trouble ahead and mostly because of her. "All right then," Jo said, "girl power! Girl power!" Jo knew tragedy was just around the corner.

The chairman did not like what was going on, how this smug sheriff seemed to think that he was as smart as he was. He ran a billion-dollar corporation and here he was, across from this simple sheriff with a smile on his face as if, as if he was in control. "Well Sheriff, as you know," the chairman began, "we've had a few problems here at the plant, which we have addressed. We have let you into our plant to inspect the property and to see that the company has nothing to hide, so if I may," the chairman said, "exactly what are your concerns?"

Right to the point, the sheriff thought, *he wants to know what the hell I am doing here wasting his time.* "Well," the sheriff began, "I still have a little problem I have to solve,"

"Yes, yes," the chairman said. "What is that?"

The sheriff's eyes hardened as he said, "I still have two dead bodies and no suspects, well excuse me ." The sheriff raises his finger in the air and wiggles it. "There actually are three dead bodies, though one is in another county that are tied to this company." The sheriff smiled as he let down his arm. "Why do you suppose that is?"

The chairman didn't smile or even appear nervous as he reached across his desk and opened a box on his desk. He reached in and pulled out a Cuban cigar and offered it to the sheriff. "Have one, Sheriff?" the chairman asked. The sheriff shook his head no. The chairman took a cigar cutter off his desk and cut off one end of the cigar then laid the cutter back on his desk. "I'm sorry, Sheriff," the chairman said. "But this one bad habit I picked up from my many travels that I am quite fond of." He lit his cigar, inhaled it, and slowly blew the smoke out.

"You know," he began, "I came to this country as a college student and I attended M.I.T." He stopped and took another puff on his cigar. "As a young man I used to go out with my friends to one of the many bars in the area, one called The Muddy Charles Pub." The chairman smiled as he remembered his youth. "Me and my friends use to drink pitcher after pitcher of beer and one or two of my friends would get especially rowdy and well, one thing lead to another and a fight would ensue, that is when," the chairman raised his finger, "I realized what effect alcohol had on people, how normally peaceful people would resort to violence when under its direction, wouldn't you agree, Sheriff?"

The sheriff nodded his head in agreement.

"It was payday, they were friends, they were young, who's to say that they didn't get into some disagreement that led to their tragic circumstances, Sheriff? The company, after all, has no control over what an employee does in their free time, now do we?" The chairman, who had sat up in his chair as he was spinning his tale, sat back in his chair, and took another puff on his cigar.

The sheriff, who had listened to this incredible version of pure bullshit, just shook his head and stood up. "Chairman," the sheriff said as he put on his hat. "I came here, trying in good faith to work with you and try and solve these problems, but since I can't. I'll guess I'll just talk to couple of these media folks about your company's involvement and…" The sheriff turned and walked toward the double doors.

"Follow the girl, Sheriff," the chairman said as the sheriff started to exit the room. "Follow the girl." The sheriff stopped as if hit by a truck, then he turned and looked at the chairman and tipped his hat before turning again and opening the double doors. He managed to contain his smile as he thought to himself, *Knockout*!

Red fired up the blunt he had just rolled as he thought about his state of affairs. It wasn't good. Every time some shit happened around here, they were trying to put it on him. Red looked at Shorty Low and said, "You ever thought what it would be like to be someplace else?"

Shorty looked at Red and, knowing him, knew he had to be cautious in what he said. "What you mean, Red?" Shorty asked.

Red took another hit on his blunt and exhaled laying back on the couch looking at the TV "I mean we sit here every day looking at TV and everything and the farthest we ever been is the casino or to Biloxi. I mean there's more to life, isn't there?"

There was a knock at the door. Red looked at the nine on his living room table. He was always looking toward it or one of the several guns he had stashed around his house.

It was the business. There was always someone out there trying to catch you sleeping, not looking, and trying to take your shit. It wasn't an easy existence by any means, but what other choice did he have? Work in a factory for eight dollars an hour with a boss telling you what to do or not to do? That was bullshit. He'd rather take his chances on the street, where he at least felt he had control of his life. "Get that shorty?" Red walked.

Shorty walks to the door with his nine in his waistband. The gun added about five pounds to his pants so his pants sagged extra low. "Yeah?" Shorty said.

"It's RC," the voice said.

Red shook his head yes as he looked at Shorty. "Alright RC," Red said, "hold on." Shorty unlocked one of the deadbolts on the door, then the other, then the other. Red eased back in his chair away from his nine, looking at the television. Finally, the door opened and RC entered the door, with that gap-toothed smile of his.

"Red," he said. "How you doing?" Red looked at RC and knew that he wanted something, a hit probably, but what RC didn't know was that Red wants something also. "Let me talk to you a minute, Red." RC looked at Red then at Shorty. "Alone," he emphasized.

"No, no, no," Red said. "We all family here, all family here! Me and shorty are family, anything you say to me, you can say to him," Red said.

"Well you know," RC says. "I've been doing this work for you and….,"

"And you want to get paid!" Red said as he looked at Shorty. "Shorty gives this man a hit on the house!" Shorty looked at RC and rolled his eyes. He then retreated to the back of the house. "You've been doing a good job, RC," Red said, rising up in his chair and folding his hands together. "It's just that stepdaughter of yours? You know?"

RC blinked his eyes, and then said. "Nikki? What she got to do with this?"

Shorty returned from the back with a hit for RC. He handed it to Red; Red took it and threw it on the table. RC, seeing the hit laying on the table, immediately started reaching for it. "Hold on there, RC," Red said as he reached out and pushed it toward him. "Nikki is the key to everything," Red said. "She's aware of what's going on here and though I'm not sure, she probably had something to do with those two boys' deaths."

RC's mouth dropped open. "You mean she killed them boys?" RC asked.

Red looked at RC and tossed the hit to him. "I'm not saying she did or didn't," Red said. "But I know she had something to do with it and what that is—" Red said as RC took out a shooter to put his rock in.

"Is what I want you to find out, understand? Amongst other things."

RC hurried up and put the rock in his shooter. He took out his lighter and lit it, inhaling the smoke. To RC, this was a pleasant retreat from the reality that he was in. All the arguments, the bills, the problems all left him as the high reached his brain. RC exhaled and looked at Red. "I need to know what she's doing and what time she's doing it."

RC took a long puff on the straight shooter. "Okay Red, okay, I got that. But what?" RC paused as he hurried to take another puff on the shooter. "About Blu?" RC asked as he took two quick puffs instead of the long puff on the straight shooter.

"Don't worry," Red said as he sat back in his chair. "I've got that handled."

The sheriff looked at his watch. It was ten o'clock in the morning. He had exactly nine hours until game time. Hours he needed to do something to get some of this shit solved. *Let's see*, he thought in his mind, *three murders, ties to Kwansung and the random murder, or is it? Could this also be tied to the previous three murders?* The sheriff picked up his radio and pressed the send button. "Buster, you there?" the sheriff asked.

There's a pause then "Yeah, Sheriff, come back."

"I've got a lead on a suspect, one you know."

"Who's that, Sheriff?" Buster came back.

"Nikki Flowers," the sheriff said.

Buster paused and then said, "What you want me to do, Sheriff?"

"You know her folks, right?" the sheriff asked.

"Yeah I do," Buster replied. "Well we gonna meet up over there."

"Right, Sheriff," Buster said.

"Okay Buster, see you there," the sheriff said. The sheriff thought about what the chairman said. *Follow the girl*. It could only be Nikki. It had to be, the sheriff thought. She was the only one who was all over the place yet not directly tied to anyone. The sheriff wondered if

she was working with or for Red. That would make sense, he thought, given how young she was. She had to be working with or for someone. Probably Red, he thought again. Of course Red.

The chairman's small motorcade left the sanctuary of Kwansung and headed toward his next destination, the real reason he had come here, to make contact with his son. He had kept tabs on him since he was born, provided support for him and his mother even though they lived in the north. He still deeply loved his mother even though that way was barred to him years ago. Nonetheless he still loved her as he replayed how they met and fell in love all these years ago. But they were in America now, the place was dreams came true and this dream he hoped would surely happen or so he hoped. There was the problem of his employer, however. It shouldn't be much of a problem the chairman thought, especially since he had the power of money, but again he was from the north and they unfortunately had their own agenda, their own set of rules. He really didn't know how this whole thing would shake out but he knew he had to try. He had to.

Blu closed the door as his son left. They had a good visit, even though Blu didn't really know any more now than he did before. Why he had been set up? And whose money was that that him and RC spent and lost. Was it Red's? And what did that Asian dude have to do with it? The questions danced around his head. He had wanted to ask Bang Bang those questions, but he sacrificed those questions in order to at least communicate with his son. They hadn't really spoken in two or three years and though he knew he was being used, what the hell? This was family, the only son he had, so forget about all the lies and deceit, he was just happy knowing that there was still some love there. Blu smiled and thought about him and his son, but he knew he had to get back to business.

His spot hadn't been open in two days and he knew people were looking for him so he decided he'd better go down there and reconnect. He looked around the house and headed toward the door, opened it and almost ran dead into Deandre, the lawyer. Red's lawyer. Blu tried not to look surprised. He knew who she was. He just couldn't figure out what she was doing here. "Well hello," Blu said as he looked at Deandre. She was standing there with some tight blue jeans on and a black silk hoodie with some moccasin type shoes on. Her hair weave was pulled back in a bun. Her mocha light skin and her shinny white teeth made her look like a goddess. Yes, she was a goddess Blue thought. He just wondered what this particular goddess was doing here. "Heh!" Blue said, "What brings you by?"

Deandre smiled with those pretty white teeth of hers and said, "May I come in?"

Blu stepped aside and bowed his head. "Why sure, come on. Blu looked at Deandre as she stepped into his house. *Damn*, he says in his mind, *that thang is fine.*

Deandre walked in to the room and looked around Blu's home. "When was the last time you redecorated this, the seventies?" Deandre looked around the house and sees a picture of poker-playing dogs and a couple of black lights. "When was the last time you had a woman?" Deandre asked.

"What?" Blu asked. "You don't think I got women?"

"No I don't," Deandre said, "You're just faking it."

The anger built in Blu's mind. *What five-dollar or two-children having women didn't want him*, he thought. He represented stability, money, something they could pay their light bill with. He had women or did he?

"I know you're the poor ho's dream," Deandre said. "But you don't have women, someone to stand beside you and take a hit, or take charge. That's a woman."

Blu shook his head and said, "What the fuck is you here for? Maybe I'm just like you said, but what exactly do you want?" Blu looked at Deandre as she looked at him.

"Well," Deandre said, "I have a business proposition for you." She smiled.

Blu looked at her and said, "Well whatever it is, it can wait, here come on in a take a seat." Blu led her through the entrance and into his small dining room. "Go ahead," he said. "Take a seat."

Deandre took a seat as Blu disappeared into the kitchen. "I'll be there in a minute," Blu said as Deandre took a look around.

"What is that?" she asked as she looked into the living room. *Plastic on the seats? That went out...* and before she could complete her thought, Blu returned holding a bottle and two glasses.

"How about this?" Blu said as Deandre looked at what he was holding.

"What is that?" Deandre asked. "Liquor this early? Are you kidding me?"

The smile on Blu's face disappeared as he said, "What the hell? I thought you was talking business."

"I am," Deandre said. "Well this is how I talk business: a bottle of moonshine and two people talkin' and drinking. Baby, this is the Alabama way."

Deandre looked at Blu and smiled. "Well since you say it that way," Deandre paused. "Pour it up!"

Blu pulled out a seat and sat the bottle and the two glasses down. "Yeah," he said. "That's what I'm talking about." Blu opened the bottle of moonshine and poured him and Deandre two big glasses of moonshine.

CHAPTER 26

The chairman's small convoy rolled down Highway 50, headed toward their destination. He was anxious, but yet happy with the way things were going. He was finally going to meet and see his son, his love child of so many years ago. He had children since from his first wife: three children, two boys and a girl, and from his present wife, one boy. When love is denied, however, you reflect back on what might have been. *What would my life had been if I had been with the only woman I ever truly loved?* he often wondered, instead of the women whose family had a lot of money and whose rank and privilege helped him and his family build the empire that they controlled, but left a sense of disinterest in life. Like you weren't living life you wanted but only going through the motions, the pretense of being happy but really not. He thought of these things as the convoy headed down through the Alabama countryside toward their destination.

The sheriff pulled into the driveway of Nikki's house. He expected Buster to be there, but he wasn't. He picked up his radio and pushed the send button. "Come on in, Buster," the sheriff said. As he waited for a reply, his mind raced over the day's events, the murder in town over nothing, his meeting with the chairman, and finally the connection between Nikki and the dope-house murders.

"Come on in, Sheriff," Buster said on the radio.

"Yeah Buster," the sheriff said, "where you at?"

"I had to stop at the house, Sheriff," Buster said.

"Stop at the house?" the sheriff asked. "This had better be—"

"I got to use it, Sheriff and this is right on the way."

Use it? the sheriff thought. *What in the hell is this boy...?* It finally hit him. *Oh, use the restroom.* "Okay Buster," the sheriff said. "That's fine but don't take too long."

"Alright, Sheriff I won't." Buster came back.

"Sheriff, come in," came the call.

"This is the sheriff," the sheriff said.

"Sheriff, there is all kinds of media here waiting for a statement about today's murder." It was Deputy Olivier. "Oliver," the sheriff said. "I won't be back for another hour or so." The sheriff paused. "You can hold them off that long, can't you?"

There was a long pause and Oliver comes back. "Okay, Sheriff, will do." Deputy Oliver was a veteran, a police officer with over twenty years' experience looking forward to retirement. His loyalty, his dedication could not be questioned. Whatever he said he'd do, he'd do.

"All right," the sheriff said as he returned the handset to the holder on his dashboard. *Media looking for answers, election time, and the football game*, the sheriff thought. *Not to mention the unsolved murders. Could it really get any better?*

Jo and Nikki looked at each other as the colonel left. They knew they were in the money, paid. They knew everybody and knew how to manipulate them so that everything turned in their favor, so why not celebrate? Jo moved toward her liquor cabinet. "What would you like to drink?" Jo asked.

"Drink?" Nikki had heard about drinking and alcohol, but she had never drank any alcohol ion her life, and judging what she had seen with her stepfather the good reverend, it wasn't something she had seriously thought about trying. "You got any Poweraid?" Nikki asked.

Jo laughed. "Girl, you gonna have money, you need to know about the temptations life has to offer," Jo said.

"Why?" Nikki asked.

"So that you know what to avoid," Jo said. Nikki thought that odd, what somebody twice her age would say about what she should avoid, while giving her something to drink. Jo scanned her liquor cabinet. She had some brown and white liquor. She thought what about some Hennessey with a Coke mixer? *No*, she thought. *That's too strong for...*

Suddenly, the front door burst open. Jo turned and looked and it's Buster. "I don't know what the hell all got going on, Mom, but the sheriff is looking for that girl Nikki and you had better get her gone or you because you know how he is!"

Jo looked at Nikki, trying to figure out what Buster was talking about. "We're just," Jo started, before Buster says, "Mom, I don't know what the hell you got going, but I do know the sheriff is looking for Nikki. Right now!" Buster was wide-eyed and looking exited, Jo saw.

She looked at Nikki and said, "You and I both knew this could happen so…"

Nikki looked at Jo and shook her head. "Time to go!" Nikki got up from the couch and grabbed Jo and hugged her. "Well," Nikki said, "it's time to go." Nikki hugged Jo again one last time turned and smiled and headed out the door. When the door closed, Buster looked at Jo and said. "Mom, what the fuck just happened here?"

"What are you talking about, Buster?" Jo asked.

"Mom, the sheriff is looking for that… shit," Buster began, "Mom I've got to use it!" Buster rushed out of the living room, headed toward the bathroom.

Nikki looked at Jo. "I think I better get out of here," she said.

"To where?" Jo asked.

"I don't know," Nikki said. She really didn't but she knew she had ten grand stashed and if all went according to plan she would get that quarter of a million dollars from Red. She didn't know where she was going, but she damn sure didn't worry about getting there.

Nikki moved toward the front door with Jo following close behind. Nikki got to the front door then turned and looked at Jo. "Well it's been fun Jo. It's been fun!"

Nikki turned the door handle, opened the door, and exited the house, never looking back or saying goodbye. Jo closed the door and leaned up against it, shaking her head. *Young folks,* she thought as she called out. "Buster, you alright?"

The alcohol was beginning to get to Deandre. Her speech was slurred and she was about to forget what she was there for. "Now, now," Deandre said, "enough of this drinking. I'm here about business."

Blu looked at her and laughed. "I don't know what kind of business you're here about, but you sure then went about the business of drinking my moonshine!"

Our Small Town

They both laughed as Deandre looked at Blu and said, "You know that quarter million dollars that you had? How would you like to have it back?"

Blu stopped smiling and looked at Deandre. *How does she know about that?* he thought. "I don't know what you're talking about," Blu said. Playing the fool was appropriate at this time, or so Blu thought.

"C'mon," Deandre said. "You and RC, and the ride to Biloxi?" Deandre smiled. "By the way, did y'all have fun?"

Blu thought to himself, *How did this bitch know this?* "What do you want," Blu finally asked.

"How," Deandre began, "would you like to get that money back?"

Blu looked at Deandre and said, "It's already gone. Red has it."

Deandre took another swig of the moonshine on the table and put the glass back down. "What if I told you," she began, "that I know were the money's at and that we can get it?"

Blu's eyes widened as he looked at Deandre. "What's the split?," Blu asked, "If we do get it back?"

Deandre got up from the table, almost stumbling and stands erect. "Since I'm supplying the information," Deandre said as she weaved and bobbed back and forth. "I'll get seventy five percent and you get twenty five percent." Suddenly Deandre stands as stiff as an iron board and passes out, falling face down on the floor.

Lord, Blu thinks. *I got to tell Uncle Ray to cut that shine a little more.*

The chairman's motorcade stopped at the hotel. The chairman sat in the black SUV as his men get out and look around.

The colonel's men looked out the window of the motel room and saw the three SUVs pull up. "Colonel," the fat associate said, "someone's here."

The colonel got up from his chair at the small table in the room and went to the window and looked out. He saw the SUVs and the Asian men looking around the hotel parking area, "I see," the colonel said as he closed the curtain. "It seems that we have a special visitor."

The chairman, flanked by his men, exited the vehicle and walked toward the hotel room. He was anxious, not knowing how this meeting would turn out, but this was why he was here. Why he was in some poor little town in the middle of America? He was here to see his son. The door from the hotel room swung open and out walked the colonel and his two men. Both the chairman and the colonel looked at each other, studying each other closely. Finally, the colonel said, "Well you're not from the U.S. and you're not Chinese, so of whom do I have the pleasure of meeting?"

The chairman smiled and said, "My name is of no importance to you but my mission is…" The colonel reached for his pocket to pull out his pack of cigarettes and not finding them, looks at one of his associates, the fat one and said, "In the room, my cigarettes please."

The associate turned to go and stopped and said, "Are you—" the colonel stopped him mid-sentence.

"I'm sure I'll be alright, me and this gentlemen will just take a walk down the lot and back." The associate looked at the colonel and the man next to him. The man seemed familiar to him. He was not sure why, so he dismissed it out of his head immediately, turned, and walked toward the room.

The colonel smiled as he looked at the chairman and said, "Let me introduce myself to you. I am Colonel—"

"Woo-Sung," the chairman said.

The colonel seemed amused as he put his hands behind his back and begins to walk. "And you are Chairman Kwan," the colonel said as the chairman also smilds and said, "Well I guess it's time we drop the entire pretense then and get to the reason I'm here. I have a son that is in your employ that I would very much like to talk to."

The colonel stopped and turns as he looks at the chairman. Now this did surprise him as the fat associate walked toward him with the pack of cigarettes. "Well," the colonel said, "I only have two in my employ here and…" The fat associate reached out the cigarettes to the colonel who took them from him.

The chairman took the fat associate's hand and shook it, saying, "My son, I can't tell you how long that I have wanted to meet you." The colonel who had pulled out a cigarette and was about to light it stopped as his mouth flew open in amazement.

Blu looked at Deandre lying on the couch with her drunken ass. *Her drunk fine ass*, he thought. She was fine but she definitely couldn't hold her liquor. He had pulled her up on the couch after she had passed out and even now he couldn't help but shake his head and chuckle a little bit. Suddenly she started to stir and as she fought to push herself into a sitting position on the couch, her right arm flew up and she wiped her forehead, sweat was pouring off her face. "You want a drink of water or something?" Blu asked.

Deandre shook her head yes. Blu walked toward the kitchen as Deandre undid the top button on her blouse. "What in the hell did you give me?" Deandre asked.

Blu returned from the kitchen with a glass of cold water and a cold wet rag. "Nothin' but my uncle's finest moonshine," Blu said as he handed Deandre the rag and the cold water.

She grabbed the glass of water and hurriedly drank it. The cold water immediately started to cool her off as she wiped her forehead with the cold wet rag. "Now," she said as she somewhat composed herself, "where was I?"

Blu shook his head and said, "Something about Red and his money, my money."

"Oh yeah, yeah, yeah," Deandre said, "I did tell you were the money was right?"

"No you didn't get that far," Blu said.

"Well then, let me start over," Deandre said, "I don't want to leave anything out." Deandre took another drink of the cool water, and then said, "This is it, you see everyone thinks Red keeps a lot of cash with him at the spot but he doesn't. He saves the money."

"I know that nigga ain't got no bank account."

"Bank account?" Deandre said then laughed. "You know he ain't that stupid, don't you? Anyway what he does is each month him and his boys go around to the different post offices and get postal money orders. They never get the one thousand-dollar maximum but just under, like nine fifty or nine seventy-five. That way, if they're lost or stolen, he can get his money back."

Blu shook his head. He knew that Red was smart and this again proved it. He didn't trust anyone to hold the cash so he converted it

into something so simple that no one would question it so safe that if they ever turned up missing he could get his money back. "So where does he keep these money orders?" Blu asked.

"Well, that's the tricky part," Deandre said, "He mails the money orders to a number of P.O. boxes in the different post offices and keeps them in there until he needs them."

Blu started to rub his chin. "You have to have keys to get those P.O. boxes open and you got to know what post office."

"Well that's right, but I know someone that knows where the post offices are and were the keys are at," Deandre said.

"Well of course you do," Blu said, "and I come in where?"

Deandre was wide awake now, "You, me, and some friends can go around and empty those P.O. boxes and then convert them into cash since they're blank we can cash them anywhere in the U.S. since there not made out to anybody."

Blu continued to rub his sparse grey beard. Finally he said, "What's my take and how much do you think it is?"

Deandre looked around the room and saw the moonshine bottle lying on the dining room table. "You think," Deandre said, "I might have another one of those drinks?"

Blu looked at Deandre and thought to himself, *Who would have thought? Miss High and Mighty is an alcoholic.* "Yeah," Blu said, "of course you can."

Blu walked toward the table as Deandre said, "Well he's been doing it for a while so probably close to three hundred, four hundred thousand, and I'm feeling generous. I will give you a tenth of it."

Blu thought, *that isn't enough if I got to blow town and leave everything behind and knowing Red, if the money orders were insured or not, he'd want revenge on whoever took it because they stole from him.* "No way, Deandre" Blu said, "Up that to a quarter share and I'm in."

Deandre smiled as Blu poured her another drink. "Well, what about your revenge?" Deandre asked as she sipped on the moonshine, swishing it around in her glass. "I know what he did to you and that money y'all took of all places to a casino and what about your son?"

Blu raised an eyebrow as he looked at Deandre. "Oh you know about that?" Blu asked. Deandre shook her head up and down as she

finished off the drink. "Well, yeah but, business is business and I still want a quarter percent share," Blu said.

"Okay, okay, then that's what will do," Deandre said as she sat the glass on the table. "Pour me another shot of that good shine and we'll seal the deal, as they say," Deandre said as Blu looked at her. This woman was wide awake and not showing any indication that she was going to slow down drinking. How the hell was she doing it? He didn't know and he especially didn't know what kind of deal he had just entered into, but he did know it would be something he would never forget.

CHAPTER 27

"Damn," Sheriff Johnson said. "That boy should be here by now." He had been waiting for twenty minutes and Buster still hadn't shown up. "Fuck it," he said as he opened the door to the Dodge and got out, He decided to go ahead and go it alone. Hell, how much trouble could a teenage girl be? He closed the door and headed down the drive. He had turned and taken maybe two steps when he heard, "Yo Sheriff, Sheriff?" He looked around and saw the good Reverend Clark. The reverend was smiling and he walked fast trying to catch up him.

"Why, if it isn't reverend Clark," the sheriff said as he stopped and waited for RC. RC, smiling and nearly out of breath, shook the sheriff's hand. "What can I do for you this fine fall day?" the sheriff asked.

"I should be asking you that question, Sheriff," RC said.

The sheriff looked at RC and thought a minute. He had heard that RC was seeing Nikki's mother but he didn't know it was true and he definitely didn't know he was staying here at their house but again I guess now he knew. "Well," the sheriff said, "I'm here to see Nikki? Have you seen her?"

RC immediately went from being playful to serious. "I haven't seen that girl since this morning. Why you looking for her?" RC asked.

"I just had to ask her some questions, that's all. Is the lady of the house home?" the sheriff asked.

"Yeah, yeah. I think so, I think so," RC said as the sheriff turned and the two continued walking down the drive. "Well, let's see," the sheriff said as the two of them continued walking.

Nikki walked down the street. She knew she couldn't go home. The police, the sheriff was looking for her, so she knew she couldn't go there. *What about Red's?* she thought. *Naw, naw, naw, no.* He was the only person in town hotter than her; she had to go somewhere she could get her mind right, get her a plan together, but where? She thought as she continued down the street, wondering which way to go.

"You all right in there Buster," Jo asked. No reply. "I know you're nervous an all," Jo said. "But you know what you have to do."

Buster sat on the toilet straining. He has to go but he doesn't. Every time he came under any type of stress, he had to shit. He didn't know why, he just did. "Mama here," Jo said as Buster sat on the toilet.

Damn, he thinks, *my mama's going to jail and that bitch she's hooked up with is going to lead her there. The sheriff was going to figure it out*, Buster thought. He was gonna figure out everything. "I'm all right, Mama," Buster said. "Just give me a few minutes," Buster said. Ever since he was a child, every time some stressful situation arose, Buster headed to the bathroom. He didn't know what it was. The excitement, the stress? Who knows? He just knew he had to shit.

Jo waited outside the bathroom door. All she knew was that her baby was hurting, maybe confused. She just needed to talk to him, let him know that everything was all right, that everything was gonna be alright. "Buster," she called. No reply. Ever since he was a child, every time something happened that took Buster out of his comfort zone, he ran to the bathroom. She had been through this many times before, coaxing him out of the bathroom, comforting him, trying to make everything better. Jo looked at the bathroom door and shook her head. She had done all that she could do. She'd just have to wait to he came out, and deal with it then.

"Mom," Buster said, "what have you got going on with that girl, Nikki?"

"What?" Jo said.

"Why is she over here? What has she or you got to do with each other? Three days ago, she didn't exist, now I see her every day and to top that off, the sheriff wants to question her in a murder investigation," Buster said. "Mom, does any of this strike you as strange? That she's your best friend as soon as the police investigate her?"

"She's a student," Jo said, "I'm working with her and some of the problems she's experiencing."

Buster could feel his bowels explode as the shit runs out of his ass. "Ah," he said.

"Why you asking all these questions," Jo asked.

"Because it's a murder investigation, Mom," Buster said.

"I don't want you to go to jail on the 'I'm just helping someone out' shit! And what about my career?," Buster asked.

Jo listened to her son and thought. She knew what she and Nikki had agreed to was dangerous and could have implications for Buster, but hell he was looking at things the way he wanted them, the way a young man looks at things and she was looking at things the way they were. Low pay, trying to please a lot of people with a lot of problems but when she added everything up, where did that leave her? Broke and struggling. She just knew she had to try something and ten thousand a drop was a good place to start. "Baby," Jo said, "I'm not doing nothing, just helping out a student, that's all,"

"Helping out a student? Helping out a student? How come none of the rest of them come over here? And why is it that the two of you are always smiling and giggling, Mom?" Buster asked as his bowels started to return to normal. All the pressure that had built up in him has finally been released. "Ah," he said.

"What was that, baby?" Jo asked.

"Nothing, oh nothing," Buster said.

"You know, Mommy can make it feel better, don't you?" Buster didn't know how long he'd been here, but he knew the sheriff would be asking questions about him pretty soon, he had to get out of there. Buster got up from the toilet and flushed it and pulled up his pants. "I've got to go, Mom," Buster began, "the sheriff is waiting on me!" Buster grabbed the Softsoap dispenser and ran the water to wash his hands.

The water ran as Jo leaned up against the bathroom door and said, "Please, baby. You know Mommy can make it better."

The bathroom door opened and Buster rushed out. "Bye Mom, see you later!" Buster rushed past his mother. He ran through the hallway as he headed toward the front door. Jo looked at her son as he headed out the door, wondering what in the hell was going to happen next.

Nikki knew what to do; she would get her friends together down at the schoolyard. Dre, D, Moon, and of course her boo, Joyce. She pulled out her Android and started texting them, telling them when they would meet. She still had the ten thousand dollars somebody had given her and she knew she would have to get out of town, especially

with what she knew and what she planned. Yeah, what she planned. That mutherfucker Red. He thought he was in control. But was he? Nikki would show him who the boss was, that's for sure. *Yeah*, she thought, *that's for sure.* She would show him what he had showed her: indifference to what she either thought or felt.

The sheriff had interrogated Nikki's mother about that night of the murders and the where about of her daughter that night. Nikki wasn't there but he was about to solve that right now. "Come in, Oliver?" the sheriff said. "Do you know where Buster is?"

Before Oliver could answer, Buster answered, "Here, Sheriff!"

"Buster, that was the longest shit, I think, in the history of mankind. That was what forty-five minutes ago, wasn't it?."

There was a pause then Buster said, "Sorry, Sheriff, I guess I was constipated a little."

"Constipated?" the sheriff asked. "Well I guess so."

"Sheriff," Deputy Oliver said, "The place is crawling with reporters about this morning's murder. Any idea when you'll be coming back?"

"I'm on the way back now, Oliver," the sheriff said.

"All right, Sheriff," Deputy Oliver said.

"Buster, you still there?" The sheriff asked.

"Yeah sheriff, I'm here ," Buster said.

"Well I left the girl's house and I need you to ride around to some of the teen hangouts and see if you can locate her. Got that?"

"Yes sir! I've got that," Buster said as the sheriff hung up the receiver on the radio. The sheriff took a deep breath. The storm was brewing; the players were set he thought. There was goanna be a big wind and lightning and thunder but it would all be over soon, yes very soon. He just hoped that after the storm he would still be standing, and *Damn*, he thought, *why does shit always happen on game day*?

"Nikki, Nikki," the voice called. Nikki looked up from her Android phone. It was Dre. "Hey, man," Nikki said.

"Yo, what's up Nikki?" Dre said, flashing that gold-toothed grill. "Ain't heard from you in a while," Dre said, "I thought you done left the money team behind." Dre laughed.

"No bro," Nikki said, "I've been lying low, you know?"

"Yeah, yeah, yeah," Dre said. "I can feel you."

Walking down the walk near the football stadium where they secretly met, Nikki could make out two shapes. "That looks like D and Moon," Nikki said. The two slowly approached until Nikki could make out their features. D was wearing a curly red Mohawk with a red base and then a layer of black then red. Moon was wearing dreads tied up in a bun. "My folks, my folks," Moon said as he clapped hands with Dre and snapped his fingers.

"What's up, nigga?" Dre asked. "I heard you been having that spice,"

"Yeah, yeah, I've got some," Moon said. "Holler at your boy then, I've got some…"

"'Scuse me, 'scuse me," Nikki said, "ya'll can talk about that stuff later"

Moon, D, and Dre looked at each other. "I know where we can get some money and make some money. I'm talking real money, not no twenty or fifty dollars either."

"Man," D said, "Nikki always talking shit and don't do nothing." Nikki reached into her backpack and pulled out the ten thousand dollars she has and showed it to the fellas.

"Damn, Nikki!" Dre said. Then rest of the crew looked at the money with their mouths open.

"You niggas thirsty? Ya'll want a drink?," Nikki said as she held the money out toward them, but being careful not to let them touch it. "This is what I'm talking about," Nikki said as she launched into her sales game. "Ya'll think I'm playin'. I ain't playin'," Nikki said.

"What we got to do to take a drink?" Moon asked.

"You got to step up and be the men that I know you to be," Nikki said. "Ain't no backing out, your momma called or you forego," Nikki said. "This is serious and I want to know if I can count on you. Can I?"

Dre and D shook their heads yes, but Moon remained skeptical. "What you talking about, Nikki?" Moon said. "Just last week you was trying to borrow money from me so you could get that lean." Moon pointed at her and, looking at her with one eye closed, said, "We done all came up together and ain't nobody no better than anybody else." Moon looked at the other two boys there and they all shook their heads yes.

"Naw, naw, naw," Nikki said. "I'm no better than you, that's why I need your help. I can't do none of this without—"

"Heh Nikki!" a voice called out. Nikki and the three guys looked up and see Joyce.

"Its five-oh," Joyce said. The three guys and Nikki started to move off. "I'll text y'all and let you know what's up?" Nikki said as the three guys nodded their heads and start to move off in different directions.

Nikki started toward Joyce. "No, Nikki," Joyce said. "He's coming this way!" Nikki made a sharp right and headed to exit from the bleachers. It was dark there she thought. It would be hard for anyone to see her. Just as Nikki ducked into the bleacher exit, she heard Joyce say, "Hey Officer Clearly."

Damn, Nikki thought, *I bet they're looking for me*. She turned and pressed her body up against the wall, not moving, trying to hear what was being said.

Joyce smiled as Deputy Clearly pulled up along side her in his Dodge Charger. "My father got y'all following me now?" Joyce said as Buster rolled down the window.

"Now, you know better than that Joy," Buster said. "The good taxpayers of this county wouldn't stand for the sheriff to have his children followed around, no matter how much of a T.H.O.T. see was."

"T.H.O.T.?" Joyce said. "Who you calling a T.H.O.T. with that messy momma of yours?"

Buster put the car into park and jumped out of the car. "I see you don't know who the boss is," Buster said as he grabbed Joyce and threw her on the ground and straddled her, putting his knee in her back. "I don't care if you're the boss's daughter or not, you ain't goanna talk about my mother and get away with it!" Buster flipped Joyce around so that she was face down in the grass and still straddling her, he raised his right hand back and slapped his hand down hard on her butt.

"Ow!" Joyce said. "Boy, you better quit playing!" she shouted.

"Where that bitch friend of yours?" he asked. "Nikki?"

"I don't know. Let me up! Get off me!"

Buster raised his hand back and brought it down hard again on Joyce's backside. "Ow!" Joyce said again.

Buster stood up still straddling her. Buster pointed a finger at Joyce and said, "You tell That Nikki that I'm looking for her, that…" Buster pointed at his chest. "That we are looking for her!" Buster shouted as he opened the car door and slammed it shut.

Joyce was sobbing, laying on the ground as he pointed out the window before putting his car into drive. "And don't you ever say nothing about my mother again!" Buster gunned the car and raced down the track from the stadium. Joyce turned over and propped herself up on her elbows. She wiped the tears from her eyes with her left hand as Buster pulled out of the stadium while propped up on one elbow.

"Don't worry, boo," Nikki said. Joyce hadn't heard her as Nikki had walked up. She looked up as Nikki reached out her had. "We'll make him pay. We'll make 'em all pay."

Jo hadn't felt well since Buster left. She knew what this was doing to him, to her. She just hoped he could keep it together. When he was a little boy, he had these violent outbursts. When other kids taunted him or teased him, he had these violent outbursts. Outbursts where the other children had to see the school nurse and one so severe that the other child had to go to the hospital. She had considered counseling for him, but decided against it when she feared the truth would come out about him and her. She just quietly monitored the situation and talked to him after each episode, figuring out what pushed his buttons. She then tried to keep him out of those situations, getting the kids that teased him moved to different classes, even schools. That worked as he was growing up and he was grown now and each day becoming more and more of a man.

She couldn't control him anymore and being a deputy sheriff provided its own set of difficult situations. It worried her but she had did the best that she could do and that was all anyone could ask or expect. Now was her time though. The circumstances that created the opportunity now before her and Nikki could not be passed up, so she would have to find a way to keep Buster calm, to keep him cool. In a few months she would have enough money to start her own business, a daycare, where she could at least control some of her destiny, not like now, with the teacher review system, the state cutbacks,

The paying of subsides for charter schools and home schooling. Hell she didn't know if she had a job day to day not to even speculate on years left to her retirement. No, she had to do all that she could to make her future now. Not later, now.

CHAPTER 28

"That's all I have right now, ladies and gentlemen," Sheriff Johnson said. "If you will excuse me, there's plenty of work to be done and unfortunately I'm understaffed and over budget and have plenty of work to be done." The sheriff turned from the podium set up in the squad room and attempted to exit,

"Sheriff," a voice in the crowd called out. "Have you considered calling in the state or federal authorities to help in the investigation?"

The sheriff stopped and turned and said, "They're already here. We're doing everything in our power to solve these murders and get these criminals off the streets. If that means calling out the National Guard, we'll do that too." Again, the sheriff turned to walk out of the room.

"Sheriff, sheriff," came two more voices. The sheriff ignored them and pushed through the throng of reporters and out the squad room. *Damn*, he thought, *has there ever been a news conference, where nobody asked any questions? Where everybody accepted what you said and knew how hard you were working to solve the case? Naw, probably not.* The sheriff walked quickly down the hall toward his office. He did his usual greetings to his staff and swung open the door only to find… "Sam Jackson," the sheriff said, smiling.

"I wouldn't be so quick to smile, sheriff," Sam Jackson said, not smiling. "There's lot of people in the state looking at you and these cases," Sam said, "and they're about to bring in some more people to help." The sheriff walked to his desk and threw his hat onto the desk.

"What else is new, Sam? You've got the incompetent black sheriff who's way over his head and the good white folks of Alabama want to give him a hand?" the sheriff asked. "Come on, Sam," the sheriff said as he sat down at his desk. "What are they talking about really? Is it public perception they're concerned about or money?"

"Both," Sam said. "This isn't the old south were a few white folks controlled the finances of an entire state,"

"It's not?" the sheriff said sarcastically.

"Well yes and no," Sam said. "The majority of the voting public might be white and Republican but they need money and business too. That means we have to have a broader appeal, a global appeal. We are not self-sufficient were we make and consume everything that the citizens of this state need, therefore we have to market ourselves to anyone and everyone who wants to do business here."

"Just like a prostitute, huh?" the sheriff said. "It don't matter what the size of the dick as long as it's a dick?" the sheriff asked.

Sam laughed. "I guess that's one way of putting it, but," Sam said, turning serious, "the state has spent billions of dollars, taxpayer's dollars to ensure that these companies have the cooperation and attention of the state."

"I get it," the sheriff said, "they will do anything to get rid of this stain, this hiccup in their ten-year plan?"

Sam smacked his hand on the desk. "Sheriff, I couldn't have said it any better."

The sheriff nodded his head up and down then said, "Well, what do they plan to do?"

Sam shook his head and said, "They plan on bringing in a special investigator for Birmingham. He will take charge and you will answer to him. All your evidence and all investigations will be handled by him. The sheriff rubbed his chin. "When do they plan on doing this?" the sheriff asked.

"Within the next twenty four hours," Sam said.

The sheriff sat back in his chair. He folded his hands behind his head and said, "Well, I guess I'll have to solve the case by then."

"Which case?" Sam Jackson said. "There are four dead bodies and granted one is pretty much an open and shut case."

"You know which case, the crack-house murders. That is the thing that got all this started and the case that when we solve it will settle everything," the sheriff said.

Sam nodded his head. "Do you really think that the company is involved?" Sam asked.

"Yes and no," the sheriff said. "Everybody is or was an employee and all the action originates from them, so they either knew what

was going on or staged it," the sheriff said. "Since it happened, all the substantive leads have come from them so," the sheriff paused, "I conclude that they are involved. Maybe they didn't pull a trigger but they had something to do with it."

Sam Jackson thought over what the sheriff said. "Maybe probably, but you better believe there's no smoking gun. They have covered up or left unanswered anything that would be of use to you."

The sheriff's brow began to wrinkle as he thought. "I just can't help but think," the sheriff began, "that in all this bullshit, Red is involved."

"Red," Sam said. "That small time drug dealer?,"

"Small time to you," the sheriff said, "but not to me."

Sam sat up in his chair and said, "Sheriff, I know that sometimes we can't let go of things in the past but this Red? He couldn't possibly be involved in something like this, it's above him."

The sheriff looked at Sam Jackson and smiled before he said, "The mistake we old people make when dealing with these young folk is how far advanced they are. They look at TV, the Internet, and follow Facebook where whatever they don't know, some of their friends know. Red," the sheriff continued, "has one of the best criminal minds I've ever come across, so believe me that I know whatever we're thinking, he's already done thought of it."

Sam shook his head up and down before he said, "I know what you're saying but there's one thing I've got to know."

"What's that, Sam?" the sheriff asked.

"How much Auburn is gonna beat Alabama by tonight."

The sheriff jumped forward in his chair. "I knew," he said, "that there was some reason that I didn't like you, You walk in here like you're a friend and you start talking that Auburn shit!"

Sam laughed. "It isn't shit to me. All you Alabama fans…" Sam launched into the debate that was going on all across Alabama. Who would win the Iron Bowl? Auburn or Alabama?

"Shorty Row," Bill Heard said, "Alabama gonna kick Auburn's ass. I say they beat them by at least forty points, what you say?."

"All you Alabama fans the same," Rooter said, "Y'all think the sun rises and shines with Alabama football that is until Auburn beats their ass! That's all y'all want to talk about when there's a murder on the corner and nine black people are killed in a church while worshiping God?"

The group of nine to ten black men grew silent until one, Tibbs, said, "Well the one thing we all know is that we don't decide when we go or how," He chewed on a plug of chewing tobacco. "To me, it's an honor to go while worshipping the Lord," he said while spitting. "There ain't a better way to go."

"I just think it's them white folks, still mad at Obama, that just can't accept the fact that a Black man is president," Will Jefferies said. "They say Black people got too much power while they tote that rebel flag, hell that rebel flag was for slavery, for the Southern states to defy the United States' government and it was one hundred and fifty years ago, so what's the point?"

"That is the point!" The group looked over at Cecil Daniels, a white farmer and entrepreneur who raised everything from corm to pigs and everything he owned was for sale, and I mean everything. "In this information society, everybody knows everything about everybody so is not surprising since you have Black History Month, MLK Day, and the like that us Southern white folk want something too, to show that our heritage was full of proud women and men who were willing to stand up and fight for what they believed,"

"They believed in slavery," Bill Heard said.

"I know, I know, so they took the stand that the North wasn't gonna listen to them so they fought to be heard, fought for what they thought was right and that is what American means: to fight for what you think is right, even though you might lose."

"That's the point," Alabama Shorty said. "We're the United States of America, where there are no confederate states, there are no union states; it's just us."

The older black men and the white man who had just spoken looked at each other and shook their heads yes. They knew that what he had said was true. That in this here America, pretty much everyone had a different opinion about how to do things and everyone wanted to be right but being an American means that no matter how much you and the other fellow disagreed, you would die for his right to say it.

The sheriff had turned on the box TV in his office. It was a thirteen-inch old Sanyo. Twenty years old, but it had played and showed a good picture every time he turned it on. He was looking at the pre-game show showing Alabama's strengths, Auburns weaknesses and vice versa. *The build up to the game,* he thought about how he loved it. Suddenly, the door flew open and old black woman with glasses on stood in his door followed by Deputy Oliver. "Sheriff," the old woman said, "I need to have a word with you!"

The sheriff looked up from the television screen and stood up and turned the volume down with the remote control. "I'm sorry, Miss…"

"It's Missus," the old women said, "I have been married for over forty years!" The sheriff looked at the old woman. Her bluish-gray hair and dark but powered skin gave her the look of an old woman hanging on to that beauty that once was and spending two hundred and fifty dollars a month to Mary Kay to do so. "What are you doing about the murder of my grandson?" the women demanded.

"What?" the sheriff said.

"My grandson," she said. "James Wyatt. James Wyatt the Third," she said proudly.

The sheriff shook his head yes. "I know Missus Wyatt," he said. "We are working hard on his murder and I anticipate within…"

"Sheriff?" the old woman said, "I don't want any of that bull crap that you tell the media and that's why I'm here." The sheriff looked at the old woman as she started to speak. "My grandson was a good boy. All through school, he never gave me any trouble. His daddy was in prison and his momma, my daughter, was going from man to man, searching for herself." The sheriff sat back in his chair and kept his eyes focused on the old woman. "She had two children: a boy and a girl," she said as she stared off, telling her story. "The boy, James, or Jimmy as I called him, was a good boy, he did whatever I told him to do." The old woman continued, "But his sister, she followed after her mother who, because of some man, ended up in jail. I had to take care of them children," the old woman said as she took a napkin out from her purse and wiped her nose. "Jimmy started playing sports and man was he good! He had the college recruiters calling every day, from all over the country. He would ask me, 'Granny, which school should I choose?' I

didn't know nothing about football so I tells him, pick from your heart baby, pick from your heart." The old woman stopped and looked back at the sheriff. "You know, I couldn't have been a bigger fool, I didn't know nothing about one year scholarships, NCAA rules, infractions or whatever and he just liked that school's colors, black and red."

Black and red, the sheriff thought, *that would make him...*

"Needless to say," the old woman said, "once he got hurt his freshman year, everything changed. He went from being the next best thing to washed up in a manner of months."

"Oh come on now, the school provides for—"

"The school is out to win games not look out for players," the old women said, "There two different things, but needless to say my baby was pushed aside, thrown away like a McDonald's paper bag."

"I understand, I understand," the sheriff said.

"Do you, Sheriff?," the old woman said, "All your baby's dreams, all your baby's hopes gone, smashed like an ant. Next thing you know, there are babies on the way and no job. He got to scramble to get that, but he hangs in there, never giving up, never quitting. I'm as proud of that boy and his regular life as I would have been if he were an NFL star. That's why I got to know—"

The sheriff waved his hand to cut the old woman off. "Who killed your grandson?" the sheriff asked. The sheriff looked at the old woman and smiled. "You know?" he said, "There's a lot of people out here that would bullshit you and tell you to be patient and that we have everything taken care of, but the truth is we don't know any more than you know. In fact, I need to know what you know."

The old woman wrinkled her forehead. "What are you saying?" she asked. "Who was your grandson in contact with, who were his friends? I need any information that can be helpful in our investigation."

"I thought you knew about that already," the old woman said.

"About what?" the sheriff said.

"About that young girl that they use to hang around with."

"What young girl? Describe her," the sheriff said.

"The light-skinned one, the one with the red hair,"

The sheriff sat up in his chair. "Tell me," the sheriff began, "exactly what you know about her,"

The old woman wiped her nose with her handkerchief and tilted her head back. "Well let me see," she began, "she always came around on a weekday in the afternoon before he had to go to work. She was pretty but I always thought was to young too being associated with my grandson. I mean she was a teenager and he was a father with a wife. Anyway," the old woman said, "they would talk for a few minutes and he would always give her a bag."

"What kind of bag?" the sheriff asked.

"You know," the old woman said, "one of them backpacks."

The sheriff thought about what the old woman said. They were making a money drop and Nikki was the mule. She took it to Red, who gave the two young men the drugs when they came over on their break, so what went wrong that night? The sheriff wondered did this have something to do with that other murder? The Korean killed at the gas station? "Mamie," the sheriff said, "I'm sorry for your loss and rest assured your police and sheriff's office are working hard as we can to solve this murder."

The old women wiped her lips with her handkerchief once again. She struggled to get up from her chair and, once erect, turned and headed toward the door. Before she departed, she turned and looked at the sheriff. "You know I've heard that before." The old lady turned and headed through the sheriff's office door.

CHAPTER 29

Chairman Kwan walked with his son through the driveway of the hotel. "Your mother was the love of my life," the chairman began. "We met and fell in love…" The chairman looked at his son as his son looked blankly around the driveway. His son walked as he was talking, oblivious to what the chairman is saying. His son looked at him and smiled. The chairman started to tell him about his family. "You know you have brothers and sisters?" the chairman said. His son nodded and a smile crossed his face. "Your name?" the chairman said.

"Ji-Hu," his son said.

"Ji-Hu," the chairman said. "Well Ji-Hu, we are a powerful family, a family that has great responsibility as we pay and protect over eight million employees."

Ji-Hu shook his head as he tried to comprehend what the chairman has told him. He saw two sparrows in the walkway chirping. He stopped and looked at them and reached into his pocket. He brought out a pack of nacho cheese crackers. He Unwrapped the cracker packet and crumbled them up in his hand and tossed them toward the sparrows.

The sparrows hurriedly ate the crackers as two more sparrows then three joined the feeding frenzy. The chairman looked at the smile on his son's face and wondered what kind of man has his son become.

RC looked at Blu. "I'm telling you she has a sweet plan," Blu said.

RC frowned up and shook his head. "I don't get it, money orders?"

"Yeah, money orders," Blu said. "We go to the different post offices around the area and collect them, then cash them in," Blu said.

"But don't you need keys for them post office boxes?" RC said.

"My partner got that all covered," Blu began. "You don't have to worry about that, all you got to do is be at the appointed time on the appointed date, understand?"

RC nodded his head yes. "Tell me," RC said, "how many more people are involved in this?"

"Well there's…" Blu hesitated. Why should Blu tell him the plan when he just fucked up a good plan at the casino? Blu was and always had been a fool, but he wasn't a damn fool. "Well," Blu said, "just so you know, we could make a big score with this if you're interested."

RC looked at Blu and knew he was not telling the whole story, but the life of a country preacher wasn't easy, and he certainly needed the money. "Yeah, yeah, oh yeah," the reverend shouted. "I need some time to happen." Blue looked at RC and smiled. He didn't know how this plan would turn out, but they were on the right track. It was all about that money.

The colonel looked at the chairman and his son as they walked around the courtyard. The colonel was still astounded at the fact that the head of one of South Korea's biggest companies. His son was one of his best associates. Strong and ruthless. He was quick to comply with a directive and did an excellent job. He was the muscle that there operation needed but it was true he was slow at the start, he sometimes had to be told things more than twice to understand, but once he did he did, he did a good job. In fact, between he and the other associate, the skinny one, they made an adequate team, one capable of carrying out orders from the most exaulted one. The colonel took out a cigarette and lit it. Still he thought, *this is Kwan's son?*

Blu looked at RC and thought, *it's mighty funny that every time he was on the come up, he was on the come down with RC there.* RC was fun and a pretty good friend, but friendship and money rarely went hand in hand if at all. The only friendship he had like that was from the old days, when he was just starting out, those people, and those friends. But it was a new day with all the social media and the fake friends that everyone professed to be. He knew what to do with RC: tell him what he needed to know and nothing more and to make sure you always kept an eye on him. *Yeah*, Blu thought, *always an eye on him.*

Deandre looked at her cellphone watch. It was 1:30 p.m. on game day. She had gotten drunk on Saturday morning and, with the headache she had, was starting to pay for it. She turned her head back

to the left and that's when she saw… "Nikki?" Deandre said. "Nikki?" Deandre's eyes focused in as she looked at Nikki.

There, Nikki sat with her red hair and green eyes, "What up sis?" Nikki asked.

"What in the hell are you doing Nikki, sitting there staring at me?"

Nikki smiled at Deandre and said, "I don't know if you forgot or just don't give a fuck, but we got some business to handle."

Deandre sat up in her bed and wiped her eyes. That moonshine was some powerful shit. She thought that she had handled the business but she wasn't sure. "Well you know," Deandre said, "We need to get on it."

Nikki looked at Deandre with her half sleepy drunk look and said, "You sure you don't need some more sleep or something?" Deandre shook her head, trying to wake up and be focused. "You know what we got to do," Nikki said. "You got the people lined up?"

Deandre looked at Nikki and, feeling bad with a hangover, said, "Sure you know I handle my business."

"Remember, Nikki said, everything has to go down before the game. Three o'clock before the post office closes, okay?"

"I got it baby girl, I got it."

"Well get up then," Nikki said. "We got a lot of work to do."

Deandre got up from the bed and swung her legs over to the floor. She felt like shit. *But this money*, she thought. "What are you going to do after we get it?" Deandre asked.

"Like we said I take the money and get lost for a couple of months, and then I'll contact you through Twitter, you already know the emoji that I'll use, okay?" Nikki asked.

"Yeah, I know," Deandre said as she got up off the bed.

"Well let's go then sis," Nikki said. "We got a lot of work to do."

"Yeah," Deandre said, "we do."

Red took a big puff off the blunt he just fired up. "Alright, Marshall Dillion," the television said. Red liked looking at the old Westerns on the old rerun television channel. It was good guy versus bad guy and Red always thought of himself as the good guy. He would have loved living in the world back then except for one thing: the racism. The racism back then was overt and everyone went along

with their set ways of doing things. Red, being a modern man, hadn't experienced overt racism, just the vague kind, like when he went to a job interview and he was qualified but somehow not gotten the job or when he showed up and the personnel person looked down while they interviewed him. He knew what that meant: he wasn't getting the job. This being the world that it was, racism wasn't supported if you could prove it but it sure hadn't gone away.

"Eight ball, eight ball!" Red hollered. "Where in the hell is Bang Bang?"

Eight Ball shook his head. "I don't know, he left about an hour ago."

Red lit his blunt and slowly inhaled it, thinking, *What the hell is this nigga up to?* Red's cellphone rang. He looked at it laying on his table. It rang again. Red picked it up and pushed the button. "Yeah?" he asked.

"Bro, I'm down here at Four Corners and I just ran into three bad bitches on the road to the A. Is it cool if I bring them over?," Bang Bang asked.

Red took another long hit on his blunt and said, "What kind of question is that, Bang?" he asked. "You know what to do."

"Yeah, I know," Bang Bang said as he handed up the phone.

Red looked at the phone and stared at it, then put it back down on the table. "Niggas," he said finally and resumed smoking his blunt.

Blu said, "All right everybody, you know what you're supposed to do." Blu looked at the faces of the people in his club. They were all trusted friends and associates or at least he thought so.

"Blu, Blu," Nigga Bob said, "when we gonna get some of this money we getting?"

"You gonna get it when I get it and that's the deal," Blu said. "You got to do the work first and then you get paid and you all know that I pay," Blu said, smiling. "If you need gas or something to eat or your child support, you go out and do this job and you got it. I don't need no niggas here that ain't hungry, looking for some money. If this is just something to do that day, you need to leave. If you're looking to start a Gerber baby fund, then this ain't for you."

RC laughed as he said, "This ain't no investment portfolio; this is money today and for today, period,"

Blu and RC looked at each other and nodded. RC was his right-hand man on this deal, but because of past deals, Blu wondered if he could trust him. "Look here, we all broke and if we can come up five thousand a piece, you and me done made a good score, *comprende*?" Blu said.

"Look, look, look," a voice said out of the crowd gathered in Blu's club. It was Long Dong Cheechie Chong. "There's three of for deer running around back there!"

The back of Blu's property was covered with heavy forestry. Blu often had seen deer running around his property. He wasn't a hunter, but most of these boys were and he knew what was gonna happen. "Jimmy, you got you're rifle?," RC asked.

"Sure do," Jimmy said.

"I got mine too!," Ray Goldwater said.

There was a rush for the door as Blu said, "Y'all don't forget now three o'clock be in place!" Blu knew it was hopeless to try and control or stop what was happening. These were country boys and deer meat was highly valued around here, especially if they just wandered in your yard.

"Hey, hey," Long Dong said, "they moving off." The crowd of about eight to ten of them rushed toward their weapons, each one of them being the man to kill one of those deer. With the pay at the auto factories around nine to ten dollars an hour, any free meal was welcome. Blu looked at the men rushing out the door and the remaining women five to six of them left ion the club. "Well ladies," he said, "I guess the drinks are on me!," The women squealed as Blu stepped behind the bar and started pouring drinks as the women huddled up around the bar.

Chairman Kwan thought about his past life as his son fed the sparrows. His son had his mother's features and, alas, some of his features. He had a DNA test done on him years ago, so he knew this was his son. He just didn't know what he was gonna do with him. *The past cannot rule the future,* he thought. His destiny and that of millions of people were predicated on his every move; he could not let emotion enter in to it.

"Son," the chairman asked, "tell me what your long term plans are?"

Ji-Hu continued to feed the birds and then stopped and turned toward his father. "You know, Father," he began, "one day, I would like for our two countries to live in peace, to live as one." He said this as he continued to feed the birds. "I know that you and the colonel and our two countries have had their differences," he says. "But there not my differences or my future children, so why pretend that they matter?"

The chairman looked at his son and knew what he said was true. He also knew that he must protect him, help him along his journey. He also thought that this couldn't have come from a better source, his son who lived in North Korea and agent, but also the son of one of the powerful companies in the world. For there to be any hope of his dream coming true, he would have to have help, from the north and the south. The chairman thought that there could be no better people than he and the colonel, his mentors, to get his son ready for the pratfalls of reunification. He would have to form an alliance with the colonel. *Yes*, he thought, *the colonel is the key.*

CHAPTER 30

The sheriff flipped the remote on his old box television. It was getting close to game time and he enjoyed the commentators, the pluses and the minuses of this offensive, and that defensive, the attributes of both Coach Malzahn and the imperious Nick Saban. He was just about to settle in and listen to the rhetoric when Buster burst into his office. "Hey, Sheriff," Buster said.

The sheriff glanced up from the television screen and said, "Where you been? I thought one of them girls done kidnapped you?"

"Let me explain. Let me explain," Buster said as the sheriff yawned. Hell, he had been up and on the go since early this morning. He was tired.

"Yeah what?" the sheriff said as deputy Oliver rushed into the office.

"Sheriff," Deputy Oliver said, "we got a hit back on N.I.B.I.N."

The sheriff leaned forward in his chair. "Oh yeah, from where?"

"Biloxi," Deputy Oliver said.

"Biloxi?" the sheriff asked.

"Yes it seems some Good Samaritans out snorkeling found our murder weapon." *Wow,* the sheriff said to himself, *finally, a break in the case.* "The bullet and the barrel match up perfectly," the deputy said.

"Have they found any fingerprints?" the sheriff asked.

"Yes," the deputy said, "there are."

"Any matches in our database?" The deputy shook his head no. "But the fingerprint is from a small hand."

The sheriff sat back in his chair and said, "Well the murderer was either small professional or someone young, not yet an adult."

The sheriff immediately thought of Nikki, his prime suspect at this point. "Oliver ," the sheriff said, "I want you and Buster too put out an APB on this girl Nikki. Nikki Flowers," the sheriff said. "I want you to find her and to bring her in for questioning."

The deputy and Buster looked at each other as the sheriff turned up the volume on the pregame. "Now," the sheriff said, "I want her now!"

Deputy Oliver and Buster headed out the door as the sheriff settled back and watched the pregame show.

This was game day and though she didn't care about who won, the Auburn/Alabama game was always something. It was the underdog versus the superior team. Jo Clearly didn't give a hoot who won. There was no man in house who pushed sports so she stayed away from it. She liked sports but wasn't a big follower. Jo knew she had to wash clothes and wash her car. That was what you usually do on Saturday. Take care of the basic work. Whatever was left if you had the money you took care of. If not, you waited until next week.

The doorbell rang. *What?* Jo thought to herself. *Who could this be? Buster*, she thought, *that's who it is*. It had to be, but why was he ringing the bell? Or the thought entered her mind: were the police looking to arrest her? Jo shrugged her shoulders, whoever it was was whoever it was. She went to door and opened it. "Constance," Jo said. It was Nikki's mother.

"I'm sorry to bother you Jo," Constance said. "I'm looking for RC, have you seen him?"

Jo looked at Constance and thought for a moment. What in the hell was this bitch here for really and why did she come to her h ouse?"Come on in, Constance," Jo said. Constance brushed past Jo and walked right in. Jo closed the door and smiled at Constance. "Why do you think he's here?" was Jo's first question.

Constance in a ball of energy, twisted and turned. "I just don't know where he is, Jo," Constance said. "He's been gone for the last two or three days."

Jo looked at Constance and saw the anxiety in her eyes. "I don't know where he is," Jo said.

"He went to do something for Blu," Constance said.

"What was that?" Jo asked. There was another knock at the door. "What the hell?" Jo said. "Who in the hell could this be?" She darted to the door and opened it. It was Nikki.

"Jo, Jo, Jo," Nikki said as she entered the house with her arms outstretched. "Come here and give me a hug."

Jo complied as her mother looked on. "You better watch it, Jo," Constance said, "you squeeze a serpent and it always bites you."

Nikki shot a look at her mother. "What, bitch?" Nikki asked. "What the fuck are you talking about, with your ho ass?"

Jo looked at Nikki then at Constance and thought, *Uh oh, what's about to happen*?

"What the hell you doing here, Mom?" Nikki asked. "Are you looking for me, following me?"

"You ain't nothing but a user bitch," Constance said. "Everything got to be about you, Nikki this, Nikki that. You come and go as you please!" Constance said. "You and that damn RC got so many deals going on that I can't tell who is who or what is what?" Constance stood toe-to-toe with Nikki. "You're just some selfish, evil bitch that needs to go!" Constance said.

"Oh really?" Nikki said, "That was why my father left, 'cause he was selfish and evil? Is that what's it's about? Anybody that doesn't do what you want is that?"

Constance stepped toward Nikki. "Now you look, bitch," Constance said. "From the time you were an infant to now, I have always looked out for you! I have provided some kind of home for you! This is how you repay me?" Constance asked. "You talk about me, tell all your friends, how I'm the cause of all your problems." Constance shook her head. "My mother was a crack-head, addicted to drugs, she didn't care if I was fed or not! I at least tried to raise you where you had something."

Nikki and Constance looked at each other. Nikki wanted to tear her mother up, destroy her. Constance looked at her daughter and understood the pain, how someone who was so young and didn't understand that she was dealing with the same pain and disappointment. Nikki was her daughter though, not the other way around and she was going to have to play by her rules.

Seeing her mother brought out emotions that Nikki both liked and disliked. She loved her mother but there circumstances made her think she could have done a better job, heck, do a better job. This woman still believed in hard work and sacrifice, really? Really, did that still even exist? She was wasting time, though. She had to get over to Red's house and she couldn't let their daily drama hold her up. "Whatever," Nikki finally said, "whatever you think is what it is, that's fine." Nikki walked toward the door. Nikki opened the door and started out, but not before saying, "This is what I'm talking about, Mother. You for you and you want me for you, when does it become…" Nikki paused, "me and you for us!" With that, Nikki went through the door and slammed it shut. Constance and Jo looked at each other, neither knowing what to say.

Buster drove down the highway with various thoughts running through his head. He knew he needed to make something happen, something good. He knew he was early in his career as a deputy sheriff, but he knew that the sheriff would tolerate only so many screw-ups and he didn't plan on ending his career before it began, so he knew what he had to do, what he was going to do: find that bitch Nikki!

Nikki shook her head as she exited the house. She was headed to Red's house. She only had a couple of minutes before she was supposed to be there. She hadn't expected the run-in with her mother, but fuck her, this was her life and she was about to seize control of it.

Buster turned off the highway and headed straight toward his house. He just had a feeling, a feeling that that Nikki would be there. "Come in, Buster," the page over the radio came.

Buster picked up the mic and said, "This is Buster."

"You got to Nikki's house yet?" the sheriff asked. Buster became nervous. He knew the sheriff expected him to go to Nikki's house but he knew better.

"Yeah sheriff," Buster said, "I'm about five minutes away." Buster lied.

"I need you to do this, Buster," the sheriff said. "A lot of people are depending on them to bring them some answers and hopefully some justice, do you understand?"

Buster nodded his head before saying, "Yeah, Sheriff, I understand." Buster put down the receiver. He thought about what he needed to do and the circumstances that he was involved in. "I know she was there," he finally said. Buster thought about the consequences as he raced toward his destination.

Nikki walked down the street. She was just stopping by Jo's house to kill some minutes before she went over Red's. That shit that transpired

was shit she hadn't anticipated. The old woman had some good pussy and she wanted some. She didn't know all this shit would happen. She walked toward the center of town, toward the store. All the folks she needed to talk to were up there.

I'm gonna make the sheriff proud, Buster thought. He turned down the street to his mother's house and that was when he saw her.

Nikki looked at Buster as he passed by. *Damn*, she thought. *What's he doing here*? It wasn't good, so Nikki started walking faster.

Buster passed Nikki and thinks to himself, *Yep, there she is*. He comes to a halt and put his cruiser into reverse. He looked into the rearview mirror and saw Nikki begin to run. He stopped and put the car into reverse and turned it quickly around.

"Shit," Nikki said, "he saw me." As she cut back through Big Trotter's yard, she ducked the low hanging branches of the under growth and snaked her way through Big Trotter's yard.

Buster thought, *Wow, I can catch this bitch; I know where she's going*. Buster gunned his car and headed toward the crossing of 50 and Highway 14.

Nikki ducked and dodged as she made her way through the undergrowth. The sticker bushes tore her skin as she made her way through them. "That was Buster," she said, as she kept moving forward. She didn't know why they didn't hit it off; she just knew he didn't like her or her him. Nikki heard the intersection of 50 and Highway 14. She looked in both directions before standing upright and walking to the intersection. Suddenly there was a screech of tires as she steps onto the highway.

"Yeah, yeah, yeah," Buster said. "That's my bitch, that's my bitch!" Buster saw Nikki at the intersection. Buster stopped the cruiser and was about to exit as he heard an engine. He looked up and saw a black SUV speeding toward him. Buster took a defensive position and drew his forty-caliber Glock and ducked behind his car. The SUV came to a stop between Buster and Nikki. The door to the SUV flew open and Nikki got in. The door to the SUV closed and the driver gunned the engine and sped off. Buster started taking deep breaths and putting his gun back in his holster. He said, "Shit!"

Red looked at his Rolex watch. It was exactly three o'clock. That bitch Nikki said she would be here at two. She was an hour late. He also was waiting to hear from RC. Nothing. Red sat back and said, "Fuck it. Whatever happens happens." Every broke or wannabe rich nigga in the state was looking to take his spot. He knew that. Though people had tried and people had failed, he knew they were still after him. He knew it wasn't personal; they were all about that money. Eight Ball walked toward him.

"Hey, Red," he said.

Red, still deep in thought, looked up at Eight Ball and said, "Yeah?"

"Your baby mama is up front wanting to see you," Eight Ball said.

Red shook his head and said, "Shit!" That was all he needed was for this bitch to show up, unannounced and if he knew Drekka, she wanted something. Red motioned to Eight Ball and said, "Okay, let her in."

Eight Ball nodded his head and exited the room. Red tried to get himself prepared but no matter what he tried, this bitch always made him angry, always. He would be feeling fine and after she left, he wanted to tear up the world. He heard the commotion as she entered the house. "Hey, y'all," she said cheerfully as she entered the house with a smile on her face. Drekka was a mocha chocolate-colored woman, standing about five feet, five inches tall. She was blessed with teardrop-shaped breasts that only accented her narrow waist. You add that to her thirty-eight-inch butt, and you had what some would say was a bad bitch. That was until she opened her mouth.

"Red, I need some money," she began, "your twins got to go to the dentist and that ain't cheap. I don't want them walking around with no rotted teeth in their head like most of these niggas in this town."

Red looked at her and, knowing the game they were about to play about what happened to the money he gave her two days ago, decided to avoid it and reached into his pocket and pulls out a wad of cash. He unfolded the money and counted out five hundred dollars and held it out for her, still not saying anything.

Drekka walked over and took the money and counted it herself. "Well," she said, "they might have to get braces and…" Before she could finish, Red was already counting out more money—another

five hundred and did the same thing. He held it out for her to take. Again, she took the money, but wondering this time what's wrong, why no argument?

Finally, she said, "You must be having one of your bitches over, huh?" Red looked at her, trying to contain the anger that was welling up inside of him. "Why it got to be like that, Drake?" Red asked. "You know me and you ain't never gonna be together yet you always looking to boost something up?" Red said.

"Me boost something up?" Drekka said, "While you fucking me every week and telling me how much you need me? Nigga please!" Red and Drekka looked at each other.

"Well at least I know you getting some good dick because I'm giving it to you."

Drekka laughed. "Nigga, if that's good loving, your mother then stripping at the strip club."

Red laughed. "Your mama don't know who none of her baby's daddy is!" Red said. Both of them laughed. *Yeah, this was what it was like with family*, he thought. It's give and take, with nobody no more important than anybody else.

CHAPTER 31

The chairman looked at his son then at the colonel. He knew in the next few minutes he would be making a decision that would shape his family and company. In the process it could also shape the destinies of two different worlds, of two different cultures. "Colonel," the chairman began, "it has been a very fortunate visit on my part to meet my son that I have never met and to find out that he has been in such good care." The colonel nodded as he listened. "However, I must say I am willing to go even further." The chairman paused so that his words would be listened to. "We," the chairman said, "now have the opportunity to take this farther, to bridge the gap between north and south, to…"

Suddenly, there was movement in the foreground. One of the chairman's lieutenants motioned toward him. The chairman stopped and left his son and the colonel and went over to his lieutenant. The chairman and the lieutenant conferred. The chairman shook his head and then separated and headed back to the colonel and his son. "I'm sorry, but a situation has arose. It requires my immediate attention." The chairman looked at the colonel and said, "I need for you to release him to me. I will take care of you and your family in the process but he has to come with me."

The colonel reached for his cigarette pack. He pulled it out and there was one cigarette left. He pulled it out and put it to his lips but did not light it. "Chairman," the colonel began, "you are asking a great deal of me. Too not only switch my allegiance with the great leader, but to also protect and implement your plan for both our countries." The chairman shook his head yes. "With each gain," the chairman said, "there is great risk, don't you agree?" The colonel nodded his head yes. "We each have to play our part in order for there to be change," he said. "We both know that is what both our countries need."

The colonel contemplated what the chairman had just said and nodded his head up and down. "I agree," the colonel said, "that is

why I release your son to you." The chairman smiled. The colonel motioned for the chairman's son to come forward. "Ji-Hu, it has been a great pleasure, our time together, but destiny calls before duty so." The colonel looked at Ji-Hu and said, "I would like for you to go with your father."

Ji-Hu looked at the colonel and his father. "But why must we change?" Ji-Hu asked.

The chairman looked at the colonel and said, "That is the nature of life my son. The old die off and the young take their place, my days are coming to an end and I want to help you make a better future, do you trust me?"

Ji- Hu looked at his father and the colonel. With one, he faced the unknown; with the other, he had a life he had known since he was an adolescent. He had cared for him and nurtured him and taught him. He knew what to do. "Colonel," Ji-Hu said, "what is it that you think I should do?"

The colonel smiled and, having run out of cigarettes, did not have a ready prop for what he had to say. "Ji-Hu," he said, "your service to the leader has been outstanding but now you must decide what you must do for your future. Your future because of the knowledge that you have other options, I advise you to take advantage of them."

Ji-Hu frowned as he thought. He thought of the past and then of the future. Finally, he said, "I will go with you, Father."

The chairman smiled then motioned to his men. "Time, my son, is both your greatest asset and biggest enemy. That is why we must leave quickly and move on to our next destination." The chairman's men rushed toward the chairman and his son, eagerly ready to begin the process. Ji-Hu was quickly led to a black SUV with the chairman close behind. Ji-Hu entered the vehicle followed by his father. The colonel looked with amazement as the procession moved forward. The doors closed and the colonel paused as the chairman rolled down the window and said, "Sinuiju." The colonel looked as the window rolled up. Did he hear what he thought he heard or did he misunderstand?

Buster looked at his car as it lay in the drainage ditch. He looked at the car and shook his head. "Damn," he said. He reached into the car and grabs his mic. He pressed the send button and said, "Come in, Sheriff, this is 412. Come back," Buster said. He waited for a response as he viewed the damage to his vehicle. *Well,* he thought, *if the sheriff wasn't mad at him, he sure would be mad now.*

"Yeah, Buster," came the response.

"Sheriff," Buster began. "I was over at the girl's, Nikki's, place and got run off the road," Buster waited.

"Run off the road?," the sheriff said.

"Yeah, run off the road." Buster ran his fingers through his hair, anticipating the sheriff's response.

"Are you all right?" came the sheriff's reply.

"I'm alright, I'm alright," Buster said.

"Well I'll send Oliver out there," the sheriff said. "Do you need a tow?,"

"Yeah sheriff, I need a tow," Buster said.

"Well you hold on Buster," the sheriff said, "Help is on the way."

Buster said, "All right, Sheriff." His big moment, his payback to the department ended in what? A tow? Buster shook his head in disgust and wondered what would happen next.

The sheriff shook his head and thought, *These young folks can't they get anything right.* Must he do everything himself? Now he had to send another officer to clean up the mistake of another. He pressed the button on his radio to call Deputy Oliver when lo and behold who walked through the door but Deputy Oliver.

"Sheriff," Deputy Oliver said, "we have a match on those fingerprints off the gun they found."

"Yeah, yeah," the sheriff said. "Let's have a look."

Deputy Oliver handed the results to the sheriff and he opened the folder and looked at the results. He looked at Oliver and said, "Is this some kind of joke?,"

"I'm afraid not, Sheriff, We ran the results twice."

The sheriff shook his head and said, "Well, what's got to be done gots to be done." The sheriff put on his hat and headed toward the door. He stopped and said, "You get in contact with Buster. He ran into some trouble down in the ninth ward, okay?,"

Deputy Oliver nodded his head as the sheriff headed out the door.

Blu looked at his watch. It was five o'clock. The information that he was looking for hadn't come through. The job was off until he found out what happened. Damn, he had called in all the people he trusted and nothing happened. He felt like a fool. He looked at RC sitting next to him. He thought about the adventures of the last few days. It was just mighty funny he thought, how all that money fell into their hands then out and now this. RC was there the whole time, was this all a set-up? Was he set up by Red? Or Bang Bang? Each had their own motives. Well, he decided, the best way to kill a snake was to just kill it and not let it slither around, biting folks

"RC," Blu started, "you said Bang Bang told you where to find that bag with the money, right?"

RC drained his drink. "What you talking about, Blu?" RC asked.

"The money, RC, the money. Didn't you say Bang Bang gave you the note..."

"Naw, naw, naw," RC said, "what you talking about? At the jail? I got that note from Red. He..." RC realized what he was saying and stopped. "I'm sorry, Blu," RC said, "I misspoke. I'm a little tipsy right now, I... "

Suddenly, there was a loud knock at the door. "Blu, Blu," the voice called out. Blu recognized the voice. It was the sheriff.

"Just a minute, just a minute," Blu said as he rushed toward the door. He looked at RC and nodded his head, telling him this conversation wasn't over with. Blu reached the door and unlocked it. He opened the door and saw... "Sheriff, how you doing? Come on in."

The sheriff said, "You're looking good, Blu, you're looking good!" The sheriff entered the club and looked around. The setup was the same as always, but he saw someone he didn't expect to see: RC, sitting at the bar wolfing down the whiskey in the bottle beside him.

"What can I do for you, Sheriff?," Blu asked.

The sheriff came over and stood in front of Blu and RC and said, "You know there was a shooting down at Red's place a week ago?"

"Yeah," Blu said, wondering what the hell that had to do with him.

"Well after some exhaustive police work, we finally have a suspect."

Blu and RC looked at each other, shrugging their shoulders. "What that got to do with us, Sheriff?" Blu asked.

"Well not you but…" The sheriff looked at RC, "it does with you."

RC's eyes got big as he said, "What you talking about, Sheriff? I ain't committed no murder! I might have stolen a few things but I ain't never committed no murder."

Blu, shocked, looked on as the sheriff continues. "You see, we found the murder weapon and your fingerprints are all over it."

"That's because we—"

"Shut up," Blu said. "He don't need to know that."

RC went into panic mode. "I'm a man of the cloth, what would my parishioners think if I was involved in a murder case?"

The sheriff looked at Blu then at RC. "I must admit," the sheriff said, "that I was initially shocked until I looked at the facts. I initially thought it was Red," the sheriff said. "He had the means and the motive, but why? Why would he kill his prime supplier? He was making dollars by not killing anybody so why would he screw everything up over a few hundred thousand? No, the person that killed the two young men and the company's mule needed money, he needed it desperately."

Blu thought about what the sheriff had just said. There was nobody in the town that needed or wanted money more than RC. He had a crack habit and a new family. It was all starting to add up. "It was that bitch Nikki, I tell you!" RC shouted.

The sheriff, still pacing the room, stopped and said, "I thought about that too," he said, "but two hundred thousand? Naw, whatever her true intentions are, it ain't worth two hundred thousand."

Blu thought to himself, how the hell did the sheriff know how much money was involved? So, he asked him. "How do you know how much money was involved?," Blu asked.

"Due to an informant the D.E.A. has working for them in Biloxi."

Blu shook his head. He knew this whole thing wasn't right from the rip. It all swelled through his mind: the reverend bringing his stepdaughter around the club, his stepdaughter dating the Korean to the reverend holding onto to the gun. *Damn*, he thought, *had the whole thing been set up?*

"But, but me and Blu found that money, ain't that right Blu?" RC pleaded.

"Sheriff," Blu said.

"I like you Blu and I'm going to advise you as a friend that you need to shut the fuck up! The state of Alabama today is charging Reverend Clark with first degree murder, premeditated. Now if you wish you be brought in as..."

Blu immediately shut up. "No, Sheriff," he said. "It's your ball. Roll with it."

"Reverend Clark, you are hereby charged with the murders of James Wyatt III and Ticki Barnes." The sheriff moved toward the Reverend. The reverend looked into the sheriff's eyes and his first instinct is to run. "Don't do it, Rev," the sheriff said.

There were all kinds of law enforcement people outside just waiting for a nigga to fuck up!" The sheriff paused before he said, "Do you want to fuck up?"

RC looked at the sheriff and Blu and said, "I didn't do it. I tell you it was that bitch Nikki. I was just doing what she told me to do."

The sheriff looked at Blu then laughed. "C'mon now," he said. "I'm supposed to believe that a sixteen-year-old female manipulated you, a forty four year old male, a pillar of the community?" The sheriff took his radio receiver off of his shoulder and pressed the send button. "All right, Oliver, send them in!"

Suddenly, the locked front door is blasted in by a battering ram, Law enforcement personnel swarmed the place with weapons drawn. "Take him," the sheriff commanded as Blu sat there in silence watching everything unfold. He thought about all the stuff that had transpired in the last few days. He ran it over and over in his mind. From the meeting with his son in the jail to the trip to Biloxi and them gaining money then losing it all, he wondered if the whole thing was a set-up?

The law enforcement personnel, some from the state, some from the feds, and some from his department handcuffed RC against his denials and led him out the front door. One of the senior state troopers, dressed in his SWAT gear, approached the sheriff with his assault rifle at the ready. "What about him?" the trooper said.

The sheriff looked at Blu. He waved his hand and said, "You boys go on ahead. I still got something to talk about with Blu." The law enforcement personnel hustled out of the building, leaving the sheriff and Blu alone.

Blu, sitting there looking at the sheriff, finally said, "Well what do you do with me, Sheriff? I was there through some of this but not all of it. I simply did not know."

The sheriff nodded his head up and down and said, "Mind if I take a seat?"

Blu nodded his head yes before saying, "Go ahead, Sheriff."

"Does that television work?," the sheriff asked, pointing toward the television above the bar.

"Yeah sure," Blu said, somewhat confused.

"Well the game is on," the sheriff said.

"Yeah, well, I guess it is," Blu said.

"I'll tell you what?," the sheriff began. "If Alabama wins, I'll take you in for charges and if Auburn wins you can at least spend this night free."

Blu looked at the sheriff and said, "Just like an Alabama fan, always trying to show your superiority before the ball is snapped! Bring it on!" Blu pressed the remote control button and…

CHAPTER 32

The chairman stepped out of his SUV and was quickly converged on by a platoon of assistants. One grabbed him by the arm and hustled him toward the plane. He let the young man lead him to the steps of the Gulf Stream jet then waved him off and he climbed the stairs. Once inside, he went toward his seat and sat down. "We'll be taking off in a few moments, sir," the assistant in the plane said, following the chairman and being led to a seat across from the chairman is his son.

His son seemed nervous. "Are you all right?," the chairman asked, looking at his son.

His son shook his head yes. The chairman turned his head and chair toward Nikki Flowers. "How about you, miss?" the chairman asked. "Are you alright?"

Nikki smiled and said, "Yes I am, but I have a bunch of questions."

"As do I," the chairman said.

The captain of the aircraft moved into the cabin and said, "Fasten your seat belt, we shall be taking off in a few minutes."

The chairman smiled at Nikki and said, "Do you know where you're going?"

Nikki laughed and said, "Yeah, away from here." Nikki had learned through the chairman's associates who he was and where they were going, she just didn't know why.

"I know, young lady," the chairman began, "that at your young age, you see everything as good and bad, black and white. I have completed the first leg of my journey, which is to bring my family, my country together. I know you know nothing of what I say but in the process I have found it necessary to add or subtract certain pieces to the puzzle."

Nikki looked at the chairman, trying to figure out what this old man was talking about. "I know you don't understand," he said, "but what I'm doing will last long past my death, and that is why you are here."

"I'm just a poor country girl." Nikki said. "What can you possibly need me for?"

The chairman laughed. "My dear, you are far from a country girl, the way you had that town of yours wrapped around your young fingers," the chairman said. "Nobody has yet surmised that you killed the two young men and controlled the deal between your Red and the North Koreans, have they?"

Nikki's eyes widened as she said, "I didn't—"

"Come, come now ," the chairman said. "You orchestrated every event, every action that occurred from the shootings to the money trail to the misdirection," the chairman said. "I applaud your every move and to encourage you. I had my people throw you ten thousand dollars, to see what else you would do."

Nikki shrugged her shoulders, deciding whether to say nothing and to see what the chairman was going or try and take control of the situation. "Suppose I did everything you said," Nikki said. "Why am I here?"

The chairman looked at his son then at Nikki. "Like I said before," the chairman began, "the two things that I wish before I die are to unite my family and my country and you shall play a role in both. What my son needs is a strong woman one who will direct him and lead him in this new century while at the same time able to bear his offspring and make sure the family continues. I could not think of a better choice than you."

Nikki looked at the chairman and thought of his crazy proposal and his son. Well, he was a man, maybe not her type but she thought about the possibilities that lay before her and the life she had and was leaving behind. Nikki turned her chair as the airplane lifted off from the runway. She sat back in her chair and thought to herself, *What the hell? Might as well enjoy the ride.* She swung her chair back around to the chairman and said, "I'm in."

The chairman smiled as the airplane leveled off and they began the long flight to Korea.

The End

www.ingramcontent.com/pod-product-compliance
Lightning Source LLC
Chambersburg PA
CBHW071813080526
44589CB00012B/781